TRACKING TOWARD

TRIBULATION

AND THE ANY-MOMENT INTERVENTION BY

JESUS CHRIST

TRACKING TOWARD
TRIBULATION
AND THE ANY-MOMENT INTERVENTION BY
JESUS CHRIST

TERRY JAMES, GENERAL EDITOR
WITH CONTRIBUTORS

Brandon Holthaus, Jonathan C. Brentner, Dr. Randall Price, Dr. Nathan E. Jones,
Jan Markell, Wilfred Hahn, Daymond Duck, Pete Garcia, Mondo Gonzales, Jim Fletcher,
Mike Gendron, Tim Moore, Bill Salus, Tom Hughes, Allie Anderson, & Donna Howell

DEFENDER
CRANE, MO

Tracking Toward Tribulation:
And the Any-Moment Intervention by Jesus Christ

By Terry James, General Editor

Defender Publishing
Crane, MO 65633

2024 Terry James
All rights reserved. Published 2024

ISBN: 978-1-948014-84-7

Printed in the United States of America.

A CIP catalog record of this book is available from the Library of Congress

Cover designer: Jeffrey Mardis
Interior designer: Katherine Lloyd

In tribute to my great friend Tom Horn,
whose profound contributions to the magnificent cause
of our Lord Jesus Christ continue to live on while we look
forward to meeting them both in the clouds of Glory.

CONTENTS

ACKNOWLEDGMENTS

To the authors of *Tracking Toward Tribulation*, I can scarcely find the words to fully express my gratitude. Each has been an inspiration to me over the years, and, I know, to you, the reader.

The Lord's hand is upon them in these troubling although exciting days, as they speak truth to this generation—truth that all they discern from observing today's issues and events, overlaid by the prism of God's prophetic Word, points to the any-moment call to all believers by the Lord Jesus Christ.

My deep love and thanks to Angie Peters for her usual editorial expertise, and to the rest of my family, Margaret, Terry Jr., Nathan, Kerry, Dana, and Jeanie, as well as all my "grandkids" for just being there for "Pops."

A special thanks and love to Todd Strandberg, my partner and founder of our website, Raptureready.com. Same to my great friend Mike Hile, my traveling partner who keeps me between the ditches as we traverse the country for speaking obligations.

Thanks, too, to Donna Howell, Joe Horn, Allie Anderson, Nita Horn, and all others at Defender Publishing and SkyWatch TV. They continue to bless my life with their family-close treatment as we work together to publish these books for our Lord's service.

To you the reader, our thanks and prayerful best wishes while we, with you, watch for our Lord's return (Mark 13:37).

And to our Lord Jesus Christ, my love and thankfulness, the deserved praise of whom I am woefully incapable of adequately expressing.

—*Terry James*

INTRODUCTION

By Terry James

God Himself gave the formula for knowing just how close is His coming to receive unto Himself those who believe:

> And when you shall see all these things begin to come to pass, then look up and lift up your head, for your redemption draweth nigh. (Luke 21:28)

Key in this statement by the Creator of all that exists are the words, "all these things."

There are many things to consider included within this framework given by Jesus Christ in answering His immediate disciples' question: "What shall be the sign of thy coming and of the end of the age?"

We who have determined to enter this examination titled *Tracking Toward Tribulation* prayerfully intend to look at each of "all these things" to give readers a picture as accurate as possible of where this generation stands on God's prophetic timeline.

Most who observe these times as Jesus commanded—"What I say unto one, I say unto all, watch" (Mark 13:34) agree. "All these things" we are to "watch" have accelerated significantly within the recent months, weeks, and days. The ominous foreshadows of the Tribulation—Daniel's seventieth week—hang heavily above every point on earth.

Yet the gathering darkness that closes in gives those who are in God's family the opportunity to shine the light of His truth—that Jesus Christ alone is the hope for humankind. Christians are to be the light that reflects from our Savior's heavenly luminescence. We are to be both salt and light to a decaying, darkening world.

We are to be looking up all the while for our redemption, which is growing ever nearer.

The words I hear when talking to believers about the Rapture of the Church is that while they hope it will happen soon, they are afraid it's way out there in the future. This is a common thread I find in the thinking of fellow Christians these days. That's not to say all are thinking in this direction. Many who come to our website, Raptureready. com, and to my personal website, Terryjamesprophecyline.com, look around at all that is happening and express that they don't see how the Rapture could be meant for any generation other than ours. They see all the collateral cultural and societal prerequisites for that stunning event to occur.

So what is the probability that the Rapture is scheduled in God's plan for humanity in either a *sooner* or *later* timeframe? Is there any one signal on the prophetic horizon that might give a clue to answering that question? I believe one area to look at might provide insight.

Believers and nonbelievers alike are being fed a daily diet of doomsday fodder. COVID-19 more or less suctioned the attention of the world's populations into its orbit of terror. This, I sense, was done deliberately. That is, it was an intentionally created, worldwide, pathogenic assault specifically designed to bring people under the cloud of gloom and doom. As a matter of fact, documentation being unveiled is beginning to point in that direction, providing proof that it was spawned to control the minds and movements of the earth's populations.

Added to the pandemic was the intent to radically change cultures and societies through the *wokism* we've all been subject to in recent times. Overall, it's been an effort to move people's focus away from the God of Heaven and toward anti-God thinking. That effort to totally corrupt humankind has been largely successful, and governments of the world have become, as Romans 1:28 tells us, "reprobate" at every level. That is, our leaders can't and/or won't think rationally. Every thought is only on evil continually, it seems.

This is exactly the mindset of the antediluvian world of Genesis 6, the one Jesus said would be prevalent at the moment of His catastrophic intervention into the affairs of humanity. He said it would be "as it was in the days of Noah."

We see not only the anti-God attitude, but violence that fills the whole earth, exactly as described in Noah's day. Consider that with the upside-down thinking of the legislators and city councils of the so-called blue states and cities, murder rates are up exponentially in some areas. The catch-and-release policies of the blue cities have validated those policies' wrongheadedness, their insanity. The reprobate thinking of governors, mayors, and legislators are manifest for anyone who cares to see.

America has at least half a population and half a Congress with the same deadly disease—Romans 28-level, reprobate thinking. The president of the United States in charge during all this madness seemed to be at the apex of present American leadership manifesting upside-down or reprobate thinking. This isn't just the ranting of some prophecy nut. Joe Biden's wrongheadedness during the most recent years has been evident, and we have seen his handlers closely guarding his movements daily, keeping him from press conferences and having him avoid most questions of substance by White House and other reporters.

While wars and rumors of wars ratchet up to the point of threatening to break into World War III, according to some, the American military, led by the present chiefs of staff, advise the president to concentrate on creating a culture of wokism within the ranks. Some in our military even wear rainbow symbols, indicating their awareness that the transsexual movement is front and center in their midst. The chairman of the Joint Chiefs of Staff seems to be all in regarding his support for this LGBTQ+ incursion into the American military. This is, to my thinking, Sodom and Gomorrah-level, reprobate manifestations in these days that look forever more like the days of Noah and Lot about which Jesus prophesied.

All of the above constitutes substantial evidence that the world of rebellious, anti-God forces against Heaven's governance is indeed *Tracking Toward Tribulation*. The Rapture of the Church might be close to fulfillment. But one particular symptom of our time stands out significantly. And it is much more than just a symptom; it is a growing monster created by "evil men and seducers" who deceive and are themselves deceived. Those greedy creators of the monster have reached the point that they can no longer control its voraciousness.

The people to whom I refer are the money powers that be. These are the men and women whose only desire, it seems, is to create larger and larger debt among those they force to do their bidding, financially speaking. These globalist, fiscal elitists' evil economic shenanigans have brought this generation to a moment I believe Jesus, Himself, was speaking about, regarding His next intervention into this doomed, rebellious world. More about this in due course.

The following excerpt defines the uncontrollable monster, I think:

> For years I have been clear that the world is reaching the end of an economic, financial and monetary era which will detrimentally affect the world for probably decades.
>
> It is unequivocal that all currencies will finish the 100+ year fall to ZERO in the next few years. It is also crystal clear that all the asset bubbles—stocks, bonds and property—will implode at the same time leading to a long and deep depression.
>
> We had the warning in 2006–2009 but central banks ignored it and just added new worthless debt to existing worthless debt to create worthless debt squared—an obvious recipe for disaster.
>
> So as is often typical for the end of an economic era, the catalyst is totally unexpected and worse than anyone could have forecast....
>
> If a miracle doesn't stop this war [Russia and Ukraine] very quickly (which is extremely unlikely), the world will soon

be entering a hyperinflationary commodity explosion (think energy, metals and food) combined with a cataclysmic deflationary asset implosion (think debt, stocks and property).

The world will be experiencing totally unknown consequences without the ability to solve any of them for a very long time.

All the above will most likely happen even without a global war.[1]

Inflation is burgeoning. Prices at the gas pumps and in the grocery stores—the shelves of which are growing increasingly sparse in products—continue to rise quickly. The above expert analyst and others predict the whole world economic system is about to experience a crash of apocalyptic dimension. If this happens, the world will again have to gather up the shambles and bring things back to a relatively normal way of conducting life. This would take many decades if it could ever be reconfigured in getting things back to how they are now.

Jesus' words tell us that when He comes again, people will be like they were in Noah's day. That is, it will be a totally evil period of violence. Well, we are there at present, aren't we?

But the Lord foretold something else. And it is what makes me think the Rapture of believers will be *sooner*, not *later*.

Jesus said the generation will be like it was in the days of Lot and his vexation in Sodom and Gomorrah. That means, of course, that it will be a totally debauched, sexually perverted, and wicked time. Are we not there?

But He said one more thing: People will be buying, selling, building, marrying, planting—carrying out normal activities. He predicted no worldwide financial collapse. "It's the economy, stupid," we might say to those who believe we are going through the Tribulation. (Although I would never use those words issued by James Carville those years ago while he was managing Bill Clinton's election.)

But it is, in fact, the world economic situation we should look at in wonder. It is still held up in spite of the any-second collapse the experts have been predicting for some time.

The collapse is being held up by God, the *Restrainer*, I have no doubt. It will be the Rapture that will pierce that enormous, constantly building economic bubble.

That moment is indeed imminent!

There is one and only one way to go to Jesus in this glorious event when He calls—the one and only way of escaping the coming time of trouble such as people of the earth have never endured:

That if thou shalt confess with thy mouth the Lord Jesus, and shalt believe in thine heart that God hath raised him from the dead, thou shalt be saved. For with the heart man believeth unto righteousness; and with the mouth confession is made unto salvation. (Romans 10:9–10)

So this is not a volume of gloom and doom, only pointing out the proliferating wickedness of this judgment-bound planet. We intend this to be an encouragement to all who name the name that is above every other—that of the Lord Jesus Christ. My friends, the tremendously gifted and spiritually attuned observers of these prophetic times who present their thoughts in this volume, prayerfully hope the book is an incentive to God's people to "look up and lift the head" and be salt and light as we await that Blessed Hope, our Savior, as He comes to Rapture all who have lived during this Age of Grace.

SECTION I

PHENOMENAL PROPHETIC PROGRESSION

General Editor's note: There can be no plausible deniability about the troubled times from those who observe from the pretribulational view of Bible prophecy. This is the view that Jesus Christ will call believers—those who have died and those who are living at the time—unto Himself in the Rapture before the great and terrible Day of the Lord comes. That is, those who have been saved from sin's dread sway by Christ's sacrifice on the cross more than two thousand years ago will vanish in the twinkling of an eye, and this will be followed soon thereafter by the seven-years era of wrath and judgment termed "the Tribulation."

Things of tremendous prophetic import are bursting upon this end-times world that are indeed phenomenal. From the deception being foisted upon humanity at every angle by governments, religious prevaricators, and media to wickedness beginning to dominate society and culture like in the days of Sodom and Gomorrah to astonishing geopolitical movements that are setting the stage for Antichrist's New World Order, the earth's inhabitants are tracking toward the worst times in human history, according to Jesus, Himself (Matthew 24:21).

Israel is front and center in the crosshairs of satanic rage just as the prophet Zechariah described for the last of the last days (Zechariah 12:1–3). We authors encourage you to "watch," as instructed by the Lord Jesus (Mark 13:37). If you will do so from the view that the Bible plainly teaches that Christians will not go through the Tribulation (Revelation 3:10), you will be brought to Holy Spirit understanding of things to come.

Most importantly, if you haven't done so, accept Christ this moment so God the Holy Spirit can indwell your soul and provide that understanding.

PHENOMENAL
PROPHETIC PROGRESSION

Chapter 1

END-OF-DAYS DECEPTION AND DEMONS

By Jan Markell

General Editor's note: Jan Markell hosts the most-listened-to Christian radio program in America—through more than one thousand stations—and her podcast is heard and watched by millions around the world. She is host of Olive Tree Ministries, a ministry dedicated to understanding the times through overlaying the Bible upon issues and events of these days so near the call of Christ to believers in the Rapture.

Deception is the first sign the Lord Jesus gave that will, as the end of the age approaches, point to the worst time of human history—the Tribulation (Daniel's seventieth week). It will be an invasion from the demonic realm that will be so obvious as to make clear the evil and wickedness surrounding us.

Can there be any doubt that this invasion is already taking place, after witnessing the opening ceremonies of the 2024 Olympic Games in Paris? We believe we are at that time now. The portal from the evil sphere is observably open, based upon the wickedness manifesting, and Jan's chapter brings great clarity to the strange things affecting this generation.

+ + +

As you see this title and read a few opening paragraphs, you may wonder what on earth I have in mind for a prophecy-oriented book. But remember, the key to Bible prophecy is the disappearance of believers and the rise of an evil, scheming man called Antichrist. He will be the architect of diabolical deeds once the Church is gone. *He will be the master occultist.*

Babylon, representing the false religious system of the last days, will deceive "all nations" with sorcery (Revelation 18:23). People will use practices and spells, and will exercise supernatural powers through the aid of the devil to deceive all nations during the Tribulation. Pharmaceuticals will also be involved, as they enhance an occult experience.

Is it any wonder that in the last twenty years, paranormal activity has accelerated many times over? I want to have a look at that in the next few pages. This is not to discourage or make anyone depressed, but to look to a phenomenon near the top of the list of the so-called signs of the times. It is truly a herald of His coming and a clear indication that *we are trending towards the Tribulation.*

Arch of Baal Visits America

In 2017, the Satanic Arch of Baal, also known as the Arch of Palmyra, was planted in the heart of Washington, DC. ISIS (the Islamic State of Iraq) destroyed the original Temple of Baal in Syria in 2015. Its history goes back to the books of Kings and the times of Ahab and Jezebel. Unspeakable activity went on in this pagan temple. *It is the essence of evil and rebellion.*

Why would anybody want to bring back a replica of it and honor it? Yet the replica began a global tour in 2015.

America welcomed it and had a "celebration" under it with the US Capitol building in the background. It was at the same time the US was embroiled in the Judge Brett Kavanaugh controversy. Is it any wonder his confirmation was consumed in turmoil when such a monument to evil was just a few miles away?

T-Shirts for Satan

Spencer's gift store inside a Chicago mall is featuring items for teens, including t-shirts encouraging them to summon demons. A local pastor intervened. "We're so close to being Sodom and Gomorrah," he lamented. "We're living in a place where just anything goes. Do whatever you want, whatever you feel. All I'm going to say is, 'Repent, for the Kingdom of God is at hand.'"

I give this man credit for taking a stand for righteousness when wickedness wants to abound.

Minnesota's Paganicon in My Neighborhood!

Pagan festivals are nothing new. People love to glory in wickedness, and they suggest their nature worship is harmless. But I live in one of the occult capitols of the world here in Minneapolis/St. Paul, Minnesota. We are the site of the famous Paganicon, where revelers celebrate pagan pride. This is literally in my neighborhood…and it *may be coming to yours.*

I walked into the event just to mingle with attendees and find out their backgrounds. Talk about confused people of all ages: They wanted to believe in a higher power, but looked toward the dark side. I asked one person about faith in Jesus Christ, and he admitted that, at some point in his background, he had considered it.

Life is filled with choices. This man's was not the best; he chose the dark over the light. Paganicon was the highlight of his year, just as Christmas might be for a believer. He simply wanted to spend one weekend a year—over the summer solstice—with equally lost people reflecting on pagan practices. Each to their own.

Unholy Act at the Grammys

The 2023 Grammy Awards included a satanic performance by Sam Smith and Kim Petras. Their song, titled "Unholy," featured British singer-songwriter Smith wearing a red devil costume and a hat with horns. He and German singer-songwriter Petras were surrounded by performers—some in cages—who were also wearing red costumes and dancing seductively. Flames surrounded them in a spectacle that was clearly intended to be satanic. *Anyone watching would think they were peering into Hell.*

The Super Bowl's Super Darkness

The 2023 Super Bowl halftime lived up to its outrageous reputation just like the Grammys. It opened with the filth merchant Rihanna descending from the sky, surrounded by what could be described as *dancing fallen angels!* This actually generated more complaints than the debacle at the Grammys.

Baal Worship at the Commonwealth Games

A few years ago, the Commonwealth Games in Birmingham, England, had seventy-two nations participating. Then Prince Charles, now King Charles, was an honorary guest. *It included ritualistic Baal worship in plain sight!* But before that, dancers placed fingers on their heads to represent satanic horns as they were announcing the coming of the horned beast!

The ceremony was blatant luciferian worship. A woman eventually climbed a gigantic bull and *the crowd celebrated the woman riding the beast*—right out of Revelation 17. I wish I were making this up, but I am not. This was seen by tens of millions of people around the world.

Baphomet Honored at Gotthard Tunnel Ceremony

We can't leave out the Gotthard Base Tunnel opening ceremony of 2016, which was attended by many of Europe's most powerful leaders. The event was *a dark, disturbing, and weirdly satanic ritual.*

The Gotthard Tunnel, the world's longest tunnel project in history, runs through the Swiss Alps; it took seventeen years to complete. It is considered the symbol of European unification, but does this require honoring Satan? I guess so.

During the eight-hour ceremony, eventually a goat man, or Baphomet, appeared, and was *the star of the show!* People bowed down to him and, at the end of the long production, the goat man was declared "king of the world." This, too, was televised to the world for hours.

Brazil Carnival Attacks Jesus

Let's head to Brazil. Recently, their annual Carnival celebration took a controversial turn with its planners calling the event "Satan's Carnival." Held in Rio de Janeiro, the parade featured participants dressed in black and red costumes, many wearing devil horns and carrying pitchforks. *A figure representing Jesus was attacked and God was mocked.*

God will not be mocked much longer!

Some would say such practices have gone on forever—they're just more sophisticated now. That may be true, but now they are celebrated, glorified, and broadcast to the ends of the earth thanks to modern communication.

Walker Art Center Summons Demons!

In the summer of 2023, the Walker Art Center in Minneapolis, Minnesota, held a "demon-summoning session" for kids. Families were invited to create a vessel to trap the demon that knows them best, then participate in a playful ceremony to summon and befriend their demon. Yes, I said "families," so that means children were targeted.

"Demons have a bad reputation, but maybe we're just not very good at getting to know them," an event description stated. "After designing your trap, Lilit the Empathic Demon will come from the dark side of the moon to lead you in locating your feelings using ancient Babylonian techniques.

"This collective and playful demon-summoning session will conclude with a somatic movement meditation, designed to help you befriend your shadows."

Pictured in the promotion materials for this outrageous occult extravaganza were children ages two, three, and four. This is outright indoctrination into the dark arts. The young are already blitzed by Hollywood and the music industry, but now an art center has *tapped into their inner demons*, trying to market them to unsuspecting parents and children.

After-School Satan Clubs and More

I haven't even described the 2016 Fox TV production titled *Lucifer*, a program that painted the main character as a really good guy, or, rapper Lil Nas X grossing out some of his closest fans by appearing to slide down a pole to Hell. Neither have I touched on another cable TV series titled *Little Demon*, and I haven't described the after-school Satan clubs designed to counter child evangelism Bible classes in the schools! And, sadly, there's so much more.

What's Spirit Cooking?

Occult "Spirit Cooking" dinners are hosted by Hillary Clinton's Satanist friend, Marina Abramovic, and attended by political consultant John Podesta. But if you think they are the only ones doing it, think again.

Can you imagine the highest leaders of the land celebrating the darkness? Yes, indeed, and it's just one reason America is on a downward slide. Again, the Church remains here to push back the darkness, and it is. *Can you imagine what will happen when believers are taken?*

Witches Are Now Spiritual Experts?

The practice of witchcraft in America is growing by leaps and bounds. No longer are the traditionally highly secret activities being kept in the closet. In fact, today's witches aren't at risk of getting burned at the stake at all; rather, they're honored and revered.

Further, witches are increasingly being accepted as spiritual experts who meet the needs of clients inclined to embrace and tap into their extensive access to supernatural spirit powers and hidden knowledge.

Wicca, the key umbrella organization for formalized witchcraft and New Age practice in general, has finally come out of the shadows. Social media is now a hotbed of supernaturalism and New Age practices. Promoters attract millions of followers.

Targeting Christians and Jews

I am told by fellow contributor to this book, Brandon Holthaus, that solid Christians are being oppressed to the point that they cry, "Deliver us from evil!" Dark forces are clearly stepping up their game here in the last days, and the target seems to be Christians who are telling the truth about God's plan for the end of the Church Age.

Be assured that the name of Jesus Christ drives away the demonic. We don't have to fear!

Does anybody think the rise of diabolical anti-Semitism isn't driven by demonic spirits? They're fueling a global phenomenon. It is likely not politically correct to suggest that the mantra, "From the river to the Sea, Palestine will be free" is inspired by the demonic. This whole topic requires a chapter of its own!

I also believe demons were unleashed on Israel on October 7, 2023, when Hamas perpetrated a twenty-first-century holocaust of the Jews. Jew-hating demons. Something supernatural happened and was unleashed that day. Our world changed—forever.

Demons may have been unleashed, but God's end-time clock went from one minute until midnight to ten seconds until midnight as we rush towards the Tribulation.

Darkness Precedes Christ's Return

But even as the shadow of darkness blankets our landscape, there is an ever-increasing number of embassies of the kingdom of light. We read in the Bible that there will be unspeakable darkness and a great falling away in the last days before Christ returns, but most of us probably *never thought we would live to see a day quite like this.*

I'm trusting that you will push back against the darkness with me! Satan gets some glory now, but remember his ultimate destination: *an eternal lake of fire for him and all his angels and cohorts, where their diabolical celebrations will come to an ignominious end.*

Destination: Lake of Fire

The unbelieving element is racing toward the kingdom of the Antichrist. *It is the spirit of Antichrist that inspires these glorifications of darkness.* You wouldn't like to be present when they are cast into eternal darkness and the eternal lake of fire. *Finally, they will no longer be celebrating.* They will no longer be mocking. They will be wailing and begging for a second chance.

Make no mistake: This is war. It will not get better; it will not go away in the Church Age; and we are all in it. The spirit of the age cannot be ignored. "This know also, that in the last days perilous times shall come" (2 Timothy 3:1).

Lifting Up a Standard Against It

The Bible says "when darkness comes in like a flood, the Spirit of the Lord will lift up a standard against it" (Isaiah 59:19). The Lord will cause our lives to impact the rampant evil surrounding us! This may be one of the very reasons God has allowed us to be born...*for such a time as this.*

The Bible is clear that the last days will be characterized by a demonic outpouring. Demons are real, and the battle we wage is real. Evil is to become worse and worse (2 Timothy 3:13). *When we see these things increasing, we are to know His return is very near.*

Jesus Came to Destroy the Devil and His Work

I could fill many more paragraphs with further proof of this encroaching evil, but I want to end on a note reminding you of a pending trumpet blast instead. Jesus came to destroy the devil's work, and He will (1 John 3:8).

As full as the day is now with evil and devils, it will someday soon be filled thousands of times over with God's glory and beauty. Yes, the earth has to go through much pain before that happens, but it will take place.

All of those who wish to exalt themselves above God will be crushed.

We should not be surprised by this level of evil or be afraid of its power. The Bible tells us we will judge the angels, and they know it. They are terrified of the great power we have as children of the Most High God.

We are facing the end of this world, and Satan does not want to quietly leave! His retirement plan is lacking. He has no benefits or perks in Hell.

Ye are of God, little children, and have overcome them: because greater is he that is in you, than he that is in the world. (1 John 4:4)

Chapter 2

ISRAEL'S PROPHESIED POSITIONING

By Brandon Holthaus

General Editor's note: Brandon Holthaus, senior pastor of Rock Harbor Church, presents crucial thoughts on the number-one signal of where this generation stands on God's prophetic timeline. That premiere signal is, of course, Israel and its critical position within Bible prophecy yet future.

Brandon's clear and in-depth presentation brings into focus exactly what all the evil being perpetrated against God's chosen people at this time means in terms of Bible prophecy. His video presentations on *Tip of the Spear* TV programs keep viewers up to date on the swiftly moving issues and events of these darkening times. At the same time, Pastor Holthaus presents the truth of Jesus Christ, the Light of the World who will soon intervene to bring to an end the wickedness plaguing humanity.

+++

Since the horrific and demonic attack on Israel's innocent civilians by the Hamas terrorist organization on October 7, 2023, Israel now appears to be heading in the direction of a setup spiritually, politically, economically, and militarily for the predicted "covenant with death" with Antichrist.[2] Several contributing factors have come to light since that attack, pushing Israel in the prophetic direction of needing a rescuer. Consider the following:

1. America's weak leadership has caused rogue nations and the enemies of Israel to take advantage of this situation.
2. We have seen an ever-increasing hatred of Israel and a rise of global anti-Semitism after October 7.
3. Israel's dependency on America for weapons that have strings attached has threatened Israel's survival.
4. The Israel Defense Forces' (IDF's) intelligence failure concerning the October 7 attack has caused destabilization among the Jewish people in Israel.
5. There is a possibility of Israel splitting from the United States in order to survive.

I believe these conditions are creating a trajectory for Israel that will send it right into the hands of Antichrist in the future.

But, before I go any further, let me note that I am a Christian Zionist, which means I support the Jewish people and the nation of Israel due to the Abrahamic, Land, Davidic, and New Covenants of Israel. This means I believe the Jews have a right to their land, a right to exist as free people, and the right to self-determination; further, I believe God has a purpose and plan for the future of Israel that extends into the Messianic Kingdom and beyond. I hold that the declaration of the State of Israel in 1948 was a birth pain and is a fulfillment of the prophecies that describe the first worldwide regathering of Israel in unbelief.[3] However, this doesn't mean we must agree with everything Israel's government, the IDF, or media says or does. We, as Bible students, love Israel, but that doesn't prevent us from critiquing and disagreeing with decisions Israel makes that run counter to Scripture. For example, when Israel gave up the Gaza Strip in 2005, it was a violation of the Land Covenant,[4] and when Israel builds its non-sanctioned Tribulation Temple in the future, that will be a violation of the Lord's words recorded in Isaiah 66:1–4. Therefore, one should not take my critique of Israel's government or the IDF as some anti-Semitic rant. I am very concerned for Israel because its leadership seems to be making mistakes that will prove to be biblically fatal going forward.

Weak American Leadership

It is evident to anyone who observed the Biden administration's foreign policy that it failed to deter enemies since it exhibited serial appeasement, inaction, and a lack of retribution toward bad actors. Therefore, the enemies of America and Israel have exploited this state of affairs because they don't fear any consequences for their actions. There has been a continuous and intentional show of weakness in America's foreign policy. For example, the Biden administration abruptly pulled the American military out of Afghanistan, which left eighty-five billion dollars' worth of military equipment behind for the Taliban. The United States is currently fighting a proxy war against Russia in Ukraine, which has cost $113 billion to date and has caused the US to run out of its munitions supplies. Does anyone believe Vladimir Putin would have invaded Ukraine had there been strong leadership in the White House? Would a Chinese spy balloon have been allowed to cross America with no repercussions? The US military warned about and tracked the balloon crossing our nation, but the leadership in Washington ignored it. When China sees this kind of response, does anyone think it deters that nation from annexing Taiwan? Since October 7, 2023, the Biden administration has allowed Iran-aligned militias and proxies to attack US troops and American installations in the Middle East with rockets, missiles, and drones more than 170 times.

Yet the Biden administration disproportionally responds (or doesn't respond at all, in some cases), which only emboldens these proxies and militias to attack again. Also, the Biden administration refuses to rescue the *remaining* American hostages taken by Hamas on October 7. Why isn't one of our special forces units, such as our Army Rangers, Delta Force, Green Berets, or SEAL teams being sent in to free them? How about when the United States refuses to control its southern border and allows illegal aliens into America in record-setting numbers that could eventually collapse the system? Do any of America or Israel's enemies quake in their boots when they see an invasion take place that America does nothing to stop? Or how about when the Houthis block the Red Sea and attack ships, and the US only responds by taking out the Houthis' tactical capabilities but not the terrorists themselves to avoid upsetting Iran? Does anyone believe this deters Iran and its proxies, such as Hamas, Hezbollah, or the Houthis themselves? Our enemies are watching, and they notice the United States' passive behavior, which encourages them to exploit the weakness.

Why is America acting like this? Strategic analyst David Wurmser explained the reason to journalist Caroline Glick when he said:

> America does not want to be the superpower in the world. The feeling is America is the problem in the world. And we have to show the world that we are not the problem. That we have to establish our credentials.[5]

In other words, America's leaders are intentionally bringing America's role in the world to that of a second-rate nation with no power or influence. Many of America's leftist leaders hate the country and want to knock it off its pedestal to appease the globalist elites. Therefore, weak leadership in the US affects Israel because that nation's enemies now know they can exploit Israel without fear of reprisals from the United States. However, according to military historian and commentator Victor Davis Hanson, America's policy of appeasement and avoiding a Middle East war at all costs will guarantee that war will take place in the Middle East.[6] Israel is now vulnerable to every nation that hates it and wants to wipe it off the face of the planet. Weak American leadership will send Israel looking for an ally to protect it instead of leaving it vulnerable.

Global Anti-Semitism

Anyone with a shred of discernment understands that the United Nations (UN) and other globalist organizations hate Israel. There is a long history of this hostility, especially when considering how the UN constantly and libelously condemns Israel more than it does all other countries combined for violating human rights.[7] However, the global anti-Semitism we witnessed after October 7 was shocking, to say the least. It seems like the Lord allowed us to see the undercurrent of a hidden hatred of Jewish people we didn't know existed. Anti-Semitism has been around ever since God created the nation of Israel, and it has existed in countries, regions, and pockets around the world. It is the oldest hatred on the planet today, and it is due primarily to: 1) Satan's desire to prevent God's promises from coming to fruition and 2) the Gentiles' spiritual jealousy of Israel, as seen in Cain's relationship with Abel. And, just to be clear: anti-Zionism and anti-Israelism are anti-Semitism.

However, what the Lord has revealed is global anti-Semitism. Three hundred eighty-four leaders from around the world demanded a ceasefire as they claimed Israel was violating human rights in its war against Hamas.[8] To understand this insane and asinine demand for a ceasefire, one only has to realize that such a cessation of hostilities allows Hamas to win, regroup, never pay for what it did, and attack Israel's civilians in the future. A ceasefire is anti-Semitic to its core. Then there was South Africa, which outrageously accused Israel of committing genocide to the United Nations International Court of Justice in its war against Hamas.[9] We also saw people from all over the world support the Hamas terrorists as oppressed victims and chant anti-Israel and anti-Semitic slurs all over the world from the streets in places such as London, Paris, New York, and Sydney. It was reprehensible to hear cries of "Gas the Jews!" and the evil slogan, "From the river to the sea, Palestine will be free," which means the annihilation of every living Jew from the Jordan River to the Mediterranean Sea.

This anti-Semitic environment is what it must have felt like to be in Nazi Germany.

This new trend is unsettling because we, as prophecy students, know where this deep hatred of Jews is heading. It will not stay regional, but will become global, as we're already witnessing in real time. Israel will become a "burdensome stone" during the Tribulation, just as Zechariah 12:3 predicts.

However, the trend lines of anti-Semitism are already setting the stage for this to happen. In fact, according to the 2023 anti-Semitism report, there was a 235 percent increase in anti-Semitism incidents worldwide after October 7.[10] The report claims "hatred of Jews has skyrocketed worldwide in the wake of the October 7 invasion."[11] It also states that there was a "1,200 percent increase in antisemitic social media posts calling for violence against Jews, Israelis, and Zionists" and "at least 74 percent of the online antisemitic material is comprised of the 'anti-Israel' antisemitism."[12] The report also indicated a significant increase in Holocaust denial and distortion, with most (68 percent) of the content published between November and December 2023 appearing on the X social media platform and the rest showing up on TikTok as well as Facebook, Instagram (both owned by Meta), and Telegram.[13] Further, the report revealed:

> In the two months following October 7, there was a 337 percent increase in antisemitic incidents in the United States compared with the same period in 2022—the highest number of antisemitic incidents recorded in two months since 1979, when documentation of such incidents began.[14]

The publication also points out that there were around 200 anti-Semitic/anti-Zionism/support for terrorism posts online, which is a 919 percent increase, and a 540 percent increase in false bomb threats directed at Jewish institutions and synagogues.[15] Lastly, when we observe campuses in the West, particularly in the United States, we can only have the gut-wrenching feeling that our young people have been thoroughly brainwashed at these indoctrination centers we call universities and colleges. According to the report, there was a 700 percent rise in the number of anti-Semitic events at US colleges and universities, which have become the epicenter of anti-Semitism due to their "woke" ideology and populations of Middle Eastern students.[16] This caused 54.5 percent of Jewish students in the America to say they don't feel physically safe on campuses and 33 percent of those students to hide their Jewish identity.[17]

Unfortunately, Bible prophecy indicates global anti-Semitism will continue to build to the point that the only place safe for any Jewish person is to live in the land of Israel, where at least the government and population will not come against them. As we connect the prophetic dots, it appears that anti-Semitism will continue to be one of several motivating factors for the Jewish people to return to their homeland. Further, as hatred toward Israel and the Jewish people increases, and once the Rapture of the Church has occurred, Antichrist will appear on the scene and pretend to be Israel's only friend in the world; he will promise to protect them. Satan never lets a crisis go to waste, especially one he creates. Satan is creating a global crisis of anti-Semitism in order to drive Israel into the hands of the Antichrist.

Israel's Dependency on America for Weapons

Israel has made a crucial military strategy mistake by depending upon America to supply its military. Israel's political left has accepted dependency upon America for weapons. Israel's left reduced the stockpiling of the nation's military weapons. It also reduced the size of the Israeli military to reinvent it to be "small, technological, [and] smart, but lethal" instead of being powerful, according to Ehud Barak and IDF Chiefs of the General staff.[18] According to journalist Caroline Glick, who cites Major General Yitzhak Brick:

The IDF shut down multiple divisions, cut artillery forces by 50%, armored brigades were shut down, [and] the reserve force was reduced by 80% between 2003–2017. The noncommissioned officer corps was gutted. It shut down its domestic production from uniforms to rifles to bullets, to artillery and tank shells.[19]

This unhealthy situation has caused Israel to lean heavily on the US to support it militarily. The Biden administration, in turn, believes it can tell Israel how to conduct its war with Hamas since Israel cannot fight without America's weapons. The unsaid threat from the Biden administration is: "If you do not do what you're told, then we will pull the supply of weapons." Therefore, the Biden administration has demanded that Israel end the war before Hamas is eliminated, which is a victory for Hamas. The US is pushing for unilateral recognition of a Palestinian state at the end of the war—regardless of the opposition of Israel's prime minister and 74 percent of the population.[20] With 150,000 rockets aimed at Israel and continued rocket launches into the Jewish civilian population from Hezbollah in the north, the US has only allowed Israel strategic strikes on Hezbollah. It has told Israel not to start a war to eradicate Hezbollah, but to seek a diplomatic solution. This diplomatic solution would include creating a buffer zone where Israel would give up sovereign land to Lebanon and rely on the Lebanese Army Forces to control Hezbollah. This strategy, of course, is delusional, because it puts Israel in a situation where they would face a threat to their existence, not to mention a violation of Israel's land covenant.

The question on everyone's mind is why the Biden administration is demanding that Israel put itself into dangerous positions with other nations and groups that would potentially destroy it. The answer may shock you, but the Biden administration is carrying out the legacy of the Barack Obama administration since many in the Deep State, the "Swamp," the bureaucracy, or whatever you want to call it, hate Israel. Biden's staffers are anti-Israeli and have adopted a pro-Iranian and pro-Palestinian policy for the Middle East theatre. The Biden administration revived the Obama pro-Iranian policy and believes if it can appease Iran, then Iran can rein in the terrorist proxies and establish stability in the region. Therefore, the US will allow Iran strategic wins, such development of their nuclear program and not responding to proxy attacks on American troops and American installations in the Middle East. According an article in the *Wall Street Journal,* "the United States showed its continued subservience to Iran when it unfroze ten billion dollars in Iranian revenue, which had been frozen under U.S. sanctions."[21] Since October 7, the United States has unfrozen another six billion dollars, with the grand total of sixteen billion dollars to Iran.[22] Lastly, Iran has made eighty billion dollars in illicit oil sales as the Biden administration has turned a blind eye to their dealings.[23] This pro-Iranian policy is antithetical to the Jewish state since Iran wants to obliterate Israel, as their leaders have indicated time and again.

The Biden administration has a pro-Palestinian policy as well. It wants a Palestinian state regardless of opposition coming from Prime Minister Benjamin Netanyahu, the rank-and-file IDF soldiers, and 74 percent of Israel's population, as noted earlier. The US insanely believes that since Hamas has been cut down in power and influence, then Mahmoud Abbas, a member of the Fatah party, can run the Palestinian Authority unencumbered with some alliance with the Hamas terrorist leftovers and other terror organizations like Palestinian Islamic Jihad, the Popular Front for the Liberation of Palestine, Bisan, Al-Haq, and others to achieve a "harmonious" Palestinian state. Honestly, this is Romans 1:18–28-type thinking. The US wants Israel to stop its war with Hamas and agree to a senseless hostage deal brokered by Egypt, Qatar, and the US, which makes Israel give up 100 to 250 Palestinian terrorists released from jail for every one Jewish hostage.[24] The US wants more humanitarian aid, which means Hamas is resupplied to continue to fight against Israel. These kinds of policies are suicide for Israel. To force Israel into a two-state deal poses another existential threat.

America's foreign policies with the Middle East leave Israel at a crossroads. America believes it can force Israel into situations that pose an existential threat because it supplies weapons, which is foreign-policy blackmail. Netanyahu and many in Israel understand what the Biden administration is doing and are surprisingly saying "No!" to this ungodly American foreign policy. Israel is not going to accept a Palestinian state run by the same people who attacked them, nor are they going to stand around and let Hezbollah or Iran destroy them. The people in Israel who are not controlled by the political left know Hamas and Hezbollah must be eliminated for Israel's survival, and this runs counter to what the Biden administration wants. Bible prophecy students can discern that the inevitable split of Israel from the United States is approaching. Netanyahu has even stated, "And if we have to take action both in the South and in the North...we'll just have to do it alone."[25] We will watch and see how this plays out.

IDF's Intelligence Failure on October 7

I have traveled to Israel multiple times post-October 7 and have seen and heard the emotions of the Jewish people who are both devastated and shocked. I have interviewed IDF soldiers, families of hostages, and many Jewish people in Israel, and it is clear that the intelligence failure of October 7 has destabilized them mentally, emotionally, and spiritually. Many had put their faith and trust in the IDF's protection, and the reality of the Hamas attack shattered that. This destabilization is why the number of requests for gun permits have skyrocketed, with 236,000 new requests after October 7.[26] The Jewish people are tough and have a spirit made of steel that helps them persevere through the hardest of times. They've been trained by the harshness of their reality as the chosen people. However, that spirit to survive also includes a trust factor for their protection, and their trust factor in Israel's IDF General Staff to protect them was greatly diminished. For example, in an interview with Channel 12 of Israel, Amit Yerushalmi, a former IDF surveillance soldier, expressed this sentiment: "What the survivors of the massacre feel is a complete failure of the IDF to protect them after failing to take their warnings seriously."[27]

Once the dust settles, the IDF's General Staff members and others must be held accountable for their actions. For example, Intelligence Directorate Chief Major General Aharon Halivav, IDF Chief of General Staff Lieutenant General Herzi Halevy, the Southern Command Commander Major General Yaron Finkelman, and others like Shin Bet's (Israel's Security Agency) Director Ronen Bar, and their close subordinates were warned repeatedly about Hamas invading…and they did nothing. These individuals and their close subordinates dismissed multiple warnings that Hamas was going to attack, but were convinced that providing economic prosperity to Gaza would prevent it. They also believed Hamas did not possess the capabilities to attack despite repeated warnings from IDF surveillance soldiers who monitored Hamas practicing their attack. Channel 11 news of Israel revealed that two female survivors, Yael Rotenberg and Maya Desiatnik, who were part of a unit of field observers at Nahal Oz base, had warned months before that they frequently saw "many Palestinians dressed in civilian clothing approach the border fence with maps, examining the ground around it and digging holes. One time, when she passed the information on, she was told that they were farmers, and there was nothing to worry about."[28] According to Channel 12 in Israel, another set of female soldiers, Amit Yerushalmi and Noa Melman, relayed the same accounts. These female soldiers also indicated Hamas was constantly training at the border fence, where they practiced driving tanks and taking them over. The females watched Hamas practice how to cross into Israel via a tunnel and how to shoot and roll.[29] They watched Hamas conduct patrols along the border fence and observed them detonating explosives along the fence.[30] They even watched Hamas construct a mock border fence to practice blowing it up and crossing into Israeli territory.[31] Unfortunately, Yerushalmi passed on what she observed up the chain of command, but said "nobody seemed to take it seriously. I saw what was happening; I wrote everything down on the computer and passed it on. I don't know what happened with it; we don't actually know what they do with the information."[32] Rotenberg also expressed that her surveillance information of Hamas was dismissed as well. As the *Times of Israel* reported:

> In the weeks before October 7, Rotenberg noticed that the efforts of the Hamas soldiers were concentrated at two specific points of the area she was responsible for tracking. However, she continued to hear from her commanders that it wasn't important and that there was nothing that could be done about it.[33]

"It's infuriating," Desiatnik explained. "We saw what was happening, we told them about it, and we were the ones who were murdered."[34]

According to Glick, these IDF women reported that "unnamed top-level officers in the intelligence corps ordered them to stop. When they continued reporting, the observers were warned that they would be disciplined and removed from the unit if they kept raising their concerns."[35]

Glick, in her article, *Aharon Haliva Has Got to Go*, also mentions a civilian hacker, Rafael Hayun, who reported that Hamas was engaging in training exercises that involved "invading Israel, penetrating the security fence at multiple points, taking over communities, committing mass murder and kidnapping."[36] Glick notes that Hayun alerted the IDF, but instead of thanking him and using this information, the IDF's "senior leadership" issued an order to seize his equipment and stopped working with Hyun five months before October 7.[37]

Even on the day of the attack, the IDF General Staff and Israel's intelligence failed to heed the warnings. Glick reported:

> At 4 a.m. on October 7, due to warnings of increased Hamas movement near the border fence, the senior security leadership, including IDF Chief of General Staff Lt. Gen. Herzi Halevy, Shin Bet Director Ronen Bar, Southern Command

Commander Maj. Gen. Yaron Finkelman and Haliva's assistant (Haliva was apparently asleep) discussed the movements and decided to go back to bed. Bar sent a small team of fighters to the border area, but that was all. The group didn't inform the Gaza division commander, Prime Minister Benjamin Netanyahu, or Defense Minister Yoav Gallant. Instead, they agreed to speak again at 8 a.m. Hamas invaded at 6:30.[38]

Dr. Mordechai Kedar also warned on April 17, 2023, that he was told by a source:

> The invasion of ground forces from Syria, Lebanon, and Gaza will focus on Israeli settlements, with the aim of demoralizing the Israeli public and forcing the government to surrender in order to save the lives of the many Israeli civilians who will be captured by the Arab and Iranian militias.[39]

The *New York Times* reported that Israeli officials had obtained a forty-page document of Hamas' battle plan (code named "Jericho Wall") concerning the October 7 attack more than a year before it happened.[40] The document "outlined, point by point...a methodical assault designed to overwhelm the fortifications around the Gaza Strip, take over Israeli cities and storm key military bases, including a division headquarters."[41] However, according to the *New York Times*, "Israeli officials dismissed it as aspirational and ignored specific warnings."[42] Israeli historian and political commentator Gadi Taub and Michael Doran, a senior fellow of the Hudson Institute in Washington, DC, also noted that the IDF had Hamas' Jericho Wall plan. They noted:

> The IDF made erroneous speculations about Hamas' intentions. The IDF had Hamas' whole plan (operation Jericho

Wall). They believed Hamas was deterred. And did not have a plan of action.[43]

According to Betsy Reed of *The Guardian*, Channel 12 of Israel claimed:

Israel's military and intelligence officials were given a highly detailed warning that Hamas was actively training to take over kibbutzim on the Gaza border and overrun military posts with the aim of inflicting substantial fatalities...based on leaked emails from the Israeli military's 8200 cyber-intelligence unit discussing the warnings....The leaked emails revealed that a senior officer who reviewed the intelligence considered the danger of a massive surprise attack by Hamas across the Gaza border to be "an imaginary scenario."[44]

Amir Avivi, a retired Israeli general, said:

The failure extends beyond just intelligence gathering and Israel's security services failed to put together an accurate picture from the intelligence they were receiving, based on what he said was a misconception surrounding Hamas' intentions.[45]

Prime Minister Benjamin Netanyahu also blamed Israel's military intelligence:

Under no circumstances and at no stage was the prime minister warned of war intentions on the part of Hamas. On the contrary, all the security officials, including the head of military Intelligence and the head of the Shin Bet, estimated that Hamas was deterred and looking for a settlement (with Israel). This was the assessment that was submitted time and time again to the Prime Minister and the Cabinet by all the security forces and the intelligence community, including up until the outbreak of the war.[46]

As many have noted, this was one of Israel's biggest intelligence failures since the Yom Kippur War in 1973. People need to be held accountable for the lives that were lost and ruined by failing to take seriously the abundance of warnings.

Why was intelligence ignored, dismissed, and not taken seriously? The General Staff and intelligence have a progressive leftist ideology that runs counter to the mindset of the rank-and-file IDF soldiers, the Israeli public at large, and conservative political leaders such as Benjamin Netanyahu and his coalition.

Caroline Glick noted:

For the past generation, the General Staff has undergone radical politicization. In successive appointment cycles in the past 30 years, colonels and brigadier generals unwilling to toe the political left's line have been blocked from appointments to strategically significant postings, and have generally found themselves out of the IDF before reaching the rank of major general.[47]

Therefore, the General Staff uses the paradigm of appeasing enemies for deterrence. For example, the General Staff, along with the political left, naively thought and continues to believe giving the Palestinians an economic boost by allowing them to work in Israel with work visas would prevent hostilities. As Glick stated:

Members of the General Staff, like their fellow leftists, are convinced that all they need is to appease the Palestinians to resolve their conflict with Israel. Give them money or jobs, let them build illegal villages and neighborhoods in commanding positions along highways or adjacent to Israeli cities, as well as villages on both sides of the 1949 Armistice Line, and they will be appeased. Give Hamas-ruled Gaza cash from Qatar and jobs in Israel, and prosperity will trump jihad.[48]

This left-wing mindset ignores the fact that anti-Semitism in the Middle East and surrounding Israel is primarily driven by religion and not economics. Islam informs its followers through the Qur'an and other writings that Israel has a hatred for Muslims; Jews lie; and Jews claim Allah's power is limited. Further, the writings state that Jews disobey Allah, mislead people, wish evil on people, devour people's wealth through subterfuge, slander Islam, are cursed by Allah, are merciless and heartless, never keep their promises, commit unrestrained sins, are cowardly and miserly, and have been transformed into apes and pigs.[49] Therefore, the Muslims must wage war against the Jews and either subjugate them or eliminate them. For obvious reasons, this religious motivation is always ignored by the left and progressives and is never considered when they design foreign policy for Islamic-controlled nations or groups.

The leftists of the Biden administration and the leftist Israeli General Staff, who owe their positions to the political left in Israel and want America's protection and supply of weaponry, are working together with the same foreign-policy paradigm of appeasement to Islamic countries and groups like Iran, Hamas, Hezbollah, or the Houthis. The policy of appeasement is, in essence, pro-Iranian/pro-Palestinian, which results in an anti-Israel policy. Many ask why leftist/progressive Jewish people would make decisions that are not in the best interests of the Jewish people or the state of Israel. It appears to be counterintuitive. However, we must realize that ideologies drive people. Leftism or progressivism is an ideology that acts as a religion for people. Ideology causes people to do things that would hurt them or the societies in which they live. We see it all the time here in America, such as collapsing the system by having open borders, destroying the economy for the global-warming hoax, or pushing wokeism's "diversity, equity, and inclusion" paradigm on such things as being an airline pilot or a doctor instead of meritocracy. Appeasing enemies is not how any nation should function, but this is how people who do not have a biblical worldview think. Appeasement doesn't deter anyone.

Disproportionate retaliation and victory do! History has proved that over and over again. These Israeli generals better wake up soon, or they will find themselves relieved of their posts since the political climate has changed in Israel since October 7. Israel is done with appeasing terrorist monsters.

Coming Split Between Israel and the US

Israel must finish this war with Hamas to survive, and that includes dealing with Hezbollah in the north and eventually dealing with the head of the snake, Iran. This means Israel will be forced to go in the opposite direction of the United States' strategic policies for the Middle East for its survival. This split will leave Israel alone in the world without any allies to protect it and supply it with weapons. It will be strategically vulnerable without the United States and, based on current military conditions, it will need another source of help. Furthermore, without the United States, Israel will be hurt economically. Israel has received $260 billion from the US since World War II.[50] Currently, the economy of Israel is down 20 percent due to the Hamas war.[51] It has affected tourism, which produces billions of dollars and is almost half of Israel's GDP.[52] Many of the reservist IDF soldiers are not working since they are serving in the IDF, also contributing to the economic downturn. If this continues, Israel will be placed in a major financial bind. The Bible mentions Israel will have two more massive invasions that I believe will occur before the Tribulation: The invasion described in Psalm 83 and the Gog of Magog invasion of Ezekiel 39–39. There is room for debate on the timing of these, but if they do occur before the Tribulation, Israel could face war fatigue, heavy casualties, the destruction of their economy, and loss of weaponry, etc.

Prophetic Trajectory

These converging events put Israel in a position of being alone and needing help militarily and economically. It will need a protector if a great divorce happens between the United States and Israel. The Jewish nation will need someone who is on its side and will provide "peace and security." Unfortunately, Israel will not turn to the Jewish Messiah, Jesus, at this time; the Jews will be deceived by the lawless one into a covenant that protects the nation from military invasion. Daniel 9:27 describes this deal with Antichrist as a seven-year covenant, which he breaks at the three-half-year mark. Isaiah 28:14–22 describes the contents of the covenant, which are pertinent to our discussion. Isaiah indicates this "covenant of death" Israel makes with Antichrist is primarily due to protecting itself from military invasion. Notice Isaiah 28:15:

> Because you have said, "We have made a covenant with death, and with Sheol we are in agreement. When the overflowing scourge passes through, it will not come to us."

The term "overflowing scourge" is a Jewish idiom that means "military invasion."[53] In essence, the invasion is like water that overflows into an area and sweeps away or drowns its victims. The term "scourge" refers to being whipped, which indicates affliction, suffering, punishment, or vengeance. Another passage that uses similar language is Revelation 12:15, where the term "flood" is used as an idiom for a military incursion by Antichrist.

The key idea is that Israel makes a covenant with Antichrist to protect itself from another assault. It is easy to see how Israel, after successive military invasions not only throughout recent history, but also in the future with the Psalm 83 and the Gog of Magog invasion, would be set up to make a deal with the devil. Antichrist can and will promise Israel protection—militarily and financially. According to Daniel 11:36–39, Antichrist worships the "god of fortresses," meaning he will have the military backing to protect Israel, implying he will also have the finances to support his military endeavors. The logic goes like this: To have a strong military, you must have the finances to supply it. Furthermore, add the supernatural empowerment from Satan, and Antichrist will appear as one of the most powerful military leaders in all of history, since he is accompanied by "all power, signs, and lying wonders" (2 Thessalonians 2:9). Israel will unfortunately be duped into thinking they have finally found the one who will give them rest from their enemies.

The trajectory cannot be stopped. This convergence of events is part of God's plan for Israel. The good news is that, according to Daniel 12:7, the Tribulation will break Israel's pride and they'll eventually believe in their Jewish Messiah, Yeshua. Then Messiah will come back to rescue the remnant (the believing element) of Israel from the hand of Antichrist at the Second Coming.

In light of all this, therefore, what can we do?

Zechariah 13:7–9 describes that one-third of Israel (the remnant) will come to faith in the Messiah during the Tribulation. Unfortunately, two-thirds of Israel will not believe in the Lord Jesus and will perish at the hands of Antichrist. As my good friend Olivier Melnick has said, "The two-thirds of Israel that the Antichrist will destroy is a percentage and not a number. We can reduce that number if we would evangelize our Jewish friends before it's too late." As I mentioned at the beginning of the chapter, Israel is destabilized emotionally, mentally, and spiritually. What I have witnessed in Israel post-October 7 is a spiritual openness. The LORD is bringing good out of the evil perpetrated by Hamas. Despite this horrific atrocity happening to the Jewish people, many are now spiritually open like never before. Many secular Jews are returning to the Bible. The younger people of Israel are becoming more religious. What I have witnessed in Israel is receptivity to the Gospel. The LORD is calling His people, Israel, to salvation through Yeshua. As we see the birth pangs increasing, let us be faithful in warning, contending, discipling, and sharing the Gospel "to the Jew first and also for the Gentile" (Romans 1:16).

Chapter 3

PROLIFERATING PROPHETIC PROOF

By Jonathan C. Brentner

General Editor's note: Jonathan C. Brentner is qualified like few others to explore the issues and events of these times from a biblically prophetic viewpoint. He does so in-depth in his contribution to this book, a volume through which Jonathan, like all other authors, desires to show just where the world stands on God's prophetic timeline.

Through his ministry, www.jonathanbrentner.com, and as regular contributor to the Rapture Ready and Harbinger's Daily websites, Jonathan brings valuable insights to tens of thousands of those seeking the truth about issues and events of prophetic importance. America and the world indeed face unprecedented times of turmoil in the immediate future. This chapter helps make understandable what it all means.

✦✦✦

Many people claim that today is no different than any other time in history. "Sure, things look bad now, but wasn't this also the case during World Wars I and II? Things have a way of working out so that things eventually return to some semblance of normal."

I understand why so many folks question Jesus' soon return, given the fact that it's been two thousand years since He promised to come back. In spite of the long wait, however, I'm convinced that Jesus' appearing is imminent because of myriad signs telling us that the Tribulation period is right on our doorstep. I have compiled a list of ten signs that tell us we are rapidly running out of what the world refers to as "normal."

If you are weary of waiting and long for the day when you will meet Jesus in the air, I am writing to encourage you: He's coming soon. *This is the season of His return.*

If you doubt the Rapture will happen in your lifetime, please take time to consider the following biblical evidence that tells us it's altogether possible to happen soon.

1. Israel's Miraculous Rebirth

Did you know Isaac Newton predicted Israel would reappear as a nation before the Tribulation? Based on his in-depth study of the books of Daniel and Revelation, he made that startling claim more than 250 years before Israel sprang into existence in 1948.54

Newton correctly recognized that the fulfillment of many biblical prophecies requires Israel to exist as a nation prior to the start of the Tribulation. On May 14, 1948, the miraculous rebirth of Israel fulfilled the words of Isaiah 66:8, which told us that rebirth would happen in a "day." Only God could in one day resurrect a nation that hadn't existed for the previous two thousand years, supernaturally protect it amid countless attacks and wars, and later bring it into economic prosperity.

President Harry Truman faced enormous pressure from his cabinet to deny recognition of Israel. The US administration knew many months in advance that on May 14, 1948, David Ben-Gurion would declare Israel an independent sovereign state. However, within minutes of the announcement, President Truman formally recognized Israel as sovereign state, and his letter to that effect led the United Nations to do the same.

Israel's miraculous return to being a nation after two millennia, with its original language, alone makes today more prophetically significant than any other time since the first century AD.

Isaac Newton also wrote that Israel would build a third temple before Jesus' Second Coming at the end of the Tribulation.[55] Do we see any signs that Israel plans to do this?

2. Third-Temple Fever in Israel

Scripture tells us Antichrist will defile a still-future Jewish temple. This prophecy, first recorded in the book of Daniel, finds its way into the New Testament as Jesus and the apostles Paul and John refer to it as future event.

In a one of my blog posts, "The Biblical Necessity of a Third Jewish Temple," I demonstrate why building the third Jewish temple is a necessity for the fulfillment of biblical prophecy. If we can trust the words of Scripture, and we can, there must be a third temple in Jerusalem by the midpoint of the Tribulation.

Do we see evidence pointing to this future reality? Absolutely!

Just ten years ago, few people could have imagined today's passion in Israel for the building of their temple. The Levitical law requires the sacrifice of one perfect red heifer for the purification of the temple and its priests; even one small hair of a different color disqualifies the creature. This makes such a find a rarity. Yet, in 2022, after many years of searching, the arrival in Israel of five perfect red heifers from Texas sparked a jubilant celebration throughout Jerusalem. As of March 2024, it appeared that one of the recently appointed temple priests would soon sacrifice one of the heifers as preparation for the purification of the temple that's set to be built in the near future.

The Temple Institute in Jerusalem has spent more than thirty years researching and preparing furnishings for the temple. They are even now training Levites to serve as priests there.

The Israeli government is planning the infrastructure for the coming temple, which includes a rail system completed in 2023 running between the Ben Gurion Airport and the Temple Mount, as a great many are expected to visit the holy site. This train will also carry animals to the temple for the sacrificial rites.

As we watch biblical prophecy coming to life before our eyes, can there be any doubt that we live in the last days of human history as we know it?

3. The Riders of the Apocalypse

I purchased evangelist Billy Graham's book, *Approaching Hoofbeats*, not long after its publication in 1983. I can't remember all I thought of the book, since I read it about forty years ago, but I do know it sparked hope regarding the nearness of the Rapture. As a young pastor at the time, I loved preaching about Bible prophecy and Jesus' appearing.

As I recently skimmed its chapters again, the stark differences between what Graham wrote about then and the issues and events that are occurring now leapt off the pages. Some of the signs that seemed so indicative of the nearing Rapture all those years ago pale by comparison to all we witness today in our world.

The Antichrist Rides

It's only been in the past six years or so that Klaus Schwab and the World Economic Forum (WEF) came out of the shadows and revealed their true intentions to the world. They have invited the news media into their once-secret meetings and revealed their plans to enslave the world under the slogan "Build Back Better," a euphemism for their efforts to create a Marxist, totalitarian world government.

I'm not suggesting Schwab is the coming "man of lawlessness" Paul describes in 2 Thessalonians 2:3–10. However, the WEF founder does provide an apt illustration of how Antichrist will gain control of our world under the cloak of promoting peace.

By 1983, I had heard of a group called the "trilateralists" who were pushing for a one-world government at the time. Today, however, the emerging framework for the type of world domination we read about in the book of Revelation is front and center for everyone to see, yet few are paying attention to nearness of the time when the white horse will ride across the earth.

The Threat of Nuclear War

In *Approaching Hoofbeats*, Graham wrote about the threat of a devastating nuclear war, which was a major concern at the time. Today, however, this danger has reached the point that most analysts believe it's likely to occur in the next few years.

Citing the significant risk for a nuclear war, the nonprofit organization called Bulletin of the Atomic Scientists made headlines on January 23, 2024, by resetting its Doomsday Clock back to ninety seconds before midnight. Below is a quote the website posted that day:

> A durable end to Russia's war in Ukraine seems distant, and the use of nuclear weapons by Russia in that conflict remains a serious possibility. In February 2023, Russian President Vladimir Putin announced his decision to "suspend" the New Strategic Arms Reduction Treaty (New START). In March, he announced the deployment of tactical nuclear weapons in Belarus. In June, Sergei Karaganov, an advisor to Russian President Vladimir Putin, urged Moscow to consider launching limited nuclear strikes on Western Europe as a way to bring the war in Ukraine to a favorable conclusion.[56]

Today's world is exceedingly more dangerous than it was in 1983. The prospect of a nuclear war was a possibility back then, but now it's become a matter of *when* rather than *if* it will happen.

Economic Peril

In January of 2024, the national debt level of the United States reached $34 trillion, and by the end of month it stood at an astounding $34.1 trillion. The US is adding one trillion dollars to its debt every one hundred days. Its Congress and president are rapidly spending the country into oblivion.

The current trend of rising red ink is not only unsustainable, but signifies that the black horse of economic peril (Revelation 6:5–6) will soon ride across America as well as the entire world. The rapidly increasing debt level in America will bring economic catastrophe; there's no other possible outcome for what's already happened.

The Lord's restraining hand is the only reason America hasn't yet experienced the worst level of inflation in its history. Twelve years ago, economic experts predicted imminent doom for the American economy. Their reasoning was entirely sound, but the patience of the Lord has allowed more time for people to come to faith in Him and thus escape the wrath of the rapidly approaching Day of the Lord.

The Pale Horse

A radio interviewer once asked if I thought the riders of the Apocalypse were already active in our world. I replied with a firm "no." First, the Bible tells us that the Rapture will happen before the Lord Jesus releases the seal judgments as recorded in Revelation 6. Second, although there's violence, pestilence, and a substantial number of deaths occurring in our world, the totals fall far short of the horrific conditions described in connection with the hoof beats of the pale horse.

Revelation 6:7–8 says "over a fourth of the earth" will perish as the result of Jesus opening the seals. Even considering the disappearance of people at Jesus' appearing, that's still a vast number: it will exceed one and a half billion people. The total death toll that resulted from World War II, which some place as high as seventy-five million, is horrific, of course, but it pales in comparison to what's ahead.

4. Digital Currency

Another sign that shouts to us the nearness of the Tribulation is the push for digital currencies.

During the September 2023 meeting of the G20 nations in New Delhi, India, the leaders "agreed to a plan to eventually impose digital currencies and digital IDs on their respective populations, amid concern that governments might use them to monitor their people's spending and crush dissent." This pact includes a pledge "to build the necessary infrastructure to implement digital currencies and IDs."[57]

Antichrist needs such a system in place by the midpoint of the Tribulation in order to control buying and selling throughout the world (Revelation 13:16–18). He won't be able to do this if it's possible for people to use cash or write checks for their purchases.

In America, the Central Bank Digital Currency (CBDC) is coming by way of the Federal Reserve's FedNow, which went live in 2023. Many major banks are now participating in the program, which enables the immediate transferring of money.

David Bowen, in his article, "FedNow Goes Live, Paving the Way to a Central Bank Digital Currency" on the Harbingers Daily website, wrote the following:

> The Federal Reserve claims this is the alternative to a CBDC—a Central Bank Digital Currency. But really, what this is a steppingstone to a CBDC. Once the public gets more comfortable with the speed of FedNow and the system is accepted as the standard procedure, you'll get a Central Bank Digital Currency.[58]

The inevitable collapse of the economy in the US will speed up the path to a CBDC in America, which will quickly become a unified worldwide currency during the Tribulation (if not before it even starts).

5. Mark-of-the-Beast Technology

Prior to the technical advancements of the past fifteen years, Antichrist would have needed an exceedingly large army in every nation on earth to enforce the requirement of his mark for all buying and selling as Revelation 13:16–18 says will happen in the middle of the seven-year Tribulation. Before this century, it would have been impossible for one person to exert such control over global commerce.

However, with today's artificial intelligence (AI), gigantic databases, and the 5G network, technology exists for one person to set the parameters and thus control commerce everywhere in the world. These innovations make the fulfillment of Revelation 13:16–18 not only possible, but increasingly likely when considering the agenda of the globalists!

By the midpoint of the Tribulation, Antichrist will be able to "flip the switch" and begin his murderous control of all buying and selling on the planet. This was impossible during prior times of distress and wickedness.

6. UFOs and Aliens

This may seem like an unusual sign of the end times; however, the wide acceptance of extraterrestrial life, along with many governments acknowledging their existence, demonstrates the increased activity of Satan as he seeks ways to explain our sudden disappearance via the Rapture.

I recently heard a short clip on X (previously Twitter) of an interview with Yuval Noah Harari, a bestselling author and confidant of World Economic Forum (WEF) founder Klaus Schwab. Harari confirmed the acceptance of alien life among the elite of our day—or, more likely, their willingness to perpetuate the deception. Harari also predicted the end of human-dominated history because of an upcoming alien invasion. "History will continue with somebody else in control," he said.

This set off alarm bells for several reasons. I've listened to many of Harari's interviews and read many things he has written in which he has pointed to AI and transhumanism as the future of the human race. Why is he now saying extraterrestrials will dictate humankind's future?

Doesn't Harari's apparent change in thinking show just how far the luciferian globalists are willing to go in preparing the world for our disappearance?

Did you also notice that Harari naturally assumes the aliens are far more advanced than humans in both intelligence and technology?

They must foster such an illusion of superiority for people to believe alien lifeforms are capable of making tens of millions instantly disappear from all over the world.

7. The Seven-Year Commitment

On September 18–19, 2023, a majority of member nations at the UN committed to a seven-year plan of accelerated growth to implement the 17 Strategic Development Goals (SDGs) of the 2030 Agenda for Sustainable Development. Although it is significant, let me quickly point out that this is NOT the covenant Antichrist will make with Israel as prophesied in Daniel 9:27.

What this demonstrates is the determination of the world's leaders to set up a one-world government that controls the lives of those it will enslave. It's abundantly clear that both the WEF and UN long for this totalitarian regime and want it in place by 2030.

It also tells us things are going as well as the globalists would like. Although they achieved some progress through the COVID-19 scare and are seeking to make climate change a factor in bringing the nations together, things are not progressing as well as they had hoped.

On the fifth page of the document, we're told there is an "urgent need to take the actions necessary to reverse declines and accelerate progress to achieve the 2030 Agenda and implement the SDGs."[59]

Author and friend Terry James addressed this shortfall in his excellent article, "The Crisis." He credits the Lord's resistance with stalling the elites' objectives to achieve their desired dominance and thus their panicked recommitment to the Marxists' goals embodied in Agenda 2030.

The disappearance of so many people will give globalists the emergency they crave. In the interview referenced earlier, Harari stated a united world would have a much better chance of resisting an extraterrestrial invasion. The globalists seek to create a common enemy by which they can unite the world under their totalitarian regime.

There's a sense of urgency in the statements coming from the UN. Is it because they're falling behind with their goals? Or do they know a great crisis, the Rapture, looms in the future, for which they need to prepare?

Many prophecies in Scripture point to the existence of a world government during the last days leading up to Jesus' Second Coming. The clamor of world leaders to put this plan in place by the year 2030 should set off alarms within us. Today is most certainly unlike any other time in the past several centuries, and it's not even close.

8. Scoffing

One of my favorite Peanuts cartoons pictures a troubled Charlie Brown seeking Lucy's five-cent psychiatric help. After Lucy provides several cautions about worrying, she says, "If you have to worry, you should worry about this very moment."

In response, a puzzled Charlie Brown asks, "This moment? Why this moment?" It's then that a soccer ball comes flying through the air, bonks him in the head, and sends him flying to the ground.

Lucy then explains her diagnosis: "I saw this ball heading this way, see, and...."

In his second letter, the Apostle Peter warns us about people in the last days who, unlike Lucy, will fail to accurately diagnose the *moment* in which they live. They will see the same signs of the approaching Tribulation that we see, but interpret them far differently, reject our diagnosis of them, and ridicule our hope.

> Knowing this first of all, that scoffers will come in the last days with scoffing, following their own sinful desires. They will say, "Where is the promise of his coming?" (2 Peter 3:3–4a)

The apostle's words accurately describe our day. The Rapture has become the object of scorn in many churches, even in places that once taught it as a core belief. And, of course, those outside of Christ give us much grief regarding our hope in Jesus' imminent appearing, but we expect that from those who don't believe the Bible.

What's behind the scoffing of our day? As the apostle explains, it stems from a wrong interpretation of the day in which we live. Those who mock our hope fail to recognize the imminent danger of a world in the shadow of the Tribulation.

These scoffers fulfill Bible prophecy regarding the last days, thus providing an additional witness to the fact that our world is rapidly running out of normal.

9. The Epidemic of Deception

As the spirit of Antichrist grows stronger in our world every day, it helps to remember what Jesus said about the one behind it: the devil himself.

In John 8:44, Jesus characterized Satan as "a murderer from the beginning" and "a liar and the father of lies." Our headlines bear witness to the truth of Jesus' words. The killing of innocents goes hand in hand with deceitfulness.

After the disciples asked Jesus about the signs of the end of the age and of His coming, the first words He spoke were: "Take heed that no man deceive you" (Matthew 24:4). A little later in the same discourse, the Lord described the great deception that will happen during the Tribulation period (Matthew 24:24):

> For there shall arise false Christs, and false prophets, and shall shew great signs and wonders; insomuch that, if it were possible, they shall deceive the very elect.

The Apostle Paul, when he began to speak of the appearance of Antichrist in the last days, echoed the words of Jesus in 2 Thessalonians 2:3: "Let no one deceive you in any way." A little later in the same chapter, He wrote this about the coming "man of lawlessness":

> The coming of the lawless one is by the activity of Satan with all power and false signs and wonders, and with all wicked

deception for those who are perishing, because they refused to love the truth and so be saved. (2:9–10).

Scripture is remarkably clear about the increase in deception during the last days. The time leading up to the Tribulation, as well as the period itself, will include overwhelming and widespread deceit. As we look around, we see that this deceit has reached epidemic levels, signifying that we live in the shadow of the coming Tribulation. More than that, it suggests the world has already run out of normal.

In my post, "Deadly Delusions: 5 Lies the Globalists Want You to Believe," I demonstrate that while the globalists claim they want "democracy and freedom," their goal is a Marxist-Communist state that will enslave the people of the world under the worst bondage ever experienced.

10. Days of Lot and Noah

The Lord predicted the end times would resemble the days of Noah (Matthew 24:36–39) and of Lot (Luke 17:28–29), and that's precisely what we see today.

The Bible doesn't provide us with details of the violence in Noah's day, which was a key factor that led to the worldwide Flood (Genesis 6:13). However, I believe the abortions, sex trafficking, and sacrificing of young children in satanic rituals in the US rival the violence prevalent in the world before the Flood.

Not only that, but the wickedness of our day also at least equals and likely exceeds that found in Sodom and Gomorrah. Didn't Jesus say the days just before His return would resemble the days of Lot? This alone argues for the lateness of the hour leading up to the judgments of the Day of the Lord.

Terry James also wrote a book depicting our nearness to the days of Lot and hence the time of the Rapture before the Tribulation period. Referring to what's happening now in America, he wrote the following in *Nearing Midnight*:

Yes, at the present, there is a movement in wickedness that rivals that in ancient Sodom. With all the evil taking place, while it's business as usual on the surface of society and culture, the finger of guilt must, like when Daniel read the handwriting on the wall before the drunken group of Babylonians (see Daniel chapter 5), even now indicating the nation has been weighed in the balance and found wanting.[60]

There's coming a day when all of us who trust Jesus as Savior will instantly vanish, and not long after that, all of God's current restraints will evaporate and sudden destruction will fall upon the earth (1 Thessalonians 5:1–10).

How much longer can it be before we appear in Glory with our Savior (Colossians 3:4)? I believe it's remarkably close. I'm surprised it hasn't already happened.

The Handwriting on the Wall

Just as with King Belshazzar of Babylon, the handwriting is indeed on the wall (see Daniel chapter 5). The end may not arrive as swiftly as it did for that ancient king (the Medes and Persians were already on their way to kill him when Daniel interpreted God's message).

The signs we see reveal that God's judgment will soon fall. After the Rapture of the church, God's wrath will devastate the world.

When Jesus returns and reigns over the earth from Jerusalem, we will experience life in a glorious kingdom as we reign with Him for a thousand years. This will be a "new normal" worth celebrating, but the future is even brighter and more joyous! Revelation 21–22 describes the most blissful set of circumstances imaginable. *This new normal will last forever. Wow!*

Refuse to be satisfied with the fake "new normal" the world offers. Once we meet Jesus in the air and return to Glory with Him, what we experience after that will make even our very best days in this life seem mundane and boring.

SECTION II

COMPREHENDING ACCUMULATING CALAMITIES

Chapter 4

ENDURING EVIL TIMES

By Mike Gendron

General Editor's note: Mike Gendron powerfully presents the gospel message while pointing to these times in which God's truth is attacked and dismissed at every level of human interaction. His is a spiritually attuned voice that made his invitation to write for *Tracking Toward Tribulation* one that was essential, not merely a request to add content.

Mike's deep insight into these troubled times through his ministry, proclaiming the Gospel, and preaching throughout the world in seminaries, churches, and conferences is a vital part of Heaven's outreach in these days so near the Tribulation era.

Christians face increasing persecution and opposition, not in just foreign lands where martyrdom is the norm, but in America, where hatred for all mention of Jesus Christ in the national discourse is on the rise. Mike addresses what God's Word has to say about cutting through the evil in order to serve as royal ambassadors for the King of all kings.

✦✦✦

We are living in a world where truth is being twisted, manipulated, and suppressed by hypocritical politicians, government agencies, religious leaders, corrupt scientists, and the liberal media. Our debased culture is redefining truth and reality. No one knows who to trust or how to avoid being misled or deceived. The only way we can be victorious is to fight the good fight of faith against worldly ideologies. We can never let a lie of the devil go unabated, and we must be discerning. This means we must examine everything and hold onto what is good (1 Thessalonians 5:21).

What Is Discernment?

Discernment distinguishes truth from error to prevent false teaching from infiltrating the Church. The Hebrew word *bin* and the Greek word *diakrino* are used hundreds of times in Scripture to make distinctions, to separate things at their points of difference. It calls for black-and-white thinking and a refusal to color issues gray. Those who apply discernment consistently in every area of life are sure to walk in the wisdom of our Lord (Proverbs 2:1–6).

Why Is Discernment Necessary?

Satan is the god of this world and the father of lies (John 8:44). We need to be aware of his schemes to deceive, corrupt, falsify, blind, destroy, devour, and kill. We need to discern good from evil and expose those who call evil "good" and good "evil." The Apostle John exhorted Christians to make judgments concerning doctrinal and spiritual issues:

> Beloved, do not believe every spirit, but test the spirits to see whether they are from God; because many false prophets have gone out into the world. (1 John 4:1)

All Christians are called to judge righteously by using the Word of God as the plumb line for discerning truth from error. And judge we must, because the father of lies deals in half-truths, and his fatal lies are often coated with a thin veneer of truth to deceive the unsuspecting.

Christians need discernment to know and prove the will of God so we will not be conformed to this world (Romans 12:2). We also need to test the veracity of every teaching (Acts 17:11). Without discernment, we could not identify the counterfeits from the genuine. Paul warned:

Satan disguises himself as an angel of light. Therefore, it is not surprising if his servants also disguise themselves as servants of righteousness. (2 Corinthians 11:13–15)

We need discernment to avoid being "tossed to and fro by every wind of doctrine by the trickery of people, by craftiness in deceitful scheming" (Ephesians 4:14).

Why Do We Need to Discern the True Gospel?

We live in a deceptive age, one that doesn't deny the gospel, but distorts and dilutes it! This is the strategy of Satan. His legions of liars use religious language to hide the deadly poison in his false and fatal gospels. Over a billion professing Christians have been woefully deceived by his gospel of works and religious rituals. That is why Paul exhorts us to "examine ourselves to see if we are in the faith" (2 Corinthians 13:5). Have we repented and believed the true gospel?

God's eternal Son left the glories of Heaven to be conceived by the Holy Spirit in the womb of a virgin to take on human flesh. He lived in perfect obedience to God's Law, then was crucified as the perfect sacrifice to satisfy divine justice for sinners. He bore humanity's sins, suffered God's wrath, died in our place, was buried, and was raised on the third day to show that divine justice was satisfied. This is the gospel that has divine power to save those who believe (Romans 1:16). It is the gospel that promises eternal life, without any fear of condemnation, because of the perpetual intercession and protection of the Good Shepherd (Hebrews 7:25; John 10:28; Romans 8:1).

Discerning the Times

Clearly, we are in the last days, when many "will not endure sound doctrine; but wanting to have their ears tickled, they will accumulate for themselves teachers in accordance to their own desires, and will turn away their ears from the truth and will turn aside to myths" (2 Timothy 4:3–4).

Too many Christians are following deceitful personalities rather than the Word of God. As truth-bearers, we must "reprove, rebuke, and exhort" those who are being deceived by using God's inspired Word as our supreme authority (2 Timothy 4:2). We may be labeled as "intolerant," "divisive," or "unloving," but there is much at stake if we are not passionate for the truth—the glory and honor of our Savior, the sanctity of His Church, and the purity of His gospel.

Our world will continue its opposition to God because of the forces of wickedness in heavenly places. We must remember that nations and cultures will come and go, but the souls of people will last throughout eternity. That's why the battle for eternal souls is the one war that really matters. It is a battle between the truth of God's Word and the damning lies of Satan. As ambassadors for our Lord Jesus Christ, we have the privilege to proclaim His gospel to an unbelieving world. It's not only a royal privilege, but an awesome responsibility, because those who are perishing need to hear the gospel of Christ (Romans 10:17). Clearly, the most difficult people to evangelize are those who are defiantly opposed to the gospel because of religious bondage and deception.

Self-Conceit Leads to Self-Deceit

As prince of this world, Satan holds undiscerning people captive with religious pride and deceitful indoctrination. When we witness to them, their stubborn arrogance exposes their willful ignorance of God's Word. Their stiff-necked self-conceit leads to their unyielding self-deceit. Whenever prideful people are confronted in their self-deceit, they dig in their heels to prove they're right. A frequent example of this is when Roman Catholics are asked to repent and believe the gospel. A common response is, "I was born a Catholic and I will die a Catholic." My reply is always the same. According to the Bible, you were born a sinner and you will die a sinner unless you repent and believe the gospel.

Religious Arrogance Blinds People

One of the most powerful tools Satan uses to "blind the minds of the unbelieving so that they might not see the light of the gospel of the glory of Christ" is religious pride and arrogance (2 Corinthians 4:4). We see a vivid example of this when "Stephen, full of grace and power, was performing great wonders and signs among the people" (Acts 6:8). Some arrogant Jews rose up and argued with him because they were unable to cope with the wisdom and Spirit he was speaking with. Stephen responded:

> You men who are stiff-necked and uncircumcised in heart and ears are always resisting the Holy Spirit; you are doing just as your fathers did. (Acts 7:51)

Because of their religious arrogance, they were brutally resistant to the truth, and with gnashing teeth, they stoned Stephen to death.

Deceitful Indoctrination Creates Pride

Some have said the Roman Catholic Church is an extension of apostate Judaism, with its altars and showbread, incense and priesthood, observing the law for salvation, and a fierce loyalty and devotion to their religion. Many Catholics are deceived into believing they belong to the one true Church. This deceitful indoctrination creates a lot of pride and a strong resistance to any teaching from non-Catholics. If Catholics were intellectually honest, they would have to acknowledge that their Church looks nothing like the first-century Church. That's because it drifted into apostasy by departing from the faith of the apostles. Paul warned that "in later times some will fall away from the faith, paying attention to deceitful spirits and doctrines of demons" (1 Timothy 4:1). Catholics need to be warned that any teaching contrary to the written Word of God is either a lie of the devil or a doctrine of demons. Every person's teaching must be tested by the supreme authority of Scripture (2 Timothy 3:16; Acts 17:11).

Catholic Responses to the Gospel

Our Proclaiming the Gospel ministry has been engaging Catholics with the gospel for thirty-three years, and we've heard some incredible responses, including the following:

- "I could no more renounce my Catholic faith than I could gouge out my eyes! What type of people are you? You have no idea what Christ teaches! I am a proud Catholic who is also proud to say that I respect all religions that seek peace in love. I am offended by your insults! They will lead to everlasting torment!"

- "You are so misinformed it is pathetic. I have the authority of Christ's Church. Protestant sects have nothing. I know the Church back to front, and I have loved the Catholic Church since I was born."

- "There is nothing in the teachings of the Catholic Church opposed to Sacred Scripture. I will ask Mary, the Queen of the Universe, to pray for you. I will offer up your soul to Her Immaculate Heart that she may present it, perfect and blameless, before God. Your ministry is inspired by Satan. The main function of the pope is to ensure that nothing is added or deleted from the Bible. The Catholic Church is the only Church that takes the Bible seriously."

God's Grace Greater Than Humans' Defiance

No matter how defiantly people respond to the gospel, we know stubborn hearts are no match for the penetrating power of God's grace. The Apostle Paul was a zealous persecutor of Christians before our Sovereign Lord knocked him off his high horse and granted him repentance. One of the thieves mocking Jesus on the cross had lived a life of sinful rebellion, but in his last hour, God granted him repentance and faith in the Savior (Luke 23:39–43). These two examples of the saving power of God's grace should encourage us to never give up hope for our friends and loved ones. Knowing God is opposed to the proud but gives grace to the humble, let us pray they will exchange their pride for humility and submit to God's Word (James 4:6). Let's also pray they will come under strong conviction by the Holy Spirit of sin, judgment, and righteousness (John 16:8–11). May God be exalted and honored as He answers our prayers for His glory and the salvation of perishing souls!

This Life Is Short, but Eternity Is Forever

As we continue tracking toward the Tribulation, we must remember our life on this earth is fleeting and temporary compared to the endless ages of eternity. Tragically, very few consider their lives with an eternal perspective. Instead, many foolishly pursue lives of pleasure, prestige, and power with little regard for what awaits them after death. The Lord Jesus Christ addressed this folly when He said, "What will it profit a man if he gains the whole world and forfeits his soul? Or what shall a man give in return for his soul?" (Matthew 16:26). Why are so many people living for the temporary and so few are preparing for eternity?

Preparing for Eternity Is Vital

God doesn't promise anyone tomorrow. Many have found this out when they met tragic, unexpected deaths at the office, a shopping mall, or a church. The certainty of death is unavoidable, but it shouldn't be our greatest concern. More sobering is what follows death. God's Word warns us: "It is appointed for men to die once and after this comes judgment" (Hebrews 9:27). Our appointment with death comes with an unavoidable judgment. Those whose sins were judged and forgiven at the cross of Christ will experience everlasting joy in Heaven, while those who die unforgiven will experience the eternal fires of Hell. This is why preparing for eternity is most important. We can be wrong about a lot of things and still survive, but if we are wrong about eternity, we will pay for that mistake forever and ever! For this reason,

Proclaiming the Gospel publishes and distributes what has become our most popular tract. It asks this most important question: "Where will you spend eternity?"

Christ: Our Only Hope in Life and Death

All humans have a serious problem that cannot be dismissed: We've all sinned against our God and Creator, who cannot let the guilty go unpunished (Romans 3:23; Exodus 34:7). He is majestic in holiness, and righteousness and justice are the foundation of His throne (Exodus 15:11; Psalm 97:2). He is also a God of love and mercy, and did not leave us in our hopeless and helpless condition. In His infinite wisdom, God devised the one and only Way He could save sinners while upholding His holiness, righteousness, and justice. As a demonstration of His love, He sent His Only Son to die as a substitute for sinners (Romans 5:8). Jesus was crucified as the perfect sacrifice to satisfy divine justice. He bore humanity's sins, suffered God's wrath, died in our place, and was raised on the third day to show that divine justice was satisfied. God "made Him who knew no sin to be sin on our behalf, so that we might become the righteousness of God in Him" (2 Corinthians 5:21). Christ "died for sins once for all, the just for the unjust, so that He might bring us to God" (1 Peter 3:18). For this reason, everyone who has trusted Christ alone as their sinless substitute looks to their physical death as a passage into His glorious presence (1 Corinthians 15:55–57).

Terrifying News for the Unforgiven

Those who have rejected the Lord Jesus Christ and His gospel will pay the penalty of eternal destruction, away from the presence of the Lord and from the glory of His power (2 Thessalonians 1:9). Hell is a real place of fiery torment where unforgiven sinners undergo the punishment they deserve for their sins. This eternal punishment is called the second death, where divine justice is meted out forever in the lake of fire (Revelation 20:15). Unrepentant sinners consciously suffer pain and thirst from an unquenchable fire, and the horror is so great they want to warn their loved ones on earth, but cannot (Luke 16:19–31; Mark 9:43). There is weeping and gnashing of teeth because the eternal state of God's just punishment is irreversible; there is no second chance, no escape, no hope, no rest, and no relief (Luke 13:28; 2 Thessalonians 1:8–9).

Only Two Things Are Eternal

Soon after I finished seminary, God's Word impressed upon me a compelling truth that gave me a new purpose for living. I realized only two things in this life are eternal: the souls of people and the Word of God. Everything else will be burned up by fire (2 Peter 3:10–12).

By God's grace, I wanted to spend my remaining years focused on the two things that will last throughout eternity. May God help us all to keep this eternal perspective firmly planted in our hearts. Soon this life will be over, and only what is done for Christ will last. May God "teach us to number our days" (Psalm 90:12). Let us be mindful of the shortness of time, the nearness of death, and the pending doom of lost sinners.

Living with an Eternal Perspective

No one knows what tomorrow will bring. Now is the day of salvation (2 Corinthians 6:2). Our life is but a vapor that appears for a little time and then vanishes (James 4:14). Living with an eternal perspective will motivate Christians to faithfully share the gospel of Christ with those who are on the broad road to destruction. One day we will all stand before our Creator, and He will either be a sin-avenging judge or a merciful Savior. Therefore, the most important question we all must consider is this: "Am I ready to meet my Creator?"

Chapter 5

SPEAKING TRUTH TO LAST DAYS

By Dr. Nathan E. Jones

General Editor's Note: Nathan Jones, a long-time personal friend as well as colleague in God's work, serves as the Internet evangelist for Lamb & Lion Ministries and cohost of the ministry's television program, *Christ in Prophecy*, and podcast, *The Truth Will Set You Free*.

His dynamic labor in the great cause of bringing souls to Jesus Christ makes his contribution to this volume a critical part of providing understanding for today's troubling but exciting times.

With most pulpits now sadly void of prophecy teaching and preaching, it is crucial that Christians be given the truth as the time of the Tribulation approaches. Nathan's clear and powerful presentation here on God's forewarnings about these current times helps fulfill the great prophet Daniel's Holy Spirit-inspired words: "The wise shall understand."

+++

The prophet Daniel had been listening intently to the angel Gabriel pronouncing a series of mind-blowing messages. God was revealing the rise and fall of great empires, leading eventually to a global realm led by a despot whom the Apostle John would later call Antichrist, with its inevitable demise at the divine hand of God.

Of course, all these great empires were still so far off in the future from Daniel's perspective that he was obviously perplexed by what

Not only has the exponential curve in all areas of computer technology increased our knowledge to stupendous levels, but computers have aided in all the major scientific discoveries of our day. We don't need to cram so many facts into our brains anymore, either, for the ability to easily store and access data means we can continue to learn like we've never learned before in human history.

The exponential curve isn't limited to computers. Other advances in biomedicine, space science, chemical engineering, human engineering, and all the other sciences have been climbing faster and steeper up their exponential curves with every passing day. It's expected that in the next five years, the world's technology will be thirty-two times more advanced than it is today. It's also been estimated that 65 percent of today's kindergarteners, once they finally graduate from college, will ultimately work in completely new types of jobs that don't even yet exist.

Consider that just a hundred years ago, all the information most people learned throughout their entire lifetime equated to the content of one Sunday edition of the *New York Times*. Our ability today to consume practically that same amount of information daily shows just how far humankind's knowledge has increased in a very short amount of time.

Today's exponential increase in knowledge points to the fact that we're living in the prophesied end times, and that Jesus the Messiah is coming soon.

2. Increase in Transportation

Notice that in the same prophecy, the angel told Daniel that, besides a great increase in knowledge, "many shall run to and fro" (Daniel 12:4). This tremendous increase in the ability to travel and in the speed of travel would occur in the same context—the end times. God was revealing that once people begin to run to and fro, both farther and faster, those final years before Christ returns to set up His Millennial Kingdom will finally be upon us.

Think how people traveled just a single century ago. Most roads weren't even paved yet and were traveled by horse-drawn wagons. A YouTube video of San Francisco recorded back in 1906 reveals far more horses than horseless carriages. People rarely, if ever, left their home-towns. Animal domestication and the early beginnings of decent roads, then bicycles, balloons, boats, and simple automobiles were being developed, but they weren't yet widely received. Since the early part of the twentieth century, humankind went on to invent airplanes and jets, and we've even left Earth's atmosphere in rockets and space shuttles. It used to take months for people to travel overseas by boat, but now we traverse that same distance abroad in mere hours. In today's world, people are always on the move, just as the angel prophesied to Daniel.

Today's exponential increase in travel points to the fact that Jesus Christ is returning soon.

3. Increase in Understanding Prophecy

Did you know Bible prophecy constitutes a whopping 31 percent of the content of the Bible? God's overall plan for the ages appears to be rather like a one-hundred-piece puzzle, and so far, He has only pro-vided seventy-five pieces. One can make out the outline of a picture, but until certain events unfold, which then add other new pieces to the puzzle, the picture remains incomplete.

Still, the seventy-five pieces we have now are far more numerous than what Daniel ever had. As Jesus explained to His disciples, "For truly I say to you that many prophets and righteous men desired to see what you see, and did not see it, and to hear what you hear, and did not hear it" (Matthew 13:17). Even then, the Apostles didn't under-stand Christ's teachings until after the Resurrection, when He openly explained them and then later sent the Holy Spirit at Pentecost to pro-vide further illumination. Then again, the apostles were expecting the imminent return of Christ, not a two thousand year-long wait.

Today, the various end-times signs related to nature, society, world politics, technology, Israel, and the spiritual signs are coming at us at such a fantastic rate that Bible prophecy teachers such as Dr. Ron Rhodes have begun to call the phenomenon "The Convergence." So many end-times signs converging at once has greatly opened our understanding of end-times Bible prophecy, just as Gabriel foretold.

Today's exponential increase in the understanding of God's prophetic Word points to the fact that Jesus Christ is returning soon.

Recognize the Times

These three major signs, along with the hundreds more provided in the Bible, being fulfilled in our day, reveal the fact that the Lord could indeed return at any moment. By looking through the filter of the Bible at all these wondrous yet frightening events playing out before us, we better recognize the times in which we are living. As a result, we should be comforted knowing God's got it all under control, He has a great big plan in place, and His children play a vital role in that plan. Christians are called to serve God in these dark times with all our unique giftedness, resources, and experience.

For those who haven't yet accepted Jesus Christ as Savior, but now recognize that we are living in the end times, the realization should act like an alarm clock buzzing you awake to the fact that the world doesn't have much time left. We're all living on borrowed time. Therefore, embrace the fact that God loves the world so much that He gave His one and Only Son, and that whoever believes in Him will not perish, but will have eternal life (John 3:16).

The Mysterious Role of Islam in the End Times

A juggernaut marches across the planet. Fueled by the rage of its fanatical death-cult religious leaders, this seemingly unstoppable force tramples over all that stands before its missile-wielding might. The nations' defenses crumble as cringing UN leaders shakily bear the ineffectual white-flagged weapons of appeasement. This steamroller force, first forged in the blood of a massacre in the far-off Arabian town of Mecca some 1,400 years ago, has since grown exponentially to become the source of terror for billions of people today. This juggernaut's ominous name is Islam.

Islam, for all intents and purposes, appears poised to conquer the world. Its growth rate has risen by 500 percent over the last fifty years as its birth rate dwarfs that of Christians, Hindus, Buddhists, and Jews. Today's 1.5 billion Muslims make up 22 percent of the world's population and control sixty-five nations. Between the twin strategies of holy war (*jihad*) and immigration, Muslims are expected to exceed 50 percent of the world's population and surpass Christianity as the largest religion by the end of the twenty-first century.

The looming threat of Islamic world dominancy has left many students of Bible prophecy to wonder how Islam's role will play out in the end times. Islam's role is a mystery, though, for it was founded more than five hundred years after the Bible was completed, leaving this force unnamed in the biblical prophetic writings. Quite a number of theories have been advanced anyway, from an Islamic Antichrist to the Mystery Babylon one-world religion, but these can only be mere conjecture. Islam, then, has become one of the great end-time mysteries.

Significance to Prophecies Related to the Jews

While Islam might not be named in Bible prophecy, its role can be gauged by its actions that help lead to the fulfillment of well-defined Bible prophecies. Take the prolific prophecy concerning God's promise that the Jews would be regathered in the land of Israel (Isaiah 11:12; Micah 2:12).

It's no secret Muslims are taught from the cradle to the grave to hate the Jewish people. The impetus comes from the Hadith, one of Islam's two holy books along with the Koran. Islam's founder, Muhammad, left this order skewed by his own particular eschatological view for his followers:

The last hour would not come unless the Muslims will fight against the Jews and the Muslims would kill them until the

Jews would hide themselves behind a stone or a tree and a stone or a tree would say: "Muslim, or the servant of Allah, there is a Jew behind me; come and kill him." (*Hadith*, Sahih of al-Bukhari: Book 041, Number 6985)

As the nations of the world become more Islamic, Muslim persecution of the Jews increases at a rapid pace. The growing wave of anti-Semitism has forced Jewish people in increasing numbers to emigrate from their countries of residence to Israel in fulfillment of what God foretold.

Significance to Prophecies Related to the Tribulation

Jesus warned that a time will come when "there shall be great tribulation, such as has not been since the beginning of the world until this time, no, nor ever shall be" (Matthew 24:21). He, of course, was referring to the Tribulation, the seven-year period referred to by the Hebrew prophets as "the great and terrible day of the LORD" and "the time of Jacob's distress" (Jeremiah 30:7; Daniel 12:1; Joel 2:11, 31). It will be "the hour of trial which shall come upon the whole world, to test those who dwell on the earth" as God's wrath is poured out on the nations for their exceeding wickedness (Revelation 3:10).

Of the eight prophetic end-times wars related to the Tribulation, the first two, if not three, deal directly with lands currently controlled by Islam. Therefore, Islam must play a key role in these conflicts.

The Bible prophesies God will draw the nations encompassing Israel to their destruction. He will focus His wrath on these nations in a series of battles from the Psalm 83 war to the Gog-Magog war of Ezekiel 38–39 to the setting up of Antichrist's kingdom, which shockingly destroys 25 percent of the world's population (Revelation 6). The aftermath of these three wars can only result in the Islamic world having been annihilated at the onset of the Tribulation. God's wrath upon the Islamic world for their hatred of Israel—the "apple of His eye"—will be fulfilled (Zechariah 2:8).

Significance to Prophecies Related to Antichrist

The power vacuum that will be left due to the fall of Islam early in the Tribulation can only contribute to the rise of Antichrist. Islam will then have one final role to play. Monotheism, which Islam has clung so tightly to, will likely be remembered as a danger to world peace. To rid the world of such fundamentalism, the Antichrist will persecute all religions that hold absolute views. Christian and Judaist monotheism will then be perceived as a direct threat to world peace and the False Prophet's new, one-world religion. Other religions will more easily integrate quickly into that ecumenical faith. Those who don't surrender to the new world order will be heavily persecuted. Revelation vividly depicts this scenario as Tribulation believers bear first-hand the persecution for their absolute faith in Jesus Christ (Revelation 6:11; 7:9–15).

So, Islam may not have a named role in end-time Bible prophecy, but other prophecies peel back the mysterious shroud that is Islam in the end times.

Extreme Weather in Prophecy

According to Genesis 1, in the beginning, everything God made was perfect. Then sin entered, corrupting it all, so He placed a curse upon the world (Genesis 3). Humankind has long been waiting for the restoration of the Creation upon Christ's return, for then "the creation itself also will be delivered from the bondage of corruption into the glorious liberty of the children of God" (Romans 8:21).

In the meantime, we live in a world where nature has been thrown into great upheaval. Because of this, extreme weather often occurs due to our out-of-kilter weather system.

At times, God uses extreme weather to underline the importance of major events. For example, we read that Mount Sinai, where God gave Moses the Ten Commandments, was covered in "thunderings and lightnings and a thick cloud" (Exodus 19:16–18). When Christ was crucified, three hours of darkness blotted out the daylight, and

Jerusalem experienced a great earthquake (Matthew 27:45, 51). God has continued to use extreme weather to punctuate significant events throughout history.

Extreme weather also works as remedial judgment for God's purpose of calling wicked nations to repentance. For example, Moses warned the Israelites that if they became exceedingly wicked, weather-related curses would "pursue and overtake you until you are destroyed because you did not obey the voice of the Lord your God" (Deuteronomy 28:18–30,45–46). Sure enough, every time the Israelites became steeped in sin, God would inflict them with extreme weather until they repented.

Likewise, when the prophet Elijah called King Ahab and Israel to repent, Ahab flat-out refused, so God sent a drought that withered the crops for more than three long years (1 Kings 17–18).

Another time, when Israel had become lethargic in their relationship with their Heavenly Father, God cursed the land with a great locust swarm that quickly consumed all of the nation's crops. As God had desired, the Israelites repented (Joel 1–3).

Also, after the Jews had returned from captivity in Babylon and were tasked with rebuilding the Temple, they only got as far as the foundation before they gave up. In response, God decimated their crops with root rot and mildew, and sent furious hailstorms to cut down the remaining plants. Again, as God had desired, the people repented and right away returned to working on the Temple's reconstruction (Haggai 1–2).

How do we know the difference between a natural disaster caused by a fallen world and God's use of nature as a remedial judgment? We must consider three points:

1. The timing of the event as it relates to the sins of the nation
2. The magnitude of the event
3. The prophet's declaration; the prophet speaking for God would say plainly, "I am doing this to get you to repent."

Weather Pointing to Christ's Return

Some may be thinking, "That's the Old Testament! Aren't we living in the Age of Grace? God doesn't use the sign of nature anymore, right?" Well, not according to Jesus Christ.

In His Olivet Discourse, Jesus provided ten signs that would point to His soon return. He added they would increase in frequency and intensity—like the birth pangs of a woman in labor—the closer we got to His return (Matthew 24:8). Some of these signs would involve "fearful sights and great signs from heaven" (Luke 21:11). Likewise, "there will be signs in the sun, in the moon, and in the stars; and on the earth distress of nations...for the powers of the heavens will be shaken" (Luke 21:25–26).

Once these signs become cataclysmically violent, "then they will see the Son of Man coming in a cloud with power and great glory" (Luke 21:27–28).

The Apostle Paul confirmed that Christians are meant to be able to discern the signs that point to Jesus' soon return so we won't be taken unaware (1 Thessalonians 5:1–5).

Today's Extreme Weather

What's happening around the world today? All sorts of weather calamities: out-of-control hurricanes, record numbers of tornadoes, devastating floods, and destructive forest fires. These storms are occurring more and more frequently and are causing greater and greater damage with every passing year. Most recognize that nature seems to have gotten out of hand—and is getting even worse.

Natural News released an article by David Gutierrez titled "Natural Disasters Up More Than 400 Percent in Two Decades." The article notes:

> Natural disasters are increasing in frequency, ravaging the world, our countries, and even our own homes. ...The number of natural disasters around the world has increased by more than four times in the last 20 years.

Approximately 500 natural disasters per year ravage the world, compared to 120 per year back in the early 1980s.

A report by The Weather Channel's Jan Wesner Childs, titled "Nine Billion-Dollar Weather Disasters So Far in 2022," cited The National Oceanic and Atmospheric Administration's (NOAA's) report about how the previous two years had seen record billion-dollar disasters, due largely to mega-droughts plus devastating wildfire and hyper-hurricane seasons. Earlier years were also active. From 1980 to 2017, there was an average of $7.7 billion-dollar weather disasters per year. But, in just the past five years, that number has gone up to $17.8 billion!

Besides severe weather, earthquakes have plagued the world with increasing destruction over the past decade. An NBC News article, "Worldwide Surge in 'Great' Earthquakes Seen in Past 10 Years," reports that the annual number of "great" earthquakes has nearly tripled over the last decade, "providing a reminder to Americans that unruptured faults like those in the northwest United States might be due for a Big One." The article notes that between 2004 and 2014, eighteen earthquakes with a magnitude of 8.0 or more rattled subduction zones around the globe. "That's an increase of 265 percent over the average rate of the previous century, which saw 71 great quakes." Normally there are only sixteen major earthquakes (M 7.0–8.0+) worldwide per year. In addition, an average of 142 strong earthquakes (M 6.0–7.0) have occurred worldwide annually.

The summer of 2022 continued to see the ongoing collapse of the Australian Reef. In recent years, Australia has suffered severe drought, historic bush fires, successive years of record-breaking floods, and six mass bleaching events of the Great Barrier Reef.

The tech and trends website Gizmodo reports on what's being called "America's Mega-Drought." The western and southwestern US is wilting under the biggest drought in 1,200 years. As the Great Salt Lake dries up, Utah faces what some are calling an "environmental nuclear bomb." Long-sunken history and even evidence of past crimes are emerging from the receding waters.

The World Gets It Wrong

What's telling is how politicians and scientists have been interpreting this extreme natural-weather phenomenon as the result of "man-made global warming." Germany's former Chancellor Angela Merkel warned:

> We have to get faster in the fight against climate change. Global leaders also have to come to the same conclusion after the UN delivered a code red for humanity.

And, as one report states, "Scientists long warned that climate change would contribute to an increase in both the frequency and the severity of freak weather." How interesting that the article notes an increase in "frequency" and "severity." Sounds rather biblical!

So, the world is interpreting these natural disasters, which they recognize are increasing in frequency and intensity, as the result of humankind's pollution problems. But, Christians know better. We know God alone—not humankind—is in control of the weather.

Remember that God doesn't want anyone to perish, but He wants all to repent (2 Peter 3:9). Therefore, He always sends a warning before He executes wrath. And, for thousands of years, God has chosen climatic and catastrophic weather to get our attention. Why? Because He controls the weather.

At least forty-seven verses in the Bible declare that God is in control of the weather, including the following:

- "What kind of man is this that even the winds and the sea obey Him?" (Matthew 8:26–27).
- "Fire and hail, snow and clouds, stormy wind, fulfilling His word" (Psalm 148:8).
- "He did not leave Himself without witness, that He did good and gave you rains from heaven, and fruitful seasons" (Acts 14:17).

- "I saw four angels standing at the four corners of the earth, holding the four winds of the earth, that the wind should not blow on the earth, on the sea, or in any tree" (Revelation 7:1).

So, again and again, at least forty-seven times, Scripture confirms that God is in control of the weather. He is sovereign, and nothing happens that He doesn't allow, either in His perfect or permissive will.

Yes, freak weather might be contributed to humankind's neglectful or destructive tendencies, but, again, it is God who controls the weather. We can take into account, of course, that certain natural disasters occur because the weather is off-track due to the curse on the world. But, God still utilizes freak weather to try to wake people up to their sins and show their need for a Savior.

He uses these end-times signs such as climatic weather to wake us up, calling the world to come back to Him. God is warning us that He's upset with our sins. Our Holy God is deeply bothered by all of humanity's evil. He's been crying out: "I love you! Repent and come back to me!"

Tribulation Judgments

The ultimate climax to all of these weather signs will be the period of judgment called the Tribulation. The Lord will rescue and take His Church out of the world before His true wrath comes upon it. Leading up to that time, God will increase the signs of nature, just as we're witnessing today, along with social, political, technological, economic, and other end-times signals. These disasters will increase in frequency and intensity leading up to the Rapture of the Church, then the world will plunge headlong into God's wrath for the seven years of the Tribulation.

As bad as the weather has gotten today, nothing compares to the disasters foretold in the book of Revelation. In reading that book, we marvel at how God's weather-related judgments will devastate the world, for He will be pouring out His wrath on its corrupt people during the most horrific era the world will have ever endured (Matthew 24:21).

The Expected Response

How does God want us to respond to these end-times signs, particularly the sign of nature as it relates to extreme weather?

First, we need to repent individually for our rebellion and selfishness. God is calling each of us to repent. We should respond in faith by surrendering to the Lord Jesus and then reading the Bible so we can be discerning.

Second, we need to repent as a nation for attempting to remove God from our society, for our idolatrous self-worship, for our sixty-three million murders in the womb, for our obsession with sexual promiscuity, for our fascination with the occult, and for our lack of support of Israel's right to exist, among a plethora of other sins. Every nation needs to practice "in God we trust," for that is the only way the nations will receive God's mercy.

Once King Jesus has at last returned, the curse on this earth will be lifted, and natural disasters will cease. Until that glorious day, we can live by this hope:

> The night is far spent, the day is at hand. Therefore, let us cast
> off the works of darkness, and let us put on the armor of light.
> (Romans 13:12–14)

Technology: Double-Edged Sword

Our society faces an existential crisis of epic proportions. And I'm not talking about rocket-high inflation, DC swamp corruption, discordant political division, or even threatening environmental concerns. While these crises all hold their rightful place in the pantheon of hazards, what we're truly confronting is the seismic collapse of the biblical worldview here in the West.

What's been the poison arrow to the Achilles' heel of our society? Humanism is the poison, technology is the arrow, and our Achilles' heel is the hearts and minds of our newest generation. We now reside in an age almost completely devoid of the fundamental teachings of the Bible and the biblical worldview, and we are reaping the whirlwind for it. Just watch the societal chaos raging across news feeds, and you'll most certainly agree.

One Side of the Sword

You may be thinking, "The humanism I can understand, but I'm not quite following you about the technology. Maybe you have some kind of grudge against technology?"

No, I assure you, I don't hate technology. Quite the contrary, I love it! After all, isn't technology just a matter of applying what we know to fix problems and make stuff? Technology can be thought of as the gadgets and devices we make, but it also includes the technical skills and creativity it initially takes to invent and forge these tools.

I've dedicated the last twenty-five years of my life to utilizing different technologies to reach people with the gospel of Jesus Christ. The communications abilities the Lord has provided His Church today have reached far more people for Jesus Christ than in any era before Itek's Richard Leghorn coined the term "The Information Age" back in 1960. Praise God!

The Other Side of the Sword

But—and you must realize this—though technology greatly benefits both individuals and society, in the wrong hands, it can produce great harm. The lord of all evil—Satan—knows this. He's been steadily following his sinister plan for thousands of years to be a corrupting influence on humanity, and it continues to this day. The only difference between then and now is that Satan utilizes technology in his insidious mission to send as many people to Hell as he can before he himself is at last cast into the lake of fire.

Satan's main use of technology is to create distraction. And, it has been working in spades. No other generation in the past has been subjected to as many distractions as the Millennials and Gen Zs of today. Gen Zs, in particular, have lived their entire lives never having known what life was like without being connected to the Internet 24/7. This characteristic has led Jean Twenge, a professor of psychology at San Diego State University, to label Millennials and Gen Zs as "Generation Me" and "iGen," respectively.[61] And reviewing two studies about classroom attention spans led columnist Victoria Barret to label the children of today as the "Distracted Generation."[62]

A great price has been paid psychologically for these endless distractions. Barret cites a Pew Research Center finding wherein nearly 90 percent of teachers surveyed said digital technologies were creating "an easily distracted generation with short attention spans."[63] In a Common Sense study, 71 percent of teachers surveyed said they thought technology was hurting attention spans somewhat or a lot, with 60 percent concluding that online distractions hindered their students' ability to write and communicate in person.[64]

Though ever-connected to their "friends" over social media, losing in-person human relationships has caused Gen Zs to find themselves increasingly homebound, jobless, dislocated, lonely, lethargic, physically weakened, depressed, and addicted to prescription pain killers. They are 35 percent more likely to commit suicide than previous less-technical generations. Twenge notes with some worry that "it's not an exaggeration to describe iGen as being on the brink of the worst mental-health crisis in decades."[65]

This abruptly negative shift in teen behaviors towards troubled emotional states is not solely a Western problem, either; it has become a global cultural phenomenon. Twenge identifies the extent of the problem:

> These changes have affected young people in every corner of the nation and in every type of household. The trends appear

among teens poor and rich; of every ethnic background; in cities, suburbs, and small towns.[66]

Technologies at Work

Computers are everywhere now. Smart devices are all the rage, and now people wear computers on their bodies in the form of smartphones and watches. Billions of people have scrambled to purchase electronic devices, filling their houses and their lives with portable technology. Statista reports that the average person owns 6.58 computer devices, adding up to nearly fifty billion devices operating worldwide.[67]

More than 4.54 billion of the 7.77 billion people in the world are connected by the Internet.[68] The average Internet user spends 6.5 hours online every day generating 88,555 gigabytes of Internet traffic every second![69] The average person will spend nearly four hours each day on their devices, dedicating 90 percent of that time engrossed in any of the five-plus million apps.[70]

Truly, the Internet has developed into today's Tower of Babel. Language barriers are even becoming a thing of the past as translation apps turn our smartphones into Star Trek-like universal translators. The networks are getting faster and more robust, as fifth-generation (5G) technology is being implemented at record speed to keep up with the exabytes of data being shared. And, the Internet continues to expand into its third phase, seeking to encompass every device into the Internet of Things.

Alphabet, the parent company that owns Google, has risen to become a monopoly, channeling 92 percent of web searches and 44 percent of all emails generated, and it now decides who sees what information.[71] Cries of Internet censorship, especially against Christian and conservative viewpoints, are on the rise. The one who controls information controls the world.[72]

In today's world of advanced technology and high-speed communication, many technologies drive visual learners to on-demand and streaming videos. As technologist John Dyer points out, "Technology has become a kind of supra-cultural phenomenon that finds its way into every aspect of our diverse lives."[73]

Craig Loscalzo notes that digital media is perfect for engaging with the mosaic style of thinking used by the postmodernist, meaning postmodernists draw conclusions from seeing the parts rather than the whole, because they are a "sound-bite driven culture" that has neither endurance nor lengthy attention spans.[74] A staggering 90 percent of US Internet users ages eighteen to forty-four years watch YouTube and TikTok.[75]

The $100 billion global gaming industry has also taken the world by storm. Gamers play an average of seven hours each week, but that has been increasing by 20–25 percent every year.[76] The global gaming community transcends national borders, living within virtual worlds, sharing common experiences, and speaking in a common vernacular.

Social media has added an average of two hours and twenty-four minutes per day spent multi-networking across an average of eight social networks.[77] Active social media users, primarily female, have passed the 3.8 billion mark on a plethora of popular platforms.[78] Social media has become the primary means of communication among youth, even alarmingly preferred over in-person conversation.

The New Cultural Identity

What characterizes today's brave new culture? Media expert Steve Turner would characterize it as "pop culture" and notes just how vastly it suffuses just about every part of the lives of everyone everywhere.[79] He warns that the driving spiritual forces behind much of pop culture are intent on altering the perceptions of the outgoing culture, often negatively towards God, the Bible, and Christianity. The result has been the transition of our society away from historical modernist, logic-based thinking to a postmodernist, relativistic, feelings-based post-Christian era.

Evangelism expert Rick Richardson describes the characteristics of this postmodern culture as including a common belief that people are their own gods, they often engage in identity politics, they're rampantly distrustful of authority, they hold a general belief that love rules, they have an overt fear of "the patriarchy," they readily discard whatever came before, and they tend to view Christians as self-serving.[80] This is Satan's new ethos, carefully indoctrinating the masses worldwide into humanism via their ever-present and ever-watching technologies, thus creating a new global culture devoid of any biblical foundation.

Pro-humanist, anti-Christian, "having a form of godliness but denying its power"—the end-of-days culture Paul warned Timothy about has at last come (2 Timothy 3:1–9). For these deniers of the One True God, Paul promises, folly will be made manifest to all.

But Christians know the Holy Scriptures that make us wise for salvation through faith in Christ Jesus. We must flip the sword of technology and use it instead to reach our lost generation with the gospel of Jesus Christ. Do so and you will change the world.

10 Reasons Bible Prophecy Exists

As mentioned earlier, nearly one-third of the Bible's content is God revealing how events will unfold before they happen. Our Heavenly Father wants His children to know what the future holds!

God's prophetic Word has excited us here at Lamb & Lion Ministries for more than forty years now. And, that excitement, it's true, will never abate in the years ahead, for the Good News and hope-filled message about our Savior's return is what energizes our passion to evangelize.

We want you to be invigorated by that same passion as well! So I called my fellow Bible prophecy teacher, Todd Hampson of the Prophecy Pros podcast, and we put a list together of some of the reasons we believe Bible prophecy exists. (There are many more reasons as well; feel free to add to the list.)

1. *Bible prophecy shows that God speaks the truth.* It shows us that God is God. He is the chief! He is the One in charge.

He exists outside of time. He knows everything. So whatever God says, we can take it as the truth and live by that truth.

2. *Bible prophecy proves the Bible is God's Word.* The Bible is the only holy book ever created that contains genuine, fulfilled prophecies. These prophecies were fulfilled to a "T"! Fulfilled prophecy proves the Bible is truly God's Word, so we can place our faith and trust in it and its Author.

3. *Bible prophecy shows that God is in control.* He is sovereign. That may sound like a big theological word, but "sovereign" means God is ultimately in control of every single detail. Bible prophecy puts that fact on display like nothing else.

4. *Bible prophecy demonstrates God's love.* He loves us and has a plan for our lives. We're not just floating around on a big spinning orb in outer space with no purpose and no meaning, as atheists claim. God has crafted a purpose for every person He has ever made because He loves His children. God has also planned a destination for the faithful. He wants us to live with Him in Heaven and on the New Earth forever. He gives us prophecy to show how world history will end with the faithful living forever with our loving, Heavenly Father in the eternal state.

5. *Bible prophecy describes God's plan.* This deals with how skeptics misconstrue biblical prophecies as being too general, or too vague, or too big. But, if you take a closer look, God provides many specific details about His plan for the ages. This plan shows how God is working to bring humanity back into a proper relationship with Him so that one day we will dwell in a blessed time of peace, righteousness, and fellowship with our Creator. Bible prophecy can be very specific and purposeful.

6. *Bible prophecy demonstrates God's might.* The fact that God the Father gave up His one and only Son to die for the penalty of our sins so those who place their faith in Jesus may be redeemed is truly praiseworthy. The fact that Jesus Christ is going to return one day as promised in might and power to victoriously defeat Satan and his minions and set up His kingdom should make us all stand up and shout "Hallelujah!" Almighty God alone is worthy of our praise and worship, and Bible prophecy shows us why.

7. *Bible prophecy proves God is worthy.* It shows us how big God is and how teeny-tiny we are in comparison. Nobody is like God. Therefore, He alone is worthy of us living our lives trying to please Him through obedience and acts of love. Even though God is far greater than we are, He still has a use for us: to serve and enjoy fellowship with Him. Why should we? Because He alone is worthy of our obedience and praise.

8. *Bible prophecy promises evil will be punished.* Evil often gets away with its crime on this earth. Bad people commit bad things, often without ever facing punishment. Yet, we are promised that swift justice is coming. The evil in this world does have an end. While we patiently wait for that glorious day, God is mercifully providing humanity this short reprieve to: a) give us an opportunity to return to Him in repentance, and b) allow us to grab hold of His gracious offer of having a right relationship with Him. Bible prophecy maps out the timeline for that long-desired day of justice.

9. *Bible prophecy prepares us to get right with God.* The ninth reason (a beautiful reason, and one we just love like crazy) concerns how biblical prophecy shows God's grace. Our

Creator lets us know what's going to happen ahead of time so we can get right with Him. If God had wanted, He could just drop the hammer on everybody because we're sinners and He isn't. We deserve to be sentenced to Hell for our rebellion against our Creator and for breaking His moral law. But, by God's grace and through His love, our Heavenly Father lets us know ahead of time what He's planning on doing. We know exactly what judgments are coming, as well as exactly what blessing and restoration are coming. He grants us the time to prepare and get right with Him.

10. *Bible prophecy gives Christians hope.* The Lord wants us to understand how the future will play out. Sure, there are valleys in life we must traverse, and terrifying times are coming like the Tribulation, which is hard to digest, but prophecy is meant to give us hope that this evil age will end. Jesus will return as promised to rapture up His Church before the Tribulation begins, He will defeat evil, and He will finally institute His thousand-year kingdom of peace, righteousness, and justice. We have hope knowing the Christian's final destination is to dwell in peace with our Creator forever in the eternal state.

So, Bible prophecy is meant to give believers hope of a great future. But, Bible prophecy is also meant as a warning to unbelievers about the eternal destiny in the lake of fire they are facing. The Bible calls us all to repent and accept Jesus Christ and His loving sacrifice so we may be reconciled with God and share in that eternal hope.

You probably agree that people sure need hope—now more than ever. So much craziness is going on in the world. People need to stop putting their hope in the things of this earth—whether political, monetary, or whatever—that have provided a false and fleeting sense of comfort and stability. As we quickly approach the glorious appearing of our great God and Savior, there has been no other time in history with a more urgent need to call people to put their faith and hope in God alone.

God is perfect. His promises are true. Bible prophecy assures us that God knows what He is doing with our lives and in this soon-passing world. We can have a certain hope in that fact.

If you don't know Jesus Christ, then today is the day to accept Him as your Savior, make Him Lord of your life, and claim that blessed hope. If you already know Jesus as your Savior, then continue to grow in your relationship with Him, exhibiting holy living and practicing evangelism. Start by opening your Bible. And, as we hope you've learned, don't skip over the prophetic parts.

Chapter 6

DELUDING DEVICES AND A WATCHMAN'S WARNING

By Pete Garcia

General Editor's Note: Pete Garcia is a servant whom I believe has been selected by the Lord to write and speak on Bible prophecy at this particular time near the end of the Church Age. Upon observing this former military major and helicopter pilot offer tremendous insights into matters of end-times matters as a writer for my great friend Jack Kinsella's *Omega Letter*, I asked Pete to be coauthor with me in our book, *The Disappearing*. A second book we wrote together, *New World Order*, was released the following year. Pete did a much larger portion of the writing in those books, and that made them truly in-depth and insightful in providing readers with valuable information in understanding the times. The material he contributes here provides the same tremendous insight.

We're bombarded literally every hour with truth and false information. Whether considering the societal and cultural slinking toward Sodom-like activity, the satanic Ephesians 6:12 "wickedness in high places" setting the stage for Antichrist's appearance, developing religious apostasy, hatred of Israel as prophesied by Zechariah, or whatsoever else the evil, Pete is on top of covering it.

+ + +

> I know your works. See, I have set before you an open door
> and, no one can shut it; for you have a little strength, have kept
> My word, and have not denied My name. (Revelation 3:8)

The watchman on the Western Wall cried with a loud voice to the crowds thronging below him, "Behold, the end of all things is at hand!"

No head turned towards him. No ear bent upwards to better hear.

After a moment, he cried out again, "Behold, now is the accepted time; behold, now is the day of salvation!"

Again, no acknowledgment. Just heads turned downward, eyes peeled to smartphones, trudging along like mindless zombies unaware of the danger ahead.

In his heart, the watchman knows this generation will not heed the warning. They are full of eyes that cannot see and ears that cannot hear. They have hearts hardened by the widespread cynicism of the age. Unlike any other generation before it, prophetic warnings these days are simply white noise in a flood of information bombarding the masses. Warnings, prophetic or otherwise, often go unheeded unless the threat is immediate and obvious. Indifference has become the normal state of affairs.

The watchman laments the state of the obstinate crowds addicted to their devices. Like lemmings marching to the cliff's edge, each passing day presses this world ever forward into the unforgiving winepress of the wrath of God.

A time of unspeakable horror is coming upon the world. The seventieth week of Daniel, often commonly referred to as the Tribulation, will be a foretaste of Hell on earth during the final seven years of humankind. It is this approaching storm the watchman on the wall warns of: a storm that will engulf the whole world into a tempest of tyranny, lawlessness, wickedness, and both natural and supernatural judgment.

Knowing the perilous times ahead and the seeming utter disregard by most in the world today, the watchman walks a lonely road.

The watchman's calling is not glamorous. Nor is it without cost.

Friendly acquaintances have abandoned him. Coworkers have begun to shun him. Even loved ones give wide berth, eventually avoiding him altogether. He has had long-term relationships severed by friends and close family. His calling has cost him his livelihood by passed-over promotions and missed positions; any semblance of upward mobility seems to have now eluded him.

Perhaps even his beloved spouse believes he has finally lost his mind and has taken to mocking and scoffing at him at every opportune time. One day, should the Lord tarry, she will leave him for another like herself. Someone equally distracted with the here and now, where an endless consumption of material things fills the time, yet never manages to satiate the appetite of the soul.

Vacuous and tone-deaf church pulpits increasingly ignore the subject of the return of Christ. With heads firmly planted in the ground, "learn-ed" clergy increasingly ignore the compounding signs that the end is racing towards them. Sadly, even the watchman's own church has begun to close ranks against him. No longer allowed to teach or serve in any meaningful way, he walks out of the hollow building to the sounds of those speaking, just above a whisper, things like, "He's crazy," "He's a prophecy nut," and "He has lost his mind."

With little strength, he turns to the shrinking remnant community of fellow watchmen for encouragement. These are those who also willingly challenge the "willful ignorance" of this age. But why then is he (and others like him) being shunned like a leper at every step?

He knows why. He might not bear the ugly sores of leprosy; however, he bears the ugly truth no one wants to hear…the truth that this world is coming to its inevitable end—and quickly.

Therefore be patient, brethren, until the coming of the Lord.
See how the farmer waits for the precious fruit of the earth,

waiting patiently for it until it receives the early and latter rain. You also be patient. Establish your hearts, for the coming of the Lord is at hand. (James 5:7–8)

But there is something else. Something even more troubling to those who profess Christ with their mouths, but not their hearts. Perhaps this division between professing and believing is what really causes them to reject the watchman's warning, especially in the "civilized" world. This love for the return of Christ exposes the hollowness of the modern-day church with all its trappings of seeker-friendly messages and kingdom-building platforms.

The truth is, the watchman is ruined by the love of Christ. For when one tastes of the glory so divine that only Christ offers, nothing else on earth will satisfy. The watchman becomes consumed by investing in the world to come, not in this present one that is quickly fading away.

Do not lay up for yourselves treasures on earth, where moth and rust destroy and where thieves break in and steal; but lay up for yourselves treasures in heaven, where neither moth nor rust destroys and where thieves do not break in and steal. For where your treasure is, there your heart will be also. (Matthew 5:19–21)

Nothing else on earth will satisfy the hunger for the true believers. Nothing else will quench their thirst. Christ has ruined their appetite for the things of this world, and they know they are all the better for it.

Spiritually awakened, the watchman's inner self has become quickened and reconnected to his Creator. Understanding what he was saved from, he is compelled to share this good news with others before time runs out.

The watchman sees the complete picture. He is not only thankful for what Christ has already done at the cross, but is thankful for what

Christ will do in the future. Thus, our "blessed hope" is bifurcated by the knowledge Scripture imparts to the discerning believer: "Worship God! For the testimony of Jesus is the spirit of prophecy" (Revelation 19:10).

This blessed hope is that Christ will come first calling for His Bride to meet Him in the air (lifted up) as an act of endearment. We purify ourselves by holding to this expectation. It is also a warning to those who are left behind, for if our removal is a blessing, then what should those who remain expect?

> For the grace of God that brings salvation has appeared to all men, teaching us that, denying ungodliness and worldly lusts, we should live soberly, righteously, and godly in the present age, *looking* for the blessed hope and glorious appearing of our great God and Savior Jesus Christ, who gave Himself for us, that He might redeem us from every lawless deed and purify for Himself *His* own special people, zealous for good works. (Titus 2:11–14, emphasis added)

And then He returns to the earth a second time *with* His Bride— this time in judgment, to vanquish His enemies once and for all.

> Behold, He is coming with clouds, and every eye will see Him, even they who pierced Him. And all the tribes of the earth will mourn because of Him. Even so, Amen. (Revelation 1:7)

In the meantime, the watchman often wanders this world alone like a nomad, a stranger in a strange land alienated by his new nature and his desire to be pleasing to God. He knows nothing in this world will satisfy him. Nothing will satiate his desire to be reconnected to his Creator. Spurred on by the boundless revelation in Scripture, he pores over every detail, every jot and tittle, allowing the Holy Spirit to illuminate his understanding of things past, present, and to come.

He knows this world is coming to an end. The signs Jesus gave are not just happening, but are being stored up like blast wave awaiting the right moment to explode. He knows the complex schemes of wicked people and angels are coming to nothing because they do not/cannot control the future.

Even the normal tasks of work, play, and life, without Christ, are empty and meaningless.

The *present world powers* in business, academia, culture, and government are attempting to create a world devoid of God (as if God doesn't exist), yet are fulfilling the Scripture exactly as it was written because it has already been foretold:

> Come now, you rich, weep and howl for your miseries that are coming upon you! Your riches are corrupted, and your garments are moth-eaten. Your gold and silver are corroded, and their corrosion will be a witness against you and will eat your flesh like fire. You have heaped up treasure in the last days. (James 5:1–3)

They act as if this world and reality are without an author or creator. They act as if this world and all therein are accidental. They've convinced themselves that they determine the future and can control its outcomes. They have successfully exorcised God from almost every facet of the public square, acting as if they don't talk about Him, He doesn't exist.

> Knowing this first: that scoffers will come in the last days, *walking according to their own lusts*, and saying, "Where is the promise of His coming? For since the fathers fell asleep, all things continue as they were from the beginning of creation." For this they *willfully forget*: that by the word of God the heavens were of old, and the earth standing out of water and in the water, by which the world that then existed perished, being flooded with water. But the heavens and the earth which are

now preserved by the same word, are reserved for fire until the day of judgment and perdition of ungodly men. (2 Peter 3:3–7, emphasis added)

They, like the empty-suited religious leaders of our day, have substituted transformative faith with absolute spiritual regeneration (i.e., being born again), for empty platitudes about how to live peaceably.

Coexistence doesn't bring peace.

Religion doesn't bring true life.

Morality doesn't bring sanctification.

Piety doesn't bring redemption.

Only believing and trusting in the finished work of Christ's death on the cross to pay for our transgressions can bring true life. As Scripture says:

So Christ was offered once to bear the sins of many. To those who eagerly wait for Him He will appear a second time, apart from sin, for salvation. (Hebrews 9:28)

Christ didn't come simply to die and be seemingly defeated by the powers of this world, for His sacrifice is intricately connected to His return:

For I received from the Lord that which I also delivered to you: that the Lord Jesus on the same night in which He was betrayed took bread; and when He had given thanks, He broke it and said, "Take, eat; this is My body which is broken for you; do this in remembrance of Me." In the same manner He also took the cup after supper, saying, "This cup is the new covenant in My blood. This do, as often as you drink it, in remembrance of Me."

For as often as you eat this bread and drink this cup, you proclaim the Lord's death till He comes. (1 Corinthians 11:23–26)

Christ must return to the same battlefield where He was seemingly defeated, conquer His enemies, and claim the victory promised to Him from before the foundation of the world:

I will declare the decree:
The Lord has said to Me,
"You are My Son,
Today I have begotten You.
Ask of Me, and I will give You
The nations for Your inheritance,
And the ends of the earth for Your possession.
You shall break them with a rod of iron;
You shall dash them to pieces like a potter's vessel." (Psalm 2:7–9)

So if you are a watchman and are feeling despondent, alone, weak, neglected, shunned, and ignored, know you are not alone. Christ knows your struggles and your walk. He is there with us through every step of the path He gave us. Knowing we're not alone, this journey is at its end, and the finish line is in sight, rejoice!

Rejoice for having the perseverance to endure this race until the end of all things.

Rejoice for knowing that as bad as this life is, it is the closest to hell you will ever be.

Rejoice for the things Christ has in store for those who love Him.

But God, who is rich in mercy, because of His great love with which He loved us, even when we were dead in trespasses, made us alive together with Christ (by grace you have been saved), and raised us up together, and made us sit together in the heavenly places in Christ Jesus, *that in the ages to come He might show the exceeding riches of His grace in His kindness toward us in Christ Jesus.* (Ephesians 2:4–7, emphasis added)

Maranatha! Come Lord Jesus!

SECTION III

CULTURAL-SOCIETAL, GEOPOLITICAL TRACKING

Chapter 7

SODOM-LIKE SUBMERGENCE

By Terry James

The book of final prophecies Daniel was told to "shut up…and seal… even to the time of the end" seems to now be open, its contents spilling across our newspapers' front pages and our television and computer screens (see Daniel 12:4).

No previous generation has experienced the number, frequency, and intensity of signals so similar to things prophesied to be witnessed by the generation alive at the consummation of human history. Daniel's last-days' floodgate indeed seems to be open now, and the foretold torrent of evil seems to be deluging the planet while the prophet's words in Daniel 12 resound hourly.

Knowledge now increases in geometric progression. With the advent of the Internet and other communications technologies, that pace continues to increase at a rate impossible to comprehend or harness. We run to and fro at breakneck speed.

We do so literally through travel that enables us to cover millions of miles of space in just a matter of days. We do so electronically, our communications running like lightning in a fraction of a second to every point on earth—and even to distant worlds.

Jesus' words about the signs of the times just before His return at the time of Armageddon are becoming reality before our eyes as we move through our daily lives.

False christs, false prophets, wars and rumors of wars, and all the other signals our Lord said will be happening concurrently in birth-pang fashion convulse our world with continuing regularity.

- Israel is being pressured from all sides to accept absurd demands in a satanically inspired pseudo-peace process.
- Russia and its neighbors are positioned precisely as Ezekiel 38 and 39 prophesy.
- China is gaining strength and exerting increasing hegemony over the Rising Sun regions from which the "kings of the east" will come.
- The European Union is in powerful flux in preparation to become the colossus that will produce the "ten-kings" power base of Revelation 17:12–13, from which Antichrist will launch his drive for world conquest.

The nations of prophecy appear ready to play out the final, violent scenes of this Earth Age.

Humankind grows worse and worse, just as the Apostle Paul prophesied. Perilous times are here, as the fierce, heady, high-minded lovers of pleasure more and more dominate societies and cultures. Current ecumenical movements to bring all religious systems together into one configuration prove Paul's prediction that end-time man will have a "form of godliness, but [deny] the power thereof" (2 Timothy 3:5). Human intellect continues to produce technology that Antichrist will no doubt use to subdue, control, and ultimately force all people to worship him or be killed.

Last-Days Deluge

No matter which way we look on the horizon, we see the thunder-heads of the approaching end-time storm. Despite rosy predictions by politicians, scientists, religionists, and philosophers that our golden age lies just over the next hill or just around the next bend, we hear rumblings and see the lightning signaling ominous things to come. While it is true that an infinitely magnificent, golden future lies just beyond earth's stormy horizon, such a future won't be produced by fallen humanity, but by Jesus Christ upon His return to put down satanic rebellion and establish His Kingdom.

No matter what the people of the World Economic Forum or any of the New World Order-builders believe, human beings will never produce Heaven on earth.

A brief examination of the direction the humanistic flood is sweeping this generation documents that we are gushing down a sin-darkened ravine toward apocalypse.

Wars and Rumors of Wars

War has been a continuing plague within human interaction since the day Cain slew Abel. Rumors of wars are always with us, because, as James wrote:

> From whence come wars and fightings among you? Come they not hence, even of your lusts that war in your members? (James 4:1).

The world's concept of peace is never true peace, but merely a lull between episodes of warfare. When so-called peace is enforced, threats of wars and murmurings of hostilities bubble just below the surface of civility. Jesus, in His Olivet Discourse on final prophecies, however, was talking about warfare that will come with greater frequency and ferocity the closer the end of this earth age comes. Wars, followed by rumors of wars, will come much like contractions increase for a woman who is about to give birth.

We don't have to go back very far in history to document that we live in an age of such convulsive activity. Wars on a global scale are the ultimate manifestations of humanity's fallen nature, which cannot find peace apart from Christ's atonement. Natural man harbors violence capable of producing great destruction. One-on-one violence, families warring against each other, gang warfare in our cities, ethnic group against ethnic group—all these confirm that ours is a generation witnessing one of the key final prophecies foretold by Jesus Christ.

The frightening fact that humankind now possesses, through nuclear weaponry, the capability of destroying all life on earth is proof that God's prophetic Word is truth (see Mark 13:20).

We are currently witnessing the floodgate of Daniel's prophecy being opened as the book the prophet was long ago told to "shut up" until "the end" is seemingly now wide open.

This generation watches while peace talks between Israel and its hate-filled enemies are in the news hourly. At the center of those talks is pressure by the nations making up the New World Order efforts that demand Israel give up God's land for a promised peace.

But it is a demand that, when met, will bring destruction, according to Joel 3:2. The Lord will not abide this taking place without great, catastrophic response. He will bring all nations of the world to the killing field called Armageddon.

All this means Jesus Christ is, perhaps very soon, going to step out upon the clouds of Glory and shout with the voice of the archangel and the trump of God, calling all believers to Himself. You don't want to be left behind on this judgment-bound planet when He takes believers out of harm's way.

America—Sheep or Goat?

Will the United States of America be a sheep nation or a goat nation? That is perhaps a Shakespearian question in the vein of "To be or not to be?".

The question, of course, is rooted in context of the Millennium, at the beginning of which Jesus Christ will judge what nations will be, symbolically, sheep or goats—based on how these entities dealt with God's chosen nation, Israel. Believers in Christ who survive the horrendous Tribulation will inhabit the sheep nations. All who survive the Tribulation but who haven't accepted Christ will be placed in the goat nations, then be cast into what is described as "outer darkness," and they will remain in that state until the white throne judgment at the end of the thousand-year reign of King Jesus upon the millennial earth.

Our quest here is to wonder just a bit about whether America is destined to be a sheep nation. You can guess without much speculation what I, personally, hope is the answer.

One thing that comes to mind in these contemporary times regarding the United States is its magnetic attraction to peoples around the world. This nation might be likened to the planet Jupiter. It is huge in most of the ways human beings see as alluring, giving it the greatest gravity—materially speaking—of any nation-state to grace the earth's surface. God has indeed blessed America "from sea to shining sea."

While all other nations orbit this one, realization about the liberty that is synonymous with the US to worship, move about, work, play, or even just be slovenly doesn't escape even those kept from knowing much about things going on around the rest of the planet. Indeed, America's gravity dynamically has drawn all peoples toward its irresistible opulence. With the exception of very few, no one makes noises about leaving this nation to live elsewhere.

Billions look in America's direction as the "shining light on the hill," as President Ronald Reagan once called it.

Even the defectors who sought to dodge the draft during the Vietnam era have since done all they could to come back to the nation they deserted. The Hollywood types—like Barbra Streisand, for example, who periodically threaten to leave America because they don't get their way, politically—decide to stay when it comes down to the moment of leaving or staying. In southern parlance, they know which side their bread is buttered on.

Perhaps to get right to the heart of what's made America the center of the universe of nations, and to try to determine its status so far as involvement in Bible prophecy might be concerned, I'd like to consider a well-known historical observation by a man outside this country—a Frenchman, no less.

French social philosopher Alexis de Tocqueville, while touring the United States in the 1800s, said about America: "America is great because America is good. If she ever ceases to be good, she will cease to be great." De Tocqueville no doubt was speaking of how he viewed cultural and societal good. But, upon observing the nation's Christian church foundation he encountered, he must have based his conclusion on the fact that America's goodness in the societal sense was a result of Christianity running throughout the country's cultural fiber. What he likely didn't understand was what "goodness" really means in God's economy.

God's Word speaks of this "good": "And Jesus said unto him, Why callest thou me good? [there is] none good but one, [that is], God" (Mark 10:18).

Jesus wasn't saying to the man who fell on his knees before the Lord that He, Jesus, was not "good," but the Lord was acclaiming that God, alone, is the only good. Jesus was—and is—the only "good" flesh-and-blood person to ever walk the earth following the Fall of Man in the Garden of Eden. That is because Jesus IS God.

De Tocqueville now looks from the past at America's once-pretty face, and his words of warning are reverberating: "If America ever ceases to be good, she will cease to be great."

America, a Golden Cup

Again, is the name "America" given anywhere in Scripture? Of course not. But, the influence this nation has exerted since coming to its full bloom as history's greatest superpower makes it a prophetic nation. The Creator of all things continues to use America in His mighty hand to accomplish two distinct, supernatural purposes. As a matter of fact, the United States, in my view, has an overwhelming presence in Bible prophecy. Its place is at the very heart of the end-times things we see developing—matters unfolding in hourly news reports. In this sense, I believe God is speaking of America—in type, if not by name, when His Word tells us the following:

> Babylon [hath been] a golden cup in the LORD's hand, that made all the earth drunken: the nations have drunken of her wine; therefore the nations are mad. (Jeremiah 51:7)

Certainly, the United States has been a "golden cup" in the Lord's hand. No other nation of modern vintage can come close to claiming that achievement.

Some nations of Europe were formative in bringing Christianity into the world, thus shedding a degree of gospel light into a world of sin-darkness. But it is America that, despite its great shortcomings and more recent degeneration, has been a shining beacon, reflecting from that golden cup in God's hand.

Being the first nation in spreading to the whole world the gospel message—that Jesus' sacrifice on the cross makes possible the only way to redemption for lost humankind—is a feat no other country can claim. This, ultimately, has been done not by the offices or under the auspices of American ingenuity, but by the omniscience and the omnipotence of the One holding the "golden cup." God's grace and mercy have put America as a beacon of God's light upon that mountain of gospel dissemination. God's providence gave this nation the industrial and technological genius—a fact that is denied, or taken for granted today.

All the grace God has shed upon America from sea to shining sea, it must now be noted, means nothing in addressing the question about whether America will be a sheep or goat nation.

The United States has been extremely generous with its wealth at every turn. Whether rebuilding war-torn nations far away, such as through the Marshall Plan, or providing billions of dollars whenever there are tragedies to be funded, our country has seemed to be the good Samaritan. But our largesse as a people also will not determine whether America is destined for sheep-nation status.

Again, according to the prophetic Word, it seems national status in this regard is to be based on how other nations have dealt with Israel. It is based upon this factor—US/Israeli relationship—that I have great hope in trying to answer our question.

America was chosen by God, Himself, to act as national midwife in Israel's rebirth into modernity. Any true reading of history will attest to this reality. The revisionists, the Marxists, the evil from the mind of Satan, cannot change this. America, despite its egregious acts lately against the God of Heaven, has been friend and protector of the fledgling Jewish state as it entered again as a nation at the middle of the twentieth century.

Will America face God's judgment? Again, there can be no doubt. We've allowed the murder of more than sixty million children in their mothers' wombs, just as a start on listing the absolute wickedness we've seen recently. God will judge this nation.

But there will be a glorious rebirth for America, I'm believing, once its sins are purged and the Lord again counts our nation as "good."

These Lot-like Days

It seems I just can't turn loose of the prophecy I believe to be the most immediately pertinent to Christ calling His Church to be with Him. And, at any rate, I wouldn't want to turn loose of it if I could bring myself to do so.

The words are from the very mouth of God, and they speak directly to the most-desired prophecy for our day from the standpoint of what we, as pre-Trib believers, look to be imminently fulfilled. I believe He is talking about the Rapture.

Jesus, while teaching about the same time frame He spoke of during the Matthew 24:36–42 Olivet Discourse, said the following:

Likewise also as it was in the days of Lot; they did eat, they drank, they bought, they sold, they planted, they builded; But the same day that Lot went out of Sodom it rained fire and brimstone from heaven, and destroyed them all. Even thus shall it be in the day when the Son of man is revealed. (Luke 17:28–30)

He was describing the characteristics that would be starkly observable before and during His next intervention into this earthly wickedness. That time will, as I study things surrounding the Rapture in context, look much like the very times we're enduring now.

One specific angle might pull into a little sharper focus just how much our darkening moments of history might be likened to Lot's time in Sodom. To begin, we must first consider God's words to Lot's uncle, Abraham.

The Lord said He would tell Abraham about things to come, because He knew Abraham would do righteously. God wanted him to know His plan to deal with Sodom's wickedness, once He determined that it was necessary. The Lord stood with Lot, then, and discussed Sodom's fate, while the Lord's angel representatives headed down toward Sodom and Gomorrah.

And the LORD said, Because the cry of Sodom and Gomorrah is great, and because their sin is very grievous; I will go down now, and see whether they have done altogether according to the cry of it, which is come unto me; and if not, I will know. And the men turned their faces from thence, and went toward Sodom: but Abraham stood yet before the LORD. And Abraham drew near, and said, Wilt thou also destroy the righteous with the wicked? (Genesis 18:20–23)

Then there was a profound back-and-forth discussion between the Lord God and a lowly human being—Abraham. God answered each of Abraham's questions as the old man asked them. Abraham was appealing to God to have those in the wicked cities spared from destruction. He asked if God would relent if fifty were found to be righteous—then forty, then thirty, then twenty.

Finally, after Abraham asked if God would spare the cities if the Lord could find even ten righteous, and ten couldn't be found, so the fate of Sodom and Gomorrah was sealed.

God had said to Abraham before the countdown began—following Abraham's initial question about the possibility of the cities being spared:

> That be far from thee to do after this manner, to slay the righteous with the wicked: and that the righteous should be as the wicked, that be far from thee: Shall not the Judge of all the earth do right? (Genesis 18:25)

It was almost as if the Lord was mildly indignant to be thought of as so unjust as to condemn righteous people along with the unrighteous.

Alas, there were not ten righteous folks left in the city of Sodom. There were only Lot and his small family. God's Word calls Lot "righteous," even though Lot dwelt among perhaps the worst culture and society biblically recorded in such detail. The detail was so graphic as to make the level of unrighteousness unmistakable.

While it was business as usual during daylight hours, with the cities being apparently prosperous, buying, selling, building, planting, etc., when the sun went down, it became a habitation of every sort of evil—particularly of debauchery, with homosexual rapaciousness leading the wickedness. The lustful males came even against the angels who visited Lot.

The raging men of the city threatened Lot with the worst possible attack if he didn't go along with them and send out his visitors. They were just on the verge of tearing down the door to get at their would-be victims. The only ones God considered *righteous* in the city were hated and threatened by the rest.

And this is the angle I would like us to consider for now.

Jesus said in Luke 17:28–30 that it will be for those alive at His next revealing or intervention like it was at that time for Lot when he was hated and threatened by the wickedness of that society and culture. We've covered many times the God-rejecting, hate-filled actions and activities of our own troubled times. Is there any question of how the evil and wickedness have increased exponentially?

One pastor has endured such assaults by the unrighteous against the righteous. He was imprisoned in Turkey for preaching about Jesus being the only way of salvation. He was finally released after the Trump administration and others pressured Turkey to release him after that government had sentenced him for the crime of preaching the gospel. He says that he sees in the United States the same sort of Sodom-like actions coming against believers.

Andrew Brunson's message is straightforward, but it is far from simple: The Church needs to brace for a dark wave of persecution that is coming.

"Most of the institutions of society are supporting things that a faithful follower of Jesus cannot embrace…and that's how they will justify persecuting us," Brunson said.

Believers who stand for this truth will be marginalized in schools, jobs, banks, and more, he added. Testing believers' resolve, the pressure to conform will manifest socially and eventually financially.

"What has emerged as the main flashpoint is gender identity and LGBT," he said. "And wherever that is intersecting with religious freedom, LGBT is winning. Now there is a requirement that people not only tolerate, but that we embrace and celebrate this ideology. And if you don't, you are seen as someone who is hateful."[81] The days (and nights) of Lot are gathering around those who hold to biblical Christianity. At the center of the threats is the same spirit of Antichrist that infected the hordes of ancient Sodom.

Jesus promised He will catastrophically intervene and execute judgment and wrath against the unrighteous when these conditions become evident at the end of the Age of Grace (Church Age).

You want to escape with those God considers righteous. You want to be removed from the gathering wickedness and the judgment that must destroy it the same as God destroyed Sodom and Gomorrah.

Here, again, is how to escape the coming judgment and wrath—through the Rapture promised by our Blessed Hope, the Lord Jesus Christ.

That if thou shalt confess with thy mouth the Lord Jesus, and shalt believe in thine heart that God hath raised him from the dead, thou shalt be saved. For with the heart man believeth unto righteousness; and with the mouth confession is made unto salvation. (Romans 10:9–10)

Chapter 8

ACCELERATING INTO APOSTASY

By Donna Howell
and Allie Anderson

General Editor's note: With Pope Francis declaring on numerous occasions that there is more than one way to God the Father and salvation, and saying even atheists will eventually be in Heaven, it's understatement to say we're in the prophesied time of "winds of strange doctrines."

Donna and Allie were closely associated with my great friend, the late Tom Horn, and his dynamic, cutting-edge vision of spiritually oriented, investigative ministry in publishing and television. Donna is the current managing editor and writer/researcher for Defender Publishing. Allie has served as overseer of the research arm of Sky-Watch TV and Defender Publishing. Both have written extensively on matters involving issues and events as they might relate to Bible prophecy.

Their treatment of this blatant symptom of apostasy leading to Daniel's seventieth week (Tribulation) brings much-needed understanding during these times of last-days confusion.

✢✢✢

The pope isn't the only leader currently preparing our land and churches for a satanic covenant of end-times proportions, and Catholics aren't the only Christians who need to open their eyes to the present-day apostasy. Protestants often stand proudly puffed up, slinging their own version of abhorrent condemnations at the "Catholic Church's spiritual failings," citing such reasons as the worship of Mary, indulgences, sin-booth confession sessions using priests as mediators, discouragement of individual Bible study, dictatorialism in the history of the hierarchy/papacy, and so on. We're not insensitive to any of these complaints, and we agree that these topics are extremely concerning. But before Protestants can congratulate themselves on being masters of the universe, we, also, are contributing to the formation of a currently leaderless cult that will be too vulnerable to recognize Antichrist for what he is when he shows up to lead. There are so many examples of how we're getting it wrong that it's difficult to know where to start. But, because readers may assume some of what's about to be discussed is "heresy in some other denomination and therefore someone else's problem," it's crucial to remember:

1. The most convincing and deceptive cult of all is one with members who "look like" and "act like" regular, everyday people who follow Christ.
2. Following Christ requires believing what the Bible says of Him, as well as strictly adhering to a list of tenets.
3. The members of the Western Church "look like"/"act like" regular, everyday people who follow Christ (with certain exceptions we will soon discuss), *but*...
4. The Western Church has forsaken both the key doctrines of Christ and central Christian tenets. *Therefore*:
5. The Western Church is the most convincing and deceptive cult of all.

As we've said, central tenets apply across the board. Both the Catholic Church with all its sects and the Protestant Church with all its denominations are bound to them, and this numbered list applies to both. However, due to the fragmented denominations in Protestantism that tend to represent seemingly countless variations of doctrine, assigning "cult" as a label for the whole of the Protestant body is a more enigmatic and complicated process.

Deeds vs. Creeds

When ruminating about the disease of the Protestant Church, truly "being" followers of Christ and not just "looking like" followers of Christ is by far the most important consideration, since any other position is a cultic counterfeit.

The *creed* of the Church says, "I follow Christ."

The *deeds* of the Church say, "I don't follow His tenets or believe what the Word says about Him."

For instance: The Christian statistics research group, Barna Group, in its definition of the term "biblical worldview," identifies six universal nonnegotiables within Christianity as a belief system, based on interdenominational tracking of central Christian tenets compiled since 1995. These essentials, which apply to *all* Protestant denominations, are:

- Absolute moral truth exists.
- The Bible is wholly reliable and accurate.
- Satan is a real being, not merely a symbol of sin.
- Simply being a good person does not send one to heaven.
- Jesus came to earth and was sinless.
- God is the all-knowing, all-powerful creator of the world who still rules the universe today.[82]

These authors (and everyone in the SkyWatch TV and Defender Publishing circle) concur with every item on this list. Though we would likely add several things, we certainly wouldn't take anything away from these fundamental components of Christian belief. However, Barna reports, *only a staggering 17 percent of practicing Christians in the US have a "biblical worldview" based upon belief in these six things.*[83]

That may come as a shock (it certainly did to us!), but it's a plausible statistic when we really dig in to see what today's Western Christians actually believe: One study reports that 45 percent of American *Christians* admit that "certainty about [Christ] is impossible," and only 34 percent believe He is "involved in their life,"[84] whereas another study states that 46 percent of born-again Christians believe Jesus sinned while He was on earth.[85] One report shows that only 41 percent of self-identified US Christian adults in the Baby Boomer generation consider Scripture to be "totally accurate in all of its teachings," and this staggeringly low number only jumps to 43 percent for the same category of believers in the Millennials, Gen-X, and "Elders" generations.[86] Between 1993 and 2018, Christians declined from 89 percent to 64 percent in their belief that witnessing to the lost is a duty of their faith,[87] whereas 47 percent of Millennial-aged, practicing Christians actually think evangelism is morally *wrong*, as it may pressure someone to change faiths![88] We don't know what's worse: the fact that so many Christians don't think the Great Commission is their responsibility, *or* the fact that, out of 1,004 *regular Christian church attenders* in the US who were asked about the Great Commission in 2017, 25 percent couldn't remember what it was and 51 percent had never even heard the term in their lives![89] This means at least 76 percent of Christians are ineffective in spreading the Gospel. Maybe the numbers would be more impressive if we knew how to pray with people, but as it currently stands, only 2 percent of praying Americans do so with another person present.[90]

As of October 2020, the latest large-scale research and statistics report reflects that 58 percent of evangelicals have "demoted the Holy Spirit to symbolic status," denying His role as a true Person of the Trinity. A lie is no longer a sin, according to 40 percent, so long as "it advances personal interests or protects one's reputation," and premarital sex is agreeable to *half* of all evangelicals. Salvation can be earned by doing good, 48 percent say. Abortion is morally acceptable to 34 percent, which makes sense when 44 percent don't think the Bible's teaching on the subject is clear and 40 percent don't believe human life is even sacred. This is probably why 39 percent don't respect anyone who holds to a different faith (which is ironic, since the entire faith system being described here isn't orthodoxically *any* religion). Pentecostals/charismatics aren't any more impressive, however: 69 percent reject absolute moral truth; 54 percent disagree that human life is sacred; 50 percent claim the Bible is ambiguous about abortion; and *45 percent are not born again!* But of all groups, mainline Protestants take the lead for syncretizing their Christianity with the secularized culture of the West: 63 percent say God is *not* the provider of truth and the Bible *cannot* be trusted to fully represent God-given principles; a shocking 81 percent believe people can be their own moral compass because humans are essentially good; only 33 percent make it a habit to confess sins and seek forgiveness from God, and a meager 13 percent read their Bibles regularly. The summary provided by the study states: "Sixty percent (60%) of mainline Protestants' beliefs directly conflict with biblical teaching."[91]

When our creeds don't match our deeds, that's called "hypocrisy." Keep that in mind.

It's not all about what data the veteran research group Barna collects, though. Ligonier Ministries conducts up-to-date surveys about the state of the Church, and researchers there have dedicated themselves to reporting every two years about how Protestant churchgoers in the West feel regarding the central doctrines of Christianity. The most recent survey, conducted in partnership with LifeWay Research, was released in September of 2020. The findings were appalling. Thousands of people of all faiths, as well as atheists and those with undisclosed or undecided positions, weighed in. In total, 48 percent agreed that the Bible was merely one of our world's historic "sacred writings" that record "ancient myths," but that it does not contain any truth, and 52 percent denied the divinity of Christ. This is sad for the public, surely, but far, *far* worse were the numbers reported specifically about the belief of evangelical Christians in the West, which start off bad and only get worse:

- 26 percent think church ministries cannot be effective to the world unless their worship services are "entertaining."
- 39 percent agree that "material blessings" are a *guaranteed* reward of faith (that evil prosperity gospel of recent decades is still clinging on…).
- 46 percent take a relaxed position on sin, agreeing that people are generally "good by nature."
- 65 percent believe Jesus is a being whom God created (as opposed to belief in the Incarnation of God, the Word made flesh, aka the way through which salvation is even possible—cf. John 1:1, 8:58; Romans 9:5; Hebrews 1:1–4).
- 30 percent agree with the statement that "Jesus was a great teacher, but was not God" (an outright denial of Christ's divinity).
- 18 percent answered that the Holy Spirit *can* tell a Christian to do something the Bible expressly forbids (folks, 18 percent may look like a small and encouraging number, but remember that it represents almost one-fifth of all evangelicals, which is alarmingly high considering how blasphemous it is to suggest that the Spirit of God would lead us in the opposite direction of His own Word!).

And, finally, the most demoralizing statistic of all is that:

- 42 percent (almost half!) of all evangelicals embrace the blatantly syncretistic/idolatrous heresy that "God accepts the worship of all religions."[92]

President and CEO of Ligonier Ministries, Chris Larson, is correct in his rebuke when he writes, "People inside the church need clear Bible teaching just as much as those outside the church."[93] Elsewhere, the ministry's chief academic officer, Stephen Nichols, who also sits as president of Reformation Bible College, offered his opinion after seeing the crushing blow of the survey: "As the culture around us increasingly abandons its moral compass, professing evangelicals are sadly drifting away from God's absolute standard in Scripture.... This is a time for Christians to study Scripture diligently."[94]

No, Stephen, that time was yesterday. Today, we are late, and the injury our tardiness has caused the Body is a festering maggot pool.

Take a moment to look at what a train-wreck statement this single study makes about what we believe as the people of God: Theologically speaking, the denial of Christ's divinity is a return to Arianism, the belief that Jesus was "created *by* God," which naturally denies that He "is" God. This heresy mostly died out in the fourth century after the Council of Constantinople in 381 when the Cappadocian Fathers—Basil of Caesarea, Gregory of Nazianus, and Gregory of Nyssa—brilliantly silenced Arius' otherwise baseless "theology." According to this survey, Arianism is now the position of *65 percent of all evangelicals!* Meanwhile, the number of people who accept within their heart that Christ's work on the cross was for "entertaining" worship or "material blessings" makes these authors gag. Even the age-old "they mean well" retort cannot be offered here. There is simply no excuse to mix any part of our Savior's mission with pop culture. On the other hand, almost half of us believe people are generally good by nature—so, meh, who needs saving, anyway? We can just save ourselves. Or maybe that Holy Spirit—who *apparently* tells us to carry out acts that contradict His own Word—can lead us to that other world religion He also accepts. Maybe *that* religion will have a messiah in it that can help us out—since a third of us don't even believe Jesus is God at all!

This is the summation of our "Christianity," readers. It's what one journalist calls "self-constructed, Build-A-Bear, buffet-style belief... [that] the Westernized, New-Agey offsprings of Eastern pantheisms" can feel comfortable with.[95] And maybe this is why, when Christians experience doubt crises in their faith in God, a "pastor or spiritual leader" is only the person they would think to seek help from a mere 18 percent of the time.[96]

Without true fruit, the Church is just a social club. What were once corporate goals of holiness, godliness, sanctification, and seeking the presence of God have been replaced with greatly rehearsed entertainment and production spectacles. Some of these places of "worship" have gone so far that (in our opinion), if Jesus were to appear in these buildings, He would overturn tables and clear them out: "And [He] said unto them, It is written, My house shall be called the house of prayer; but ye have made it a den of thieves" (Matthew 21:13). We wonder what Jesus would think of some of the churches that—after paying inflated salaries to ministers and staff, covering administrative expenses, installing flashy facility upgrades and amenities (such as espresso stands and gift shops), and establishing ostentatious "worship concert" services—delegate *less than 5 percent* of their massive, megachurch budget to the kind of charitable endeavors Jesus championed (feeding the poor, caring for widows and orphans, etc.).[97]

Astonishingly, the respected, check-before-you-donate organization, Charity Navigator, in their "Financial Efficiency Performance Metrics" analysis, states that seven of every ten charities they appraise (the majority of which are secular) give *three quarters "at least"* of all their accumulating monies on those they set out to benefit. In a slightly less impressive statistic, every nine out of ten will redirect "at least 65%" of all income to helping the needy in the area of their conviction.

You with us so far? This means only *one* out of ten listed charities in this country *outside* the Church would perform abysmally enough to donate less than 65 percent of their budget on the programs they designed to provide others some form of relief.

Charity Navigator goes on to say: "We believe that those spending less than a third of their budget [that's 33.3 percent in total] on program expenses are simply *not living up to their missions*. Charities demonstrating *such gross inefficiency receive 0 points and a 0-star rating*."[98]

Let's revisit this breakdown:

1. The foundation of today's North American Church claims—by the nature of the commands of our Chief, Jesus Christ—that charity is at the center of all we do. We exist to "be more like Jesus," who advocated relief work and humanitarian goals more than *any other religious figure in world history*, and to do this very work He would want us to do in His name. Therefore, both verbally and because of our affiliation, we promise the world to prioritize charity over any other entity or organization.

2. Only one out of every ten non-church-affiliated charities in our country would dare spend less than 65 percent of their budget to achieve their relief, assistance, or humanitarian goals. Anything less than that would place them in the minority of embarrassingly unsuccessful organizations and would utterly *destroy* any chance they had at a reputation of being able to reliably handle donors' money. But the *real* daggers in this picture are the charities that have the audacity to give less than 33.3 percent of their budget to their beneficiaries. *Tsk-tsk.* They get a *zero-star* rating. Their promises to the world are basically worthless.

3. North American churches are *frequently* guilty of giving around, even less than, 5 percent.

Do a little math. That's more than just mortifying. It's flat-out disgraceful that some of our *wealthiest* churches (what the world expects to be "Jesus Christ's Relief Organizations") can't be counted on for much, if anything, when it comes to helping the poor. We show how much we care about the destitute and the sick by rigging confetti cannons and fire-retardant curtains to our stages for the weekly worship-service productions. We honestly believe the Lord will someday require an answer about who would have used that same money to put food on tables overseas.

Yet not only are churches failing miserably in their compassion for the needy, like Christ commissioned. Theologically, there also seems to be a lack of conviction, as ministers everywhere now preach self-help and self-improvement rather than the fundamental (yet world-changing) doctrines of the apostles. Churches are more concerned with branding and advertisement than teaching Scripture and making disciples. The corporate attitude rings: "As long as our attendance is up and our offerings are good, that must mean God approves of this ministry, our feel-good sermons, and our fog-machine worship productions. Teaching a profound, theologically sound message is *nice*, but it would go over the heads of our congregation, so let's leave that to the seminaries. Sin is complicated. Our job *here* is only to let the people know that Jesus came so that we can experience love and joy more fully and life more abundantly."

Initially, this approach to ministry doesn't sound too offensive, but when it becomes a nationwide pattern for all Western churches (and it's our opinion that it has), the study of salvation and Christ is polluted with the underlying—yet far-reaching and culturally influential—concept that Jesus came to fluff our pillows and bolster our bank accounts when we behave ourselves. It's another era of the prosperity gospel all over again, just waiting to be given its own label when "progressive Christianity" gets old.

And what happens when theologically sound biblical teaching evaporates from the Church?

We land at a day when only 17 percent of Christians have a "biblical worldview."

And what happens *then*?

Stuff like *this* happens: In September of 2019, the United Presbyterian Church of Binghamton in Binghamton, New York, moved its communion table aside and erected the idol of the Slavic god, Svetovid, in its place during the celebrated Luma Festival. Known for being the pagan god of the four cardinal directions—as well as the god of fertility, war, and, of all things, *divination* (a form of witchcraft directly prohibited multiple times in the Bible)—Svetovid had no business being allowed in a Christian church to begin with, but to boot Christ's "do this in remembrance of me" sacrament tools out of the way to make the god a focus in the house of the Lord Jesus is blasphemous beyond comprehension. The leadership of this congregation knew very well that some of the people drawn in from the streets merely to see the colorful light display wouldn't have sufficient education or background to know just how anti-Christian it is to bring a pagan idol into God's holy place. Many likely assumed that Svetovid was part of some "Christian pantheon," or that this spectacle was just "how Christians do church," which is an outrageously disgraceful misrepresentation of and assault against our core doctrines and creeds.

Later, when a bold journalist had the leadership of the church cornered with a theologically sound argument for why God would forbid such a thing to occur in His house,[99] their retort was profoundly progressive and laden with New Ageism. The response was lengthy, wordy, and wove unbiblical rhetoric around an argument based on (at best) human reasoning and logic; but, to boil it down, their conclusion was that either: a) Svetovid isn't sacred or related to God's grace in any way, which makes the idol only a secular and artistic (as opposed to spiritual) concern; or b) Svetovid *is* sacred, in which case he is so as under the grace of God, who bestows upon humankind the capability of creating such works of beauty in the first place.[100] At no point was the journalist's scriptural challenge countered by the church leadership's scriptural rebuttal. Much to the contrary, the people in charge of raising that idol in God's house didn't quote one verse—not one!—to justify the act. (The only verse they did quote was entirely unrelated to idolatry.)

Guess who all reacted to this? Other than the journalist, a few people posted on their social media. Within two or three days from the initial story outbreak, nobody cared. We are "used to" this kind of "Christianity."

So used to it, in fact, that nobody cared a few years back when that whole "pole-dancing for Jesus" trend gained ground for a spell.

Because nobody explains *context* of Scripture in Church anymore, we have women using Psalm 149:3—"Let them praise his name in the dance…[and] with the timbrel and harp"—as "biblical approval" for "our temples [bodies]" to "spin without sin" using "moves once meant for strippers." When ABC News covered the story in an article called "Hallelujah! Christians Pole Dance for Jesus in Texas," it was reported that the strip-tease-for-Jesus routine is an "opportunity" for dancers "to worship God and practice their faith. The students dance to contemporary Christian music." A portion of the discussion introduced the idea that married couples within the Church could be brought closer together with this kind of excitement, though nobody pointed out the obvious side effect—that a group of people from the same church getting together to pole dance *could* lead to countless marital problems as well. Consulting a pastoral leader near a Christian pole-dancing studio as to whether he thought it was a good idea, he responded in the negative (thank the Lord, a church leader with brains!), saying that, regardless of whether clothes came off, the dance, itself, was associated with scandalous things. He suggested the women do yoga instead (ughhhh, *so* close, then he blew it…). On the other hand, this pastor saw a positive: If people could be drawn into Christianity by seeing these women dance on poles, *that* would be good. (Because, ya know, "pole-dance-ianity" is *kinda* what Jesus wants us to pull the lost into, right? [By the way, the answer to that is a hearty *no*, just so we're clear, though it's pathetic that has to be clarified.]) This particular article listed other mainstream churches throughout the US where Christ's followers could experience similar praise and worship through "sexy workout classes," including belly dancing at a Presbyterian church in Virginia.[101]

Weirdly, once the craze (translation: "crazy") took root with women, as one story reports, men began to trickle in: "What was once seen as sleazy practice is now gaining steam as a way for some women—and men, too—to get closer to God." Videos of both men and women being sexy for their Savior were uploaded online where anyone can access them. One proud male dancer, who later became an instructor of the art, boasts: "I am a very deeply spiritual follower of Christ."[102]

When gathering a bunch of women to simulate a stripping event as a form of praise and worship isn't enough, bringing in the men to join them is the natural next step. These authors hope some Christian marriage out there was inadvertently and fortuitously blessed, because this foolhardy drivel is more a recipe for a scourge of overnight infidelities to sweep through congregations. (As a byproduct of this activity, newly single, financially strapped women are then equipped with vocational training for a career in exotic dance, courtesy of their local church!) That is, of course, apart from how blasphemous this "exercise" is to begin with.

These authors wonder: How many of these men and women know about the associations between today's stripper pole and the ancient rituals to the Canaanite goddess of fertility and erotic love? Asherah—mother of Baal, wife and sister of El—was worshipped by pagans in the Old Testament; her presence in a community was marked with tree groves. In and around the trees were idols of Baal as well as tall, wooden "Asherah pole" idols, which God declared throughout the Old Testament must be burned or torn down (see Deuteronomy 12:3; 16:21; Judges 6:25, 28, 30; 2 Kings 18:4). Scholars acknowledge that these idols represented the female body at some point upon its engraving, but they were often also phallic in nature and shape, rendering an idol that celebrated all forms of deviant consummation. Do Christians who "spin without sin" know that today's "dance" takes Asherah worship to the next level with a living, breathing body upon the pole of a pagan goddess of sex? Are they aware that this "exercise" was the prostitutes' launching pad for demonic, orgiastic ecstasy-worship in the groves of God's sworn enemies?

These Christians are just lost...and how can the lost lead souls to salvation?

Is it any wonder the lost see us the way they do? Are we seriously still confused about why the media depicts us as a bunch of hypocritical, bungling clowns? When research organizations like the Barna Group report that one out of three young adults reject Christianity because of hypocrisy they see in the Church, and about 50 percent of them "still feel the Church cannot answer their questions…[because of] flaws or gaps in [our] teachings,"[103] do we feel *any* responsibility at all to react? Are we surprised when we hear about the mass exodus the Church of the West is facing today, or the literal doubling of the number of people identifying as atheists in the last decade (as the Pew Research Center reports[104])? Is there any shock value to the fact that 32 percent of American Christians left their churches and didn't return when the pandemic forced religious gatherings to close the doors for a month?[105]

It's shocking from every angle. Earlier we looked at statistics that showed how far away from core Christian doctrines Western Christians have wandered, but by further reflecting on "deeds vs. creeds," the scandalous behavior we're engaging in, the idolatry we're tolerating, we have been building to a climax. It's not just about whether every Christian believes in total biblical inerrancy or whether some allow abortion to be morally acceptable under some circumstances. Even as recently as September 22, 2020, according to the American Worldview Inventory conducted through the Culture Research Center at Arizona Christian University, only 6 percent of all adults and 2 percent of all Millennials hold a truly biblical worldview accountable to the most *basic* essentials of Christian doctrine—such as the inerrancy of Scripture, the necessity of prayer and worship, the belief that Satan is real, or the acknowledgment that sin exists and it is bad. Nevertheless, this study indicates that 61 percent of Millennials identify as Christians.[106]

This automatically introduces the logical question (and we ask with genuine respect): What *are* you, if you identify as Christian but don't believe in anything Christianity teaches about the reality of sin and the need to be cleansed of it through a Savior described in a Bible you also don't trust to be true in the first place?

Technically, this has been answered before, over a century ago, by world-renowned New Testament scholar and Princeton Theological

Seminary professor, J. Gresham Machen. All of the "Christianity" we see in the West today is nothing more than veiled liberalism—and by using "liberalism" here, we are referring not to the similar-sounding label in politics, but to a school of thought under the same name within theological study. The application of liberal conviction, as defined under the umbrella of liberalism as a theology, found its roots in the rationalism of the Enlightenment era, which recognized humanity's ability to reason as the new empirical authority over the words of the Bible. If something defied *reason*, as it was defined by each individual, it simply "wasn't true." Liberalists (though they were not called that at the time) approached Scripture with a postmodernist, "What's true to *me*?" application and either disregarded everything else or chalked the rest of the Word of God up to allegorical suggestion, rendering Christianity into a mere subjective experience. More simply put, liberalism is what happens when people call themselves "Christian" but "interpret away" the bits of the Bible they're uncomfortable with. Today, we hear it called "progressive Christianity," but before it got cute, it was acknowledged as a slap in the face of God and strengthened such false teachings as antinomianism (the idea that God's grace outweighs our responsibility to live righteously; the opposite of legalism).

Machen's writing, which was a shameless throat punch to liberalism, demanded that those who championed human reasoning use their own capabilities of logic to question the senselessness of their Christianity. By introducing new liberties to theology that contradicted basic essentials of Scripture, they repackaged their religion into an illogical, irrational box with more limitations on its own claims to reason than Christianity had prior. He wasn't shy in his attack against the logic (or lack thereof) of only accepting what parts of a religion give a person happy feelings. In his *Christianity and Liberalism*, after devoting several pages to exposing the inconsistency and absurdity of the logic liberalists so championed, Machen summarized how this approach to Jesus always leads back to the black hole of unfulfillment:

Religion cannot be made joyful simply by looking on the bright side of God. For a one-sided God is not a real God, and it is the real God alone who can satisfy the longing of the soul.... Seek joy alone, then, seek joy at any cost, and you will not find it.[107]

Though he wasn't the only theologian who has skillfully and convincingly criticized the ludicrousness of liberalism (which he occasionally referred to as the alternative "modernism"), there is a reason these authors chose to highlight Machen's work here. He called the kettle "black" in a way his contemporaries hadn't: While other scholars were attempting to entertain the massively popular liberalism shift long enough to sort out which new "theologies" were reliable and which weren't, Machen recognized the whole of liberalism as a *completely different religion* altogether: "Liberalism not only is a different religion from Christianity but belongs in a totally different class of religions."[108]

If Machen were around to lend his thoughts to the mess we're in now, his golden response to the kind of postmodern evangelicals reporting their beliefs to the Ligonier Ministries survey just discussed would likely be disregarded as an overly conservative voice from the minority. Nevertheless, for the remnant Church who cares, his historical genius lingers on the page forever...*or* until it's outlawed by the global system we're helping to form and ends up in the "propaganda burn piles" the chaos in the West is currently reserving for our Bibles. For now, we still have gems like this:

In trying to remove from Christianity everything that could possibly be objected to...in trying to bribe off the enemy by those concessions which the enemy most desires, the apologist has really abandoned what he started out to defend. Here as in many other departments of life it appears that the things that are sometimes thought to be hardest to defend are also the things that are most worth defending.[109]

Bottom line: A "picked apart" and "partially true" Christianity is *not* Christianity. It is a completely "different religion" from Christianity. It is—*once again*—a cult, regardless of how "normal" it looks on the outside.

Sometimes it becomes a bigger concern than whether one church removes Jesus to hail Svetovid for a weekend, or whether a group of tragically misled Christians worship provocatively. And sometimes it's not "normal looking" from any angle at all. More often than we would like to admit, colossal movements spread over regions of the world that affect all Christians in a negative way.

When Progressivism Meets Emotionalism

Perhaps the most glaring example is some of the witchcraft and occultism that had global attention during a well-known revival that drew multiple millions of people all over the world in the 1990s and dramatically and permanently changed the landscape of Sunday morning worship practices in the West. Because some calculable good actually came from this revival—and because several of those who perpetuated the more negative aspects of it have since repented of their involvement—we will sensitively refer to this period as the "Charisma Revival." (As a quick disclaimer: These authors have studied the Charisma Revival throughout the years, and we want to be clear that the Lord certainly met many seekers at those altars. The movement was popular enough that readers *may* recognize which revival we're writing about. If readers of this book were among those who attended and had a real encounter with God, *we are not questioning the authenticity of your experience*; we merely want to look at some of the questionable origins and goings-on of the movements that began in the area at that time.)

Some may wonder why, when so much of the discussion about Protestantism has taken place across all denominations, we're about to look back at a movement that was primarily Pentecostal/Charismatic. There are three reasons:

1. Demographically, if we don't count Catholicism, with approximately 584 million members, Pentecostals and Charismatics make up the largest population of Christianity not just in the West, but around the globe, accounting for 26.7 percent of the world's Christian population (8.5 percent of the human population).[110] Since the Catholic Church represents 50.1 percent of the Christian population of the world, that makes the remaining 26.7 percent of Pentecostals and Charismatics an *enormous* part of the Body. As a result, though not all readers are Pentecostal or Charismatic, many likely are, which makes the warnings from this movement invaluable.

2. The Charisma Revival, regardless of denominations, stands as a *great* example of what can happen when the Church forsakes her True Love (Jesus) and goes in her own direction to feed emotional phenomena. The correct teachings from the Word end, worship gets *insane*, the lost remain lost, God's heart breaks, and Christians lose patience waiting for their religious identity to iron itself out, so they eventually give up and leave the Church. Everyone loses.

3. Long-term damage inflicted upon the reputation of and theological trends within the Church can take *eons* to sort out. In this way, the Charisma Revival affected *all* Protestant denominations. It was such a grand-scale Western movement that egg was thrown on the faces of other traditional Christian faiths that were not involved, putting believers from all over the West in the uncomfortable position of answering for why *their* religion appeared absurd.

Lessons from the era of hype… Lessons learned the hard way.

This moment was marked by a resurgence of the "hellfire and brimstone"-style sermons similar to those of Jonathan Edwards' "Sinners in the Hands of an Angry God" in the mid-1700s, but this time, the messages were reprimands for not being "fired up like the folks at those Charisma Revival churches." These charges were often followed by the obligatory "get fired up" exhortation to which the congregants dutifully responded by demonstrating their (imitated) excitement...all for the sake of appearance. There was a lot of religious propagandizing to support the idea that this was the one, the only, and the last golden age of revival—that "God wouldn't wait on the lazy ones," and He would "work miracles" through those willing to "punch Satan in the face" and "reclaim our territory." But because the Holy Spirit wasn't truly behind all this "pulpiteering," no real fruit was produced. True followers of God were worshipping one day, then they blinked and found themselves in a cult the next; the lost had little reason to think that cult had any legitimate answers about how to be saved.

Right from the beginning, despite some very real demonstrations of God, something just "felt off" about the Charisma Revival. Stories from that congregation involved deeply unsettling "manifestations of God," even though there was almost never any scriptural foundation for those goings-on. This didn't seem to bother most Church leadership, though. Many people traveled to the churches that were right in the thick of it, having been instructed by their pastors to go see what's going on and "bring the revival back with them," as if they had been sent to pick up a loaf of bread. (One of these authors heard that very "bring it back" command in two different churches and by two different leaders. It was like they were suggesting that their ministry staff could just fling a revival in their backpack and feed it crackers on the plane.) In our opinion, these were pastors' efforts to try to "fix" the apathy of their home congregations because they weren't willing to do the work it would take to see a true revival of interest in following Christ.

In the following excerpt, award-winning journalist of religion, spirituality, culture, and history, Steve Rabey, describes the reputation several churches earned during this movement:

As [churchgoers] walk down the wide carpeted aisles—aisles that in a few hours' time will be filled with the lifeless bodies of stricken worshipers—some tread lightly, as if they are walking on holy ground.... All told, more than 2.5 million people have visited [one of] the church's Wednesday-through-Saturday evening revival services, where they sang rousing worship music and heard old-fashioned sermons on sin and salvation. After the sermons were over, hundreds of thousands accepted the invitation to leave their seats and rush forward to a large area in front of the stage-like altar. Here, they "get right with God.".... Untold thousands have hit the carpet, where they either writhe in ecstasy or lie stone-still in a state resembling a coma, sometimes remaining flat on the floor for hours at a time. Some participants call the experience being "slain in the Spirit." Others simply refer to receiving the touch of God. Regardless of what they call it, these people are putting the "roll" back in "holy roller."[111]

Another outside-perspective report we found particularly eye-opening is by *World Magazine* reporter Edward E. Plowman, who documented his own observations on the spot during one of the 1997 Charisma Revival services. Bob Jones of the same magazine assisted in writing the article that would appear in the December 20 issue of that year. The article begins with an account of the opening of the service, when two ministers on stage begin to jog in place and dance excitedly, while families all over the enormous room jump about wildly. One woman in the front row of the balcony seating caught the reporter's eye, and he took note:

Looking like a geriatric cheerleader, she crisscrosses her arms in front of her and chops wildly at the air above her head. When she finally falls to the floor and thrashes about for five minutes, her fellow worshippers burst into applause.[112]

The story goes on to state that this same woman, likely tired from all the physical activity, fell asleep as soon as the sermon began, staying asleep until the altar call, when she revived and resumed her frenzy.

Assigning the personnel to work specific roles in such a gathering was no small feat. For example, at one church that was centrally involved in the Charisma Revival, "catchers," designated by the red armbands they wore, were responsible for doing just that: catching people who had been touched on the forehead and proceeded to fall. These men would lower the fallers gently to the floor, ensuring there were no injuries. There was also a "modesty patrol": These folks draped cloths over the women who fell in dresses or skirts to prevent possible flashing of too much skin or undergarments to those nearby. An employee or volunteer served as a scorekeeper, responsible for seeing to the constant updates on the sign out front displaying the number of souls saved to date. *World Magazine* reporters remember the sign as a way that church could claim its bragging rights—in much the same way that 1990s McDonald's signs flaunted how many cheeseburgers they had sold.

But, for all the trouble these congregations went through to ensure God's movement had organization and boundaries, the teaching—which is the part true Christians consider the most crucial detail—lacked substance. The *World Magazine* article includes several quotes from the ministers the evening they compiled their report; their words sounded akin to the "punch the devil in the face"-style messages we mentioned earlier. What these authors find far more concerning than the record of bizarre behavior, however—and Plowman and Jones agree—is the focus on having an experience instead of edifying the Body with correct teaching and dividing (interpretation) of the Word (2 Timothy 2:15).

In the article, the writers raised the question of whether some of the dramatic falling episodes had actually been choreographed and staged. But that isn't even what bothers us the most, because that's an issue between them and God. What we find most troublesome is that, according to Plowman and Jones, *not one word* of the sermon they sat through addressed any theological concepts that could be soundly traced to Scripture, the doctrine of salvation, creeds of the faith, or anything else of that nature.[113]

Joe Horn, in his autobiographical and theologically rich book that addresses healthy use of the gifts of the Spirit, *Everyday Champions: Unleash the Gifts God Gave You, Step into Your Purpose, and Fulfill Your Destiny*, shares a telling testimony. This grand display of 1 Corinthians 14-style, chaotic occultism is only one of many examples of how, in many pop-culture, contemporary church congregations, discernment has left the building. The church Horn tells of was located near Portland, Oregon, at the height of the Charisma Revival; the leadership there had sent an agent to "bring the revival" back with them, as many were apt to do. His tale is similar to what everyone else was hearing at the time:

> People were "getting drunk in the Spirit," which [in this Oregonian congregation] meant that they would sway, stagger, and laugh out loud at everything they saw during service. A few times, married folks interacted with other people's spouses in a way that could be described as flirtatious, raising an eyebrow or two, but because their actions were the result of "something the Spirit was doing in them," the behavior wasn't questioned. On several occasions, this phenomenon engulfed twenty or more people at once, and the only thing distinguishing the altar atmosphere from a small-town bar atmosphere was the absence of liquor....
>
> I'll never forget the "birthing in the bathroom" incident. A guest speaker came to town and spoke about end-time "birthing pains of the Church Body." I can't remember his message, so I have no idea whether his conclusion was theologically sound. I also can't assume that what occurred next was or wasn't via his

influence, but I didn't need a seminary degree to immediately recognize it as bizarre heresy.

A grown man was found on the floor of the bathroom "giving birth in the Spirit." He was moaning in agony from "birthing pains," he said. That's what the story was by the time it reached me...

I was as curious as anyone to hear what the pastor would say about the bathroom incident that morning.... Surely the shepherd of the flock [read "pastor"] would either denounce the whole matter as heresy that he planned to deal with or he would justify the news with a verse.

When service began, the incident was the first thing the associate pastor addressed (the pastor never said a word that I can recall), but to my surprise, he didn't make a calculated conclusion one way or the other. He gave a quick, nervous comment... about how God works in mysterious ways, and then moved on to the announcements listed in the bulletin. I don't know if the pastoral team was simply trying to keep the peace or what, but their tolerance made the situation worse. A few weeks later, as I was still marinating on how to react, the same thing happened again—but this time, the second man "giving birth" in the bathroom went as far as to say that he was spiritually becoming Mary in labor, and that the baby "inside" him was the Son of God.

...I was disgusted that the only person questioning these odd "movements of the Spirit" was a fifteen-year-old who earned the title "Doubting Thomas" the first time she introduced logic to the discussion. The situation was already way out of hand, and just about everyone in the congregation could do anything they wanted, as long as they described what they were doing as "in the Spirit"—and it was not only allowed, but it was also celebrated! This church easily fit into the category of chaos Paul referred to in 1 Corinthians 14.[114]

If those experiences were faked, they were a sacrilegious mockery of the Holy Spirit's gifts and manifestations—nothing less than a circus in the house of God—because nowhere in the Word does Scripture suggest the Spirit would move upon His people in such a way. If those experiences were *real*, then, since it couldn't have been anything "of God," they must have been "of" something else…which is far more terrifying.

Part of what led to all of this was a war the Church was engaged in against an enemy that didn't really exist. Let us explain.

The Church was still wrestling through the "Satanic Panic" era of the 1980s—a time when its enthusiastic rebuke of underground satanic ritual activity launched little more than moral panic and witch hunts in our country. Multiple best-selling books (such as *Michelle Remembers*) flew off the printing presses and into immediate fame; their authors claimed they were involved with or were victims of secret, demonic cults that participated in all kinds of evils, including human sacrifice, rape, torture, blood-drinking, and every other dark thing the imagination could come up with. Of course, such claims as ritual murder and crimes of a similar nature won't bob around society for long before being investigated. As it turned out, most of the claims *did* materialize in the imagination, and nothing more. This was an instance of one scam after another being perpetrated by brilliant actors who found a way of exploiting the Church for attention and royalties on a few million books.

But Christians fell into a panic. They believed they were a part of a war, but while they were preaching about pushing against the devil, the real enemy used all the hype about evil to his advantage. The Church had given *so much* attention to Satan that a societal/cultural platform was built upon which Satan could introduce his symbols, music, and satanic gospel to the public. Everyone was talking about him, so everyone was learning his ways. The Church, by putting aside its focus on the Great Commission to reach the lost and instead throwing its resources into waging war against the enemy, ironically helped facilitate the enemy's publicity coverage to those who would be enticed.

This development in the Church is, *surprisingly*, only rarely discussed amidst Christians, as if believers either didn't see it for what it was, or they don't want to talk about it. The secular world, on the other hand, continues to have a good laugh at our expense. The takeaway for our purposes here is how it affected Western Protestants for many years.

Jesus never told His disciples, "Go ye, into the world, find those who oppose me and take them down." As His followers, we should remember that, lest we maim the Commission we were given by turning it into another gospel that has no power to save. At the very least, we were distracted. Consider this excerpt from *Redeemed Unredeemable*:

The "Satanic Panic." It was an era throughout the '80s and '90s when interest in the occult, especially amid teen circles, was a nationwide phenomenon. Gone were the flower children of the '60s. The twinkling disco ball of the '70s had dulled with the dawning of the new gothic age. Kids traded in their afros and bell-bottoms for mohawks and black fishnet stockings. Dark Baphomet pentagrams shamelessly appeared on necklaces and earrings in respectful jewelry shops. Drug use landed on a much younger generation and included more powerful intoxicants than the world had ever seen. Inverted crosses and "666" became typical graffiti symbols spray painted next to gang tags on buildings. Newspaper headlines heralded a new trend in murder: ritualistic human sacrifice in the name of Satan....

Satan loves a good distraction. While the Christian Church was pulling its focus together to wage war against a decoy called "the satanic underground," the enemy brought a real spiritual warfare against the people in the Church, attacking them from any vulnerable angle. So many pastors put their disapproving stares against those in their congregation for the way their flock members dressed or pierced their ears or tattooed their biceps or listened to music with "that devil's beat" that people became estranged from the Gospel, and a rebellion arose even higher and with more zeal. And what happened when people were estranged from the Gospel and feeling spiritually suffocated, losing interest in the church as a result of religious abuse, and feeling too exhausted to fight? They left their rear exposed to the dragon. When real attacks did come, sometimes now with authentic ties to the very satanic underground that the panic had assisted in establishing by this point, resulting in murder and crimes unthinkable, every fraudulent personality's "I told you this was happening; I told you so!" diatribe caught a second wind, which begat more panic and, sadly, more adherence to misdirection....

The more the flags of warning were enthusiastically waved by the Church, whether or not the flags were legitimate, the more children and teens felt it was exciting to shock the conservative world and concerned parents around them by living on the gothic edge.[115]

Then, while we were vulnerable, distracted, and too consumed by the fear-mongering control of the witch hunt to bother reading more than just the "rebuke the devil" verses of our Bibles, up sprouted the popular but theologically paper-thin prosperity gospel. So, to anyone who might have otherwise been reached by the saving Gospel message, "Give us all your money and God will bless you" was likely, and tragically, the takeaway.

What a disastrous day for the Church that was. What an appalling ball-drop. How lethargic and inadequate we were in our true purpose of reaching the lost!

And what's the result?

Well, turn back a few pages to all those inexcusable statistics we listed at the beginning of this section if you'd like to be reminded.

The "punch the devil out" services/sermons of the Charisma Revival age can be thrilling, and they do at times inspire Christians to wake up, stand against evil, and work for the Lord. But when the effort turns into a holiness competition among believers, the motivating sermon becomes a doggedly wet thing that dies under the weight of the exhausting, rote obligation of once again spending an entire Sunday afternoon swaying at the altar (on an empty stomach). And that's not to mention all the totally weird "theologies" and "Holy Spirit manifestations" that swept through the Pentecostal Church (and then clung on for some time) as a result of the Charisma Revival. Every other Sunday, it seemed, we would hear yet another story about feathers falling from rafters and gold dust producing itself miraculously on people's scalps. Once, a man we knew even joyfully testified that his silver tooth fillings had all turned to gold at the altar. The pastor at that church was usually a very sensible man, so we were surprised when, instead of finding a gentle way of redirecting the focus of the service, he led the congregation into several minutes of praising the Lord for the aesthetic work He had done in our brother's now-blingy mouth. (These authors are convinced that Rumpelstiltskin had more to do with that manifestation than God.)

When the world hears this kind of crazy talk, they wonder why Jesus' miracles went from mercy to nonsense—from raising the dead and making the blind see to transforming a gentleman's dental work into another color. To the lost, Church becomes a godless cabaret, and even the small-town shows are able to invest in their glitter cannons because God is their declared producer. It turns into a "Spirit-led" extravaganza. A contract with the high-kicking Rockettes is the only missing element from the pageant called "church." A whole world of the lost is dying out here, and the Church is a college of the performing arts, training its people to sing, dance, and act.

The greatest offense of excitable movements like these within the Body is when the purpose of the Church (the Great Commission) is corporately set aside in trade for experience, because that leads to emotionalism…which leads to religious ecstasy and counterfeit revival.

What does counterfeit revival produce?

Men giving birth in bathrooms, pole-dance worship, and other such occult nonsense that defiles the temple of God as much or more than any Svetovid light display. As a further assault to God's kingdom, the victims are *both* believers and nonbelievers.

Regardless of the level of heartfelt sincerity anyone may have about the Lord, if a "movement of God" isn't truly in line with Scripture, it introduces confusion, associates that chaos with the name of Christ, collapses into the history books as an embarrassing and short-lived behavioral phenomenon, and ends up leaving a bitter "religious" taste in everyone's mouths for decades.

Meanwhile, mock revival truly *does* lead to spiritual death.

To illustrate this point, consider the opinion of Frederick William Robertson, the famous Brighton, England, Holy Trinity Church preacher who graduated from Oxford and went on to memorize the entire New Testament in both English and Greek while producing some of the most celebrated evangelical Anglican Bible commentaries on the planet. While relating the early-1800s "camp meetings" revivals of his own time to the religious ecstasy habits the Apostle Paul repudiated in 1 Corinthians 14:24–25, Robertson writes of not only the unfruitful ministry of those caught up in the show church, but also of the spiritual death that imperceptibly creeps into their routine. (Note that Robertson isn't attacking the gift of speaking in tongues, but specifically the religious ecstasy that was a problem first in Corinth, and again in the 1990s.)

Robertson says:

> Respecting [the act of speaking in] tongues, note the following directions. 1. Repression of feeling in public. This state of ecstasy was so pleasurable [to the Corinthians], and the admiration awarded to it so easy to be procured, that numbers, instead

of steady well-doing, spent life in "showing off." The American camp meetings, etc., show how uncontrolled religious feeling may overpower reason—mere animal feeling mingling with the movements of Divine life. There is great danger in this, and just in proportion as feelings are strong do they require discipline. When religious life degenerates into mere indulgence of feeling, life wastes away, and the man or woman becomes weak, instead of strong. [Sounds similar to what Machen said about liberalism…] What a lesson! These Divine high feelings in Corinth—to what had they degenerated! A stranger coming in would pronounce the speakers mad![116]

When the Syncretized Saints Go Marching In?

Sadly, we could go on and on, giving more true "occult inside the Christian Church" news stories that have swept the Christian West of late, because the list just grows and grows. Within just the last few years, Steven Bancarz, Josh Peck, Dr. Thomas Horn, and countless other well-known and celebrated Christian authors just from within our own circle have released several titles raising awareness in this area.[117] Each has shown how today's pop-culture, contemporary Church is beginning to incorporate such evil, occult practices as cartomancy (fortune-telling with cards), under the guise of Holy Spirit-directed "destiny cards" or "prophecy cards" (other names for tarot cards); "angel boards," identical in every way to the Ouija board; yoga, which, if you didn't know, incorporates physical stretch-poses that are, in and of themselves, postures of worship to specific pagan gods of old (note there are many other alarming details the average Christian has never heard of regarding yoga); teachings about karma, which is strictly a New Age philosophy; Mother Earth-style training programs on the "God is all, and all is God" philosophy of pantheism; walking prayer labyrinths, which participants largely don't know draws its origins from sexually deviant Greek mythologies resulting in the birth of the half-man, half-beast Minotaur; "contemplative prayer" and/or "soaking sessions," which involve some variation of "Christ consciousness" or prayer-to-angels (or spirit guides) meditation originating straight from the New Age or Wicca; new and false "Jesus" gospels, based on pop-culture scriptural interpretations that paint Jesus to be anything *but* what and who He was described as in the New Testament; and other disturbing, anti-Christian, religious beliefs and practices, such as the following list taken from Bancarz' and Peck's *The Second Coming of the New Age*:

- Opening up portals with your minds for angels and energies of Heaven to come through
- "Spirit-traveling" out of body [called "astral projection" or "astral travel" in pagan circles today]
- Practicing "spiritual smell," "spiritual taste," and such
- Engaging in guided meditations
- Going through guided visualizations into one of the "Heavens"
- Using tuning forks and "sacred sounds" for energetic alignment
- Manifesting one's own destiny through visualization
- Believing that thoughts emit metaphysical vibrations and frequencies that create reality
- Practicing telepathic communication to put thoughts and images into another's mind[118]

These authors can bet many readers just went through this list and thought to themselves, Yes, this is a shame, but it's not surprising. That, in itself, is a shame. We're "used to" Western Christianity ebbing more and more toward this misdirected reality every day, so much so that we're desensitized by the level at which the precious Yeshua's house has been tarnished.

Chapter 9

PREPARING ANTICHRIST'S GEOPOLITICAL PLATFORM

By Terry James

I t has been taking place for decades, even longer. The American and world public have become anesthetized, or at the very least numbed, to the effects. At least half of this nation's population seems to be in a near-comatose state, in consideration of what is right and wrong in terms of what the founding fathers meant in establishing a constitutional republic.

I refer to the incessant propagandizing of the people by a news conglomerate that mimics in most every way the Big Brother news leviathan of George Orwell's novel *1984*. The author invented the term "doublespeak," defined as language that deliberately disguises, distorts, or reverses meaning to further an agenda, often by governments, corporations, marketers, or other power structures.

The novel tells of a socially stratified, post-nuclear war world ruled by three superstates—Oceania, Eastasia, and Eurasia. The ruling elite keep the "trolls" under their oppressive governmental thumb. These are the worker bees who are given just enough entertainment and mind-altering things to imbibe to keep their noses to the grindstone of serving the state and to keep their minds off the machinations of those who govern them.

We have, since the late 1950s, and even before then, been victims of the emergence of Orwell's 1949 vision of a dystopian, news-propaganda monster. It appears that perhaps two-thirds of the American populace has fallen into Orwell's "troll" category within today's political process.

Perhaps this figure is a bit of an exaggeration, but the astonishing disconnect is troubling. According to reactions I see in the matter of people understanding whether information they get is reality or propaganda, no other conclusion can be reached. Millions are falling for the lies that they should be allowed to do what is right in their own eyes. Anyone who holds up biblical or even constitutional founding principles as the way we should comport ourselves is met with angry protestation.

Those of us who believe abortion, homosexuality, use of illicit drugs, pornography, fornication, adultery, and other such evils are wrong, are seen by a vast section of the nation's population as the evil side of American society and culture.

We've reached the point forewarned by God's Word: Good is called "evil," and evil is called "good."

We've witnessed the Orwellian-like news organizations of our day in action. These join that vast number in pigeonholing Christians and "moralists," as they would have it, into a corner they call "hate-mongering."

A campaign planner of one political party's candidates recently called all who oppose the leftist-agenda Nazis. He then proceeded to, in Hitler-Aryan fashion, tell those around him what he will do to that opposition once his party wins. He said he would summarily kill some and put others in gulag. The rest would go into reeducation camps to get their minds right. The mainstream, Orwellian news media, so far as I can determine, said nothing to condemn this campaign planner's rhetoric.

Evil doesn't change. The rhetoric, under the right conditions, will become murderous implementation when opportunity arises.

There are still those with satanic-controlled minds who would perpetrate on Americans the same sort of atrocities the Nazi beasts inflicted upon the Jews and other victims of those days.

There is coming a time, God's Word states, when people will fall totally for the doublespeak and newspeak of those horrendous times. The ultimate Big Brother will forge a regime so powerful and evil in influence that no one, in human terms, can resist. He will have the consummate propaganda machine to brainwash and reinforce his dictatorship's absolute control. His minions are now being prepared, in my view, to carry out his inculcation of the "trolls" of that Tribulation time. They will be all who are left behind because of their unbelief when Christ calls believers in the Rapture.

Today's mainstream news organizations are acting as a prep school for inflicting the future lies of the son of perdition. So it isn't too far-fetched to see a bit into the future and apply prophetic Scripture, based upon what we see developing at present. The nation and world are being prepared for the ultimate manifestation of the Orwellian world the author forecast with the release of his 1949 novel.

> Let no man deceive you by any means: for that day shall not come, except there come a falling away first, and that man of sin be revealed, the son of perdition.... Even him, whose coming is after the working of Satan with all power and signs and lying wonders, And with all deceivableness of unrighteousness in them that perish; because they received not the love of the truth, that they might be saved. And for this cause God shall send them strong delusion, that they should believe a lie: That they all might be damned who believed not the truth, but had pleasure in unrighteousness. (2 Thessalonians 2:3, 9–12)

End-times Storm Steering Mechanism

Hurricane season brings the phenomenon known as a "steering mechanism." I'm no meteorologist, of course, but know enough to understand that, in the United States, winds aloft blowing from west to east have an effect on hurricanes approaching our mainland from the Atlantic.

These winds can "steer" those massive storm systems away from the continent and back into the Atlantic. This is usually the case.

News media play these things for all they're worth. They, with wind-blown reporters standing with their microphones on the shoreline, paint the worst-case scenarios each time a huge hurricane is being generated by warm Atlantic waters as the storm heads eastward from the Horn of Africa or somewhere over that way. More often than not, then, the storm has less effect on our coasts than anticipated. The steering mechanism—these winds aloft—have done their job and lessened the severity of the hurricanes.

However, sometimes these steering currents can force storms up the coast. They then do severe damage to places in more northern latitudes rather than on the lower coastal areas where they initially were expected to make an impact.

It seems we're now in the middle of the most severe moments of an end-times storm. This isn't the case, however. We are in the process of watching the Tribulation storm out in the proverbial roaring sea as it threatens to land full force.

The full-blown hurricane will come. Bible prophecy makes that forecast abundantly clear.

But there are winds aloft, so to speak. They are the steering mechanism that will determine when the storm will become full-blown and where it will make its full impact upon the generation that will endure the storm and all the wrath its power will generate.

I think we can look at COVID-19, or coronavirus, if you prefer, as a major steering mechanism in this end of the Church Age. It has been like that powerful wind aloft in meteorological terms, shaping things to come not only for America, but for the entire world.

One example of the way this pandemic was used to steer the great, incoming Tribulation storm is its movement being used by the globalists who are attempting to force America and the world into the model the globalists elite have been trying their best to bring about.

A news excerpt or two will illustrate.

A Rockefeller Foundation report once imagined a viral pandemic as the perfect catalyst to implement "tighter top-down government control and more authoritarian leadership," eerily similar to what's occurred during the recent coronavirus outbreak.

The report, entitled, "Scenarios for the Future of Technology and International Development," outlines several possible future global scenarios, including a "Lock Step" vision in which a "new influenza strain…infects nearly 20 percent of the global population…killing 8 million in just seven months…"

"In 2012, the pandemic that the world had been anticipating for years finally hit," the scenario begins. "Unlike 2009's H1N1, this new influenza strain—originating from wild geese—was extremely virulent and deadly."

"The pandemic also had a deadly effect on economies: international mobility of both people and goods screeched to a halt, debilitating industries like tourism and breaking global supply chains," the scenario continues, describing almost the exact events of 2020 in the wake of the coronavirus outbreak."[119]

Another news item from several years back further illustrates the effects the pandemic-steering mechanism is having even in this present hour, years after the Rockefeller Foundation Report's scenario for their globalist ambitions.

The United Kingdom's former Prime Minister Gordon Brown has called on world leaders to form a "temporary" global government to resolve both the medical and economic crises caused by the coronavirus pandemic reports the *Guardian*.

The ex-Labour prime minister stressed the need for a task force comprised of world leaders, health experts as well as leaders of the international organizations that could enjoy executive powers to execute the response.

A virtual meeting of the G-20 group of both developed and developing countries, chaired by Saudi Arabia, is scheduled to take place on Thursday. Brown lamented that the meeting didn't include the UN security council. "This is not something that can be dealt with in one country," he said. "There has to be a coordinated global response."[120]

Yet another excerpt even more dramatically illustrates the steering mechanism's effects. It is a more profound example of the supernaturally generated winds aloft, I propose, because God's prophetic time clock, the nation Israel, is directly in the path of the incoming, apocalyptic storm.

[Israel's Prime Minister] Netanyahu put out a direct public appeal while dealing with an escalating coronavirus crisis on Tuesday, saying, "Benny Gantz, this is a moment which tests leadership and national responsibility. The citizens of Israel need a unity government that will work to save their lives and their livelihoods. This is not the time for a fourth election. We both know that the gaps between us are small, and we can overcome them. Let's meet now and establish a unity government. I am waiting for you."[121]

The prime minister, in addressing the Israeli people back then, urged all to stay home, because, he said, "one who infects one person is akin to infecting the whole world."

He said he didn't know when the pandemic would end. He reminded the people, however, that during past plagues, the Jews were stuck in exile. He said:

The coronavirus joins the family of other deadly plagues throughout history—the Black Plague, cholera, and the Spanish flu. When those plagues ran their course in previous centuries, we [the Jews] didn't have a state. But today we do have a state.[122]

He encouraged his audience by saying, "This gives us unlimited options to control our destiny," adding, "we are one people, one country and now is the time for unity."

He concluded:

The Jewish] month of Nisan that begins tonight is the month of spring and of exodus from Egypt. It reminds us that our nation withstood intense storms. It gives us strength. It gives us hope. We overcame Pharaoh. And although the battle is difficult and challenging, we will overcome the coronavirus with God's help and with your help, people of Israel.[123]

While we now know that much of the COVID lockdown suffering and vaccinations were based on lies put forth to push forward the globalist agenda, Benjamin Netanyahu was correct; with God's help, the Jewish people—a remnant—will get past the storm to come.

The storm the Israeli prime minister seems to anticipate isn't yet here. It will be horrific, to be sure. The steering mechanism—the strange, supernatural winds that are blowing—are shaping things prophetically, precisely as God's Word has said.

Surging Spirit of Antichrist

Questions continue about what's going on in all of this geopolitical and cultural/societal intrigue in terms of Bible prophecy. What does it all mean? Why such a divide? Why such rage and hatred? People want answers, and the answer is spiritual. It is all there in Bible prophecy.

It is altogether a major indicator of how near we are to the end of this Age of Grace.

The spirit of Antichrist is indeed surging. It's most revealed through the globalist mantra—that anyone who is in denial about climate change is, in effect, an apostate within their worldview.

But, in fact, another spirit of denial is the true obstacle to a pristine earth.

It is those who make such accusations against Bible-believing Christian, climate-change deniers who are at the heart of earth's many problems. Chiefly, the Antichrist spirit denies the Lord Jesus Christ and His very existence. These are the true deniers—those who believe and proclaim that *they*, not Christ, have a right to control the destiny of this planet He created.

John the apostle and author of Revelation—the vision of the Apocalypse—presents what God gave Him to tell us about the Antichrist spirit.

And every spirit that confesseth not that Jesus Christ is come in the flesh is not of God: and this is that spirit of antichrist, whereof ye have heard that it should come; and even now already is it in the world. (1 John 4:3)

Deniers of Jesus Christ—the powers and principalities in high places, those human minions and supernatural minions—and their incessant strategies and determination to keep God out of things manifest the spirit of Antichrist at an accelerating rate.

Christians are battling the Antichrist spirit at the highest levels—the evil within both human and demonic minions. Our would-be rulers (those denying, through being influenced by, the anti-Christ spirit that God should reign) hold powerful positions within the top strata of globalist echelons. It all revolves around worldwide satanic influence on matters involving the so-called deep state. It is Ephesians 6:12 we've been watching in action. Nationalism must go…

boundaries must be erased. Sovereignty must be eliminated so global government by the elites might rule.

Once again, it's good to look at the Apostle Paul's warning:

> For we wrestle not against flesh and blood, but against prin-
> cipalities, against powers, against the rulers of the darkness of
> this world, against spiritual wickedness in high places. (Ephe-
> sians 6:12)

These powers that be in high places of government view the US as the problem rather than the answer to conflict throughout the world. It is the richest, most powerful national entity to ever exist, so it must be brought down, its assets given to the global elite to use for their own purposes.

The former Trump presidential administration, in the obvi-ously enraged opinion of the deep-state and leftist minions, sought to change the way things have supposed to be progressing since post World War II. The global order as run by the high echelon of the dip-lomatic types and the people with political power have had that drive for ultimate power disrupted by the nationalist-centered "Make Amer-ica Great Again" political ideology. America is, in this internationalist, no-borders view, supposed to be in place to fund the UN and all of its globalist agenda plans.

Making America great again is not in their blueprint. This nation, therefore, is the chief obstacle, nation-wise, to Satan's plans in form-ing the one-world order he wants to set up for the coming Antichrist. That's why we've endured insane rage while the powers in high places strive to get power back into the formerly established order by getting rid of this president.

The satanic assault against American society and culture can't be missed. Minions in high places have in recent years inflicted tre-mendous deleterious effects upon the nation's moral fiber established by the founding fathers and Christian church influences. America's public, and even private, educational systems have become completely corrupted, first by the evolutional model, then by the Marxist educators at every level of the public school system.

The rage makes clear the existence of the Antichrist spirit in high places that continues to do everything to bring America and the world into the configuration Satan wants to establish for his soon-coming Antichrist platform. At the heart of the minions' (both human and supernatural) effort is destruction of moral values and norms based upon Judeo-Christian precepts/concepts. Cultures and societies throughout the world—especially in America—must be altered drastically to pave the way for the coming Antichrist regime.

These minions in the high places of wickedness are even now using the so-called pandemic in their incessant drive to bring about their version of Heaven on earth. They will succeed for a time, but not until the Holy Spirit as Restrainer of evil removes as God's prophetic Word foretells in 2 Thessalonians 2.

Just as we witness the Antichrist spirit surging, we, as born-again believers, should have a surging sense of excitement and comfort. Redemption is near (Titus 2:13).

You don't have to be among the masses left behind to suffer through the coming wrath and judgment. Accept Christ right this moment. You will go instantaneously to be with Jesus Christ in an *atomos* of time—faster than the eye can blink—when He says, "Come up here!" (Revelation 4:1).

The Great Resist

Those of us who believe we are charged by the Lord to be "watchers" on the wall look at the acceleration of the stage being set for prophetic fulfillment as a wondrous thing to behold. There can be no missing the reality that we are fast approaching the dénouement of the Age of Grace.

No recent development has been more significant than the movement toward establishing a New World Order. A specific element that's most troubling within that movement is termed the "Great Reset."

This term, defined within the title of a book by the same name, means the globalization of the entire world—those who intend to establish a world under a single government must, in their view, not be thwarted. The very existence of the planet depends upon their being able to achieve their goals—goals encapsulated within what began as Agenda 21 and is now called Agenda 30. This "agenda" means they must accomplish all their shaping of this global order no later than the year 2030.

These would-be globalist masters don't see the things developing as we do by looking at them through the prism of Bible prophecy. While we see things advancing toward Antichrist's regime at an amazing and frightening pace, the globalists, such as author of the book, *The Great Reset,* see things as being slowed and inhibited by forces they must eliminate. That is, they must eliminate those like *us,* for example. And by "us," I mean both we who are Christians pointing out their evil, and this nation, the United States of America, whose people have been steeped in basic liberty and God-given rights, from a Judeo-Christian foundation, for almost three centuries.

America is the single most powerful holdup to Agenda 30 and the Great Reset. This nation, the most materially blessed in history, will not "go gentle into that good night," as Dylan Thomas would have it. We won't easily be made to ride bicycles, stay within fifteen-minute cities, and eat bugs instead of the foods we love, like the Great Resetters and their agenda insist we should do. There will be major pushback for as long as the nation exists as it is presently comprised.

Of course, the American, liberty-loving/enjoying constituency is under constant attack by the powers and principalities of Ephesians 6:12, both demonic and human. And that luciferian cabal is determined to take down America and eliminate all opposition to their agenda. These minions call the opposition they face "the retreat from globalization." The following gives more detail of Klaus Schwab and his cohorts' determination to change things so their neo-tower of Babel can be built, free of opposition.

Schwab and Theirry Malleret's book, *Covid-19: The Great Reset,* identified "the global governance free fall" as an existential challenge, and if we do not collaborate, "we are doomed."

"Nation states make global governance possible (one leads the other)," they state, continuing, "The more nationalism and isolationism pervade the global polity, the greater the chance that global governance loses its relevance and becomes ineffective. Sadly, we are now at this critical juncture. Put bluntly, we live in a world in which nobody is really in charge."

Managing director of the International Monetary Fund Kristalina Georgieva suggested "concentrating on the areas where, without working together, we are doomed." The examples she gave as "we are doomed" without globalization were "climate change," the "green transition" and debt.

The authors don't explain why there is a need for an "individual reset," they simply assumed it was a consequence of the COVID "pandemic." However, as they did throughout the book, they used collectivism as a tool of social control.

"If, as human beings, we do not collaborate to confront our existential challenges (the environment and the global governance free fall, among others), we are doomed," they claimed.... "The rise of nationalism makes the retreat of globalization inevitable in most of the world—an impulse particularly notable in the West. The vote for Bruit and the election of President Trump on a protectionist platform are two momentous markers of the Western backlash against globalization."[124]

As we've said before, the term "the common good" and its ugly sister "the greater good" represent collectivism which is found in socialist, communist and fascist movements. These movements use "the common good" as a tool for social control.[125]

This is exactly what we see happening within the American political process today. The incessant drive to bring about a Marxist collective system is at the heart of the attempted Great Reset being foisted by the human minions, assisted by the demonic, of Ephesians 6:12, in my studied opinion.

I heard a senator speaking before the Senate chamber not long ago. I like what he said, although I'm almost certain he didn't realize the true importance of his statement.

He said something like: "Instead of the un-American Great Reset, we need the Great Resist. We must resist this attempted Marxist-type tyranny."

The Great Resist is precisely what is given within God's Word as opposition to Satan and his minions' attempts to bring to power the man of sin, Antichrist, and his regime of horrors.

> And now ye know what [restrains] that [Antichrist] might be revealed in his time. For the mystery of iniquity doth already work: only [the Holy Spirit] who now [restrains] will [restrain], until [the Holy Spirit] be taken out of the way. And then shall that Wicked be revealed, whom the Lord shall consume with the spirit of his mouth, and shall destroy with the brightness of his coming. (2 Thessalonians 6–8)

We who know the Lord Jesus for salvation are part of the Great Resist. Pastors, listen up! Don't resist the Great Resist. To resist the Great Resist, you are aiding and assisting those who want to bring about the Great Reset.

Preach Bible prophecy—and from the pre-Trib view. Jesus is about to intervene in the wicked affairs of humankind. The Rapture, according to all the signs and signals of the coming Tribulation raging in every direction, is about to disrupt life on planet earth!

For those who haven't done so, here is how to be prepared, thus be assured that you will go to Jesus Christ when He calls all believers to Himself in that stupendous moment of rescue from this judgment-bound earth:

That if thou shalt confess with thy mouth the Lord Jesus, and shalt believe in thine heart that God hath raised him from the dead, thou shalt be saved. For with the heart man believeth unto righteousness; and with the mouth confession is made unto salvation. (Romans 10:9–10)

SECTION IV

TRIBULATION TRIGGERS

Chapter 10

TRACKING MIDEAST TURMOIL

By Bill Salus

General Editor's note: Dr. Bill Salus has his finger of discernment on the pulse of things happening in the Middle East and in Israel in particular. And things we watch develop there by the day is nothing short of astonishing, in consideration of what the Bible foretells for the time leading up to Christ's return.

Bill's Christ-centered Depot Ministry and his prolific writing and media involvement comprise the source to find the very latest prophetic stage-setting things going on surrounding God's chosen people. His contribution, taken from an appendix in his book entitled, *Revelation Road, Hope Beyond the Horizon*, provides understanding one can find at no better center of observation of these times. And make no mistake: Israel and the astonishing hatred coming against the Jewish people are the beginning of prophetic fulfillment leading swiftly to the worst time of all human history, according to the Lord Jesus Christ Himself.

✛✛✛

The foreign ministers of Russia, Syria, Turkey and Iran have met in Moscow for high-level talks on rebuilding ties between Ankara and Damascus after years of animosity during Syria's war.

—"Russia, Syria, Turkey and Iran Hold High-level Talks in Moscow," *Al Jazeera*, May 10, 2023[126]

Burgeoning relationships between Russia, Turkey, and Iran like the above headline suggests are among the reasons scholars are justifiably stirring over the possibility that the Ezekiel 38–39 Bible prophecy is about to find final fulfillment. The Hebrew prophet predicted approximately 2,600 years ago the coming of a Russian-Iranian led, nine-member-strong coalition seeking to destroy Israel and confiscate its great booty (Ezekiel 38:13).

These countries form into an outer ring around Israel. The outer ring map superimposes the modern-day equivalents over the ancient territories identified in Ezekiel 38:1–5.

This article develops the possibility that the Russian-Iranian led coalition of Ezekiel invaders implements a two-pronged "choke and capture" campaign. Step one involves a possible political boycott of Israel's booty, and step two matures into a military campaign to capture that booty.

International coalitions formed to level economic sanctions against a country have become politically expedient and often effective. Boycotting a country's imports and exports is a common first step to accomplish the will of a coalition. An excellent example was the Persian Gulf War of August 2, 1990–February 28, 1991.

Saddam Hussein had invaded Kuwait, and in so doing brought

down international economic sanctions upon the Iraqis. American President George H. W. Bush skillfully assembled a sizable coalition that ultimately invaded Iraq when the sanctions didn't work. The boycott matured into an invasion.

In the case of the Russian-Iranian coalition, this two-step process appears to occur. Identifying the modern-day equivalents of the Ezekiel 38:1–5 invaders suggests this coalition is strategically assembled. There are geographic and religious commonalities to consider in their case.

First, apart from Russia, all the other members hail from predominately Muslim countries. Second, locating the invaders geographically on a map provides another interesting clue into the coalition's campaign. Several of the Muslim members border the major bodies of water surrounding Israel. Is this coincidence, or calculated on Russia's part?

Israel will desperately need access through these waterways in order to export its plunder and great booty to global markets. We know with some certainty Israel will be conducting international commerce because the theme of merchants is introduced in Ezekiel 38:13.

Sheba [Yemen], Dedan [Saudi Arabia], the merchants of Tarshish [likely the UK], and all their young lions [likely including USA] will say to you, "Have you come to take plunder? Have you gathered your army to take booty, to carry away silver and gold, to take away livestock and goods, to take great plunder?" (Ezekiel 38:13, NKJV)

The merchants of Tarshish and all their young lions are listed, and they appear to be upset with Russia. A suitable modern-day translation of these merchants would be the "customers from Tarshish."

These international clients seem to abstain from joining the Russian consortia. Comments they make in Ezekiel 38:13 evidence concerns about Russian intentions to destroy Israel for its great booty. Their protests could be altruistic, but more likely show that they don't want their commercial interests invested in Israel disrupted.

The Mediterranean Sea, Red Sea, and Persian Gulf could easily be blockaded to Israel at Russia's command once the coalition is set in place. Israel would be forced to truck its exports through the Arabian Peninsula, into the Arabian Sea, on into the Indian Ocean in an effort to distribute goods to market.

All other transportation corridors would be choked off to Israel since they connect through coalition territories. The image below identifies some of the coalition and the arrows point out how Israel could become completely boxed in.

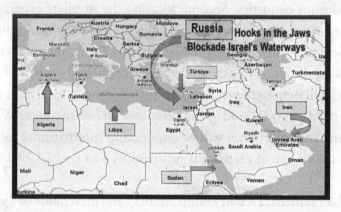

Turkey (*Türkiye*), Libya, and Algeria could choke off the Mediterranean Sea. Sudan could blockade the Red Sea, and Iran could close off the Persian Gulf.

Once Israel's economic knees buckle from disrupted commerce, the Ezekiel invaders could initiate the military portion of their campaign. Historical war campaigns have often been conducted in this fashion. First the enemy surrounds its target, prompting those under attack to circle the wagons in defense. Once surrounded, the enemy sits it out, forcing their foes to sustain themselves upon stored supplies. When fatigue sets in, the enemy attacks.

Hooks in the Jaws

I will turn you [Russia] around, put hooks into your jaws, and lead you out, with all your army [coalition], horses, and horsemen, all splendidly clothed, a great company with bucklers and shields, all of them handling swords. (Ezekiel 38:4, NKJV)

The above verse introduces the idiom of "hooks into your jaws." This might suggest a fishing typology and add credence to the blockade theory espoused above. An example would be likened to how a fisher draws a shark into his boat by putting a hook into its jaw. Perhaps this illustration pertains to the possibility that the Russian coalition has blockaded the waterways to choke off Israel's commercial exports, and the Lord will hook the coalition securely in its jaws to draw the forces into Israel for the invasion.

Why would the Lord do such a thing? Ezekiel 38:18–22 points out He will unleash His fury against the Russian coalition supernaturally. They will be defeated by a great earthquake, flooding rain, great hailstones, fire, and brimstone. This divine defeat will enable the Lord to fulfill the prophecy below:

So I will make My holy name known in the midst of My people Israel, and I will not let them profane My holy name anymore. Then the nations shall know that I am the Lord, the Holy One in Israel. (Ezekiel 39:7)

This explains that the Lord orchestrates and plans this epic prophetic event for His greater purposes. He plans to put the world on notice that He is the One True God and that His name is holy. Thus, putting hooks into the jaws of the Russian coalition to steer it into the predesignated battlefield—which, according to Ezekiel 39:2–4, is the mountains of Israel—is part of God's strategy.

Conclusion

It seems plausible that Russia will formulate a comprehensive "choke and capture" campaign, involving strategically located allies intent on invading Israel. This effort involves an outer ring of nations that do not presently share common borders with Israel. The inner circle of Arab states shown in the image below is likely not included in Russia's consortia, because they have probably been defeated previously in the Arab-Israeli war of Psalm 83.

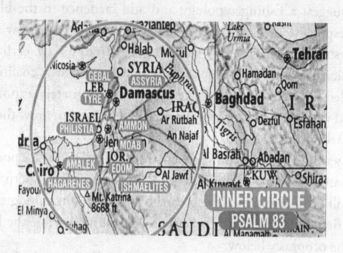

In the aftermath of the war described in Psalm 83, Israel seemingly annexes more territory and captures Arab spoils of war, making it potentially a very wealthy nation. Russia then forms its campaign and alliance to prevent Israel from burgeoning into a significant commercial goods and oil-exporting nation.

Russia strategically assembles Muslim nations sharing a hatred of Israel. This coalition seems to be strategically selected in order to blockade Israel's exports first, then destroy the Jewish state afterward. Perhaps the ominous phrase, "I will turn you around, put hooks into your jaws, and lead you out," in Ezekiel 38:4 has something to do with a waterway-related campaign against Israel. However, instead of catching fish on the seas, it may involve exporting oil and gas through them.

Chapter 11

BEWARE
THINGS TO COME

By Tom Hughes

General Editor's note: Few who watch for Christ's return more fully understand the prophetic times of this generation than Pastor Tom Hughes. He founded the prophecy ministry Hope for Our Times and has established more than four hundred churches. He has been teaching Bible prophecy for more than thirty years with his unique gift for helping people understand the last days. Tom shares weekly prophecy updates on the Hope for Our Times website, app, and YouTube channel; is in demand as a prophecy conference speaker; and conducts interviews as host of various programs. He's also frequently interviewed for his comprehensive knowledge of Bible prophecy as it might relate to current issues and events.

Tom, in his contribution, dissects these strange yet fascinating times with discernment that gives a critical heads-up on things to come. Tom helps us do as Jesus said: "When you see all these things begin to come to pass, then look up and lift your head, for your redemption draweth nigh" (Luke 21:28)

+++

I've been listening to the pronouncements and watching the posturing of political leaders and media personalities regarding the war between Israel and Hamas. A few present the idea that Israel should not respond to terror attacks. I guess Israelis are supposed to grin and bear it when such atrocities as families burned alive take place in their homeland.

One of the many obvious problems with this idea is that Israel is not the source of hatred toward Jews, especially in the Middle East. That hatred goes back many centuries before Israel became a nation in 1948. The thing they don't like about Israel is that it is a "Jewish state."

More commonly, people speak of Israel defeating Hamas in the short term, then making peace. But who will they make peace with? These people have good imaginations. They pretend there are Palestinian leaders who want to live side by side with Israel—two happy, sovereign democracies, living in harmony.

The talk of peace reminds me of false prophets in the Old Testament. Through Jeremiah, God set the record straight:

From the prophet even to the priest everyone deals falsely. For they have healed the hurt of the daughter of My people slightly, Saying, "Peace, peace!" When there is no peace. (Jeremiah 8:10–11)

Another version puts it like this:

Even my prophets and priests are...frauds. They offer superficial treatments for my people's mortal wound. They give assurances of peace when there is no peace.

Other verses repeat this idea. Please understand I'm not scorning the quest for peace. Jesus said, "Blessed are the peacemakers" (Matthew 5:9). I will not criticize those whom Jesus called blessed. In fact, I want to be numbered among the peacemakers. When war is averted, suffering is averted. Tragedies are averted. And civilization itself is maintained. The Bible admonishes us to, "Pursue peace" (Hebrews 12:14) and "live peaceably" (Romans 12:18), while reminding us that we serve "the God of love and peace" (2 Corinthians 13:11).

Psalms 122:6 says, "Pray for the peace of Jerusalem." Ultimately, to pray for the peace of Jerusalem is much the same prayer as, "Come quickly, Lord Jesus." He will return with "healing in His wings"—that is true peace and restoration. In the meantime, we are His people and we work as His agents. We should be known as peacemakers.

Even as we work for peace in Israel, we must also understand that human beings will not ultimately bring peace there. For now, "There is no peace." For Israel, it's like the situation described in Psalms 120:6–7:

> My soul has dwelt too long with one who hates peace. I am for peace; But when I speak, they are for war.

How do you make peace with those who only want war? Whatever fix comes next, it's a temporary fix, not a solution. In an article in *The Guardian*, writer Jonathan Freedland said:

> Senior Hamas official Ghazi Hamad told Lebanese TV that his organization was determined to repeat the massacre of 7 October. Hamad promised that 7 October was "just the first time, and there will be a second, a third, a fourth." He was asked if Hamas was bent on Israel's annihilation. "Yes, of course," he replied.

From the Hamas charter forward, the group has repeatedly said its religious duty is to annihilate Israel, and their actions prove that, on this issue, they've been telling the truth. That's why Israel is now determined to destroy their leadership, remove their weapons, end their war-making capabilities, and, most crucially, terminate Hamas' role in governing Gaza. These things are a matter of life and death. But the strategy won't work in the long term, because even if Hamas disappears, the hate that created it will not.

Even so, world leaders and members of the media keep pushing the idea of a two-state solution.

The headline and subhead of another *Guardian* article by Freedland said, "Once this war between Israel and Hamas is over, a deeper conflict looms: A lasting peace has to become thinkable again. And it will be—if extremists on both sides are shunned."[127]

Notice the fallacy. The phrase, "extremists on both sides," implies a moral equivalence between the Israeli and Palestinian positions. Really? How often do Israelis randomly invade Gaza with armed militants, randomly killing civilians—including babies and toddlers? Israel is on defense. When they resort to violence, it is in response to violence on the other side, and it is always a defensive action, an attempt to keep their people safe.

There are other problems with this "solution." How do you shun extremists while negotiating peace with Palestinian leaders? There would be no one to negotiate with. A person becomes a Palestinian leader by being an extremist. Do you remember Yassar Arafat of the Palestinian Liberation Organization? He was an extremist if ever an extremist existed. Israel worked hard to make peace with him because he's all the other side offered.

The Oslo Accords brought something called the Palestinian Authority (PA) into being. They gave the PA partial control of Judea and Samaria (or the West Bank) and of the Gaza Strip. In 1996, terrorist leader Yasser Arafat won a presidential election with 88 percent of the vote, and his political party, Fatah, won the parliament. Arafat died in 2004. So, in 2005, nine years after their first presidential election, they finally held another—this time electing Mahmoud Abbas.

Abbas is now in the nineteenth year of what was supposed to be a four-year term. They call him a moderate. But he leads the Palestinian Authority, an entity that rewards acts of terrorism. On October 31, The Gatestone Institute reported:

> This month alone, the Palestinian Authority will pay the families of the Hamas terrorists who were killed this month at least

11.1 million shekels ($2.7 million) "Pay-for-Slay" reward for perpetrating the atrocities against Israeli civilians.[128]

In 2015, the "moderate" Abbas said Palestinians will not allow Jews "with their filthy feet to defile our Al-Aqsa Mosque." The "moderate" also said, "We bless every drop of blood that has been spilled for Jerusalem, which is clean and pure blood, blood spilled for Allah."

The Gatestone article went on to point out:

There is absolutely no difference between the Palestinian Authority and Hamas when it comes to spreading hate against Israel and inciting the murder of Jews. It has also been proven that each time Israel cedes land or makes gestures to the PA or Hamas, they respond by increasing terror attacks against Jews.[129]

President Joe Biden is still pushing a two-state solution, but that is politics, not reality. To negotiate a two-state solution requires two partners. Right now, Israel has no one to negotiate with.

Yet, the *New York Times* reports that the terrorist action by Hamas has succeeded in bringing the "long discounted" two-state solution back to life, "As President Biden and other Western leaders promote the idea," the *Times* said, "Some diplomats and analysts say the Hamas-Israel war may breathe new life into it."[130]

Rewarding unthinkable behavior seems to be a worldwide trend with President Biden in the US, Prime Minister Rishi Sunak in Britain, and President Emmanuel Macros of France all pushing the idea.

How do these things relate to prophecy?

Among other things, the Israel-Hamas war has caused:

- A rise in hatred for Jews—as prophesied in the Bible.
- More Jews returning to the Promised Land—also as prophesied.

- A rise in reprobate thinking the world over, as described in Romans 1 and 2 Timothy 3. In this case, the reprobate thinking includes the impulse to call evil "good" and good "evil"—like standing on the side of baby-killers.
- And a world that calls evil "good" is well set up for the rise of Antichrist.

Here are seven things that are coming—as current events are preparing the whole world for Antichrist.

1. *Daniel 9 informs us the Tribulation period begins when Antichrist confirms a covenant with Israel.* Prophecy teachers have long said it would be a treaty that seems to bring peace to the Middle East. It will seem to solve the seemingly unsolvable, and the world will hail the Antichrist in messianic terms.

2. *The current turmoil increases Israel's sense of desperation for peace.* Antichrist will come on the scene with a seemingly miraculous answer to Israel's deepest longing. A false peace is coming. The current war seems to be the perfect set-up. And all the anti-Semitism currently on display may be calmed down by the leadership of Antichrist, but the hearts of the masses of people worldwide have been on display. Jesus says out of the abundance of the heart the mouth speaks. The hatred toward the Jews worldwide is on full display. And at the midpoint of the Tribulation, Antichrist will have most of the world on his side in Satan's final attempt to rid the world of Jews. Praise God the final attempt will fail, because Jesus will save them.

3. *It increases the unthinkable possibility of global thermonuclear war,* something that seems to be described in the Bible for

the last days. The fear of it is such that it will work as an incentive to give Antichrist his global power.

4. *It has brought about other threats to world peace.* For instance, Recep Erdoğan, President of Turkey, recently threatened "war between the cross and the crescent." That means a holy war between Christians and Muslims. About 2.4 billion people on earth fall under the heading of Christian and almost 2 billion under Muslim. It's hard to imagine a bigger catastrophe.

5. *Current events have increased global economic turmoil,* and Gaza might be the domino that begins the cascade of events that eventually brings the whole thing down. Antichrist will present himself not only as a peacemaker, but as the one who can bring sanity to financial markets.

6. *The Gaza war helps set up the events of Ezekiel 38.* The Ezekiel 38 coalition described in the Bible will be led by Russia and Iran, and Turkey will join them. It isn't a coincidence that Hamas leader Musa Abu Marzouk recently met with Iranian and Russian officials in Moscow. At that meeting, he said, "We look at Russia as our closest friend." And now, Turkey's Erdogan has begun to spout hatred toward Israel at a level he never had done before, even threatening to send his troops to the Holy Land.

7. *Before the Ezekiel 38 battle, I believe the Gaza war helps set up the events of Isaiah 17.* That chapter talks about the city of Damascus, Syria, being utterly destroyed in a single night. As the sun sets, it will exist whole and untouched, and by sunrise the next morning, it will be gone. That wasn't possible a hundred years ago, but today a city that size can be destroyed in a single night, and Damascus sits right in the middle of this massive conflict. More than that, Syria continues to be an active participant in that conflict.

The rockets are flying, soldiers are marching, and the hatred is deepening—just as the Bible said it would in the days leading up to the end of the age.

Hope

Here's something to offend you…

In Matthew 24, Jesus described the time just before His return. In verse 10, He drops in the phrase, "Many will be offended." It doesn't seem like much until you reach today's date; just stop and look around. Today, we live in the age of "offense."

Some relish being the perpetrators of offense. Others obsess over being the victims of offense. For the perpetrators, offending others has become a dark sport. People use their highest sense of creativity to think up new ways to offend.

Meanwhile, finding offense in the words and actions of people consumes victims. They're always on the lookout for anything that might be meant to offend them, or that they might find offensive. Being offended—being someone's victim and telling others about it—has become cool.

The Duke and Duchess of Sussex, better known as Prince Harry and Meghan Markle, have said they were the victims of racism within the royal family. They claimed to have been chased through the streets of New York City for more than two hours of harrowing escapes. This is, of course, reminiscent of the very real high-speed chase that killed Harry's mother, Diana. But video of this event shows that some of the paparazzi following the Duke and Duchess at these dangerously high speeds…were on bicycles.

Why do even the most privileged of people constantly need to depict themselves as victims? Because being a victim has become cool. Many today look for excuses to be offended as if it were gold.

The Lord's prophecy that, in the time near His return, "Many will be offended," has a specific fulfillment and a general fulfillment. Specifically, Jesus was talking about events during the seven years leading up to His return, the Tribulation. The Bible tells us specifically when that time begins and how it ends. It also teaches that the Rapture will take place before the Tribulation begins. So, we don't yet see the specific fulfillment of this prophecy. But it's crucial for us to understand the prophecy, because it is another piece of evidence that, in our day, the world continues to bend itself into the shape the Lord said it would take near the end.

At this point in His discourse, Jesus talked about a time of extreme persecution for anyone or any group who might consider following Him. The Greek word here translated as "offended" is *skandalizo*. You can probably tell from the sound of it that we get our English word "scandalize" directly from it. The Greek root has to do with tripping up or entrapping.

People have been tripped up, offended, and scandalized throughout the Christian era. But clearly it will be worse for those who consider coming to Christ after the Rapture, and especially during the intense persecution of the Tribulation.

That's the context, and in it we see the primary meaning. But here's the fascinating thing. We can also take those words at face value—"Many will be offended." When we do that, it becomes obvious it is already a major trend—even a lifestyle—among people in the world.

We already see people abandoning the faith of their parents because they're scandalized/offended by the teachings of the Bible. But they're also offended by anything that seems to restrict human behavior. They are scandalized that anyone would dare call sin "sin." Preachers—not wanting to offend—work diligently to find ways to keep people in their churches without scandalizing them. Sometimes they go to extremes and actually deny God's Word because they don't want to offend. But the Bible does offend. Bible prophecy said that would happen. And Jesus was put on a cross because He was an offense to His persecutors.

But it doesn't stop at faith. Today, comedians struggle with what to present in their acts out of their fear of offending. Advertisements trigger outrage. Sometimes they deliberately offend in an attempt to be stylish and edgy. Other times, it catches them by surprise. Announcers calling ballgames offend. Actors offend. Screenwriters offend.

While some use their creativity to intentionally offend, others use their creativity in finding offense—often where none was intended. Offending and being offended have become lifestyles.

It's a lose-lose situation for humanity, because it destroys communication while undermining friendship, family, and mutual respect. But it's a win-win for Satan, because he knows all people are members of one marginalized group or another. You can be marginalized by your skin color, your sex, your faith, or any of a thousand different characteristics. For Satan, it's a rich playground.

Adding to the environment of offense are those who offend intentionally.

The Los Angeles Dodgers created a brouhaha recently when they disinvited a group from their Pride Day celebration. The Sisters of Perpetual Indulgence repeatedly say they're not anti-Catholic. If not, then why do these people—mostly biological males—dress as nuns? Why, while wearing the outfits of nuns, do they publicly simulate sickening sex acts, repulsive to any person of good taste? They are clearly designed from the ground up to offend Catholics.

Their website brags about their ability to "raise tempers." They chant outside churches. They repeatedly make fun of prayer and blessing, and even of the Lord's resurrection. They present themselves as "the Brides of Christ."

Yet *Out Magazine* proclaims in a headline, "Dodgers Side with Religious Right, Kick Drag Group Out of Pride Night."[131] Are they kidding? If the Dodgers were siding with the religious right, they wouldn't have a Pride Night.

Jesus gave many signs of His return that are common to human history. Offending people is not new. Neither is lawlessness, war, rumors of war, persecution, deception, earthquakes, famines, pestilences, or others. They've been going on all along. Clearly, He was talking about something more—a greater intensity to these events than was seen previously, and a convergence of them. He said they would be like birth pangs, increasing in intensity and frequency.

Even though we're not yet in the Tribulation, the world seems close to it. Things Jesus said would happen during that period are intensifying right now to previously unknown levels. And they're beginning to happen all at once. We're getting an increasingly clear picture of what the Tribulation world will look like. There are two reasons: 1) With closer proximity, we can see better; and 2) As our world changes into the shape of Tribulation earth, we get new insights. Some of the blanks are filled in.

In all of this, Jesus said the opposite: "Blessed is he who is not offended because of Me" (Matthew 11:6). Jesus died on a cross, and that offends people. He died for the sins of human beings, and this offends people because it means they, too, are sinners. He gives His salvation to all who ask. This offends people because it hurts their pride. They think they can earn their way to Heaven.

In John 14, Jesus said, "No one comes to the Father but by Me." This really scandalizes folks. Is He saying He's somehow better than Mohammed or the Buddha? Well...yes.

Jesus is God the Son. John 1:3 says, "All things were made through Him, and without Him nothing was made that was made." That makes Him the Creator. I don't see Buddha or Mohammed staking out that ground. Jesus was the only man in history totally without sin. He is infinitely more than just the leader of another religious movement. He came to earth as a man, but also as God. Titus 2:13 refers to Him as "our great God and Savior Jesus Christ."

Angels sang at His birth. They weren't offended by His greatness. They were awed by it and embraced it. We should, too.

Mockers Have Come

Second Peter 3 gives both a general and a specific warning about the last days. The general warning is this: "Scoffers will come in the last days." The New American Standard Bible says, "In the last days mockers will come with their mocking."

The warning becomes more specific as it continues, but don't pass by this introductory sentence too quickly: "Scoffers will come"; "Mockers will come with their mocking."

We live in an age of mockery. It's always cool to ridicule. Sarcasm is said to be the easiest form of humor. It takes no intelligence or understanding. Just make fun of whatever you choose. The more serious and important it is, the easier it is to ridicule. Patriotism? You're humiliated. Morality—especially sexual morality—you will be made fun of. It's always good for a laugh. Mockery gives the mocker an illusion of power over the mocked.

Scoffers have been around since the days of Genesis, but not like today. Today we have mass media and social media. Kids are killing themselves because others mock them. And nothing seems able to stop it. This is the age of mockery.

Second Peter 3:3 also provides the mockers' motivation: "walking according to their own lusts."

Never in world history has lust been so commercialized. We brand it, package it, sell it, and weaponize it—especially against the young. First John 2:16 speaks of "the lust of the flesh, the lust of the eyes, and the pride of life." Billions of dollars are spent getting people to buy things. What are advertisers' favorite tools? "The lust of the flesh, the lust of the eyes, and the pride of life." And, because thousands of advertising images bombard human brains every day, those brains are being reprogrammed and rewritten.

What stands in the way of "the lust of the flesh, the lust of the eyes, and the pride of life"? God's Word. So, how does humanity respond to God's word? Mockery.

Then Scripture becomes more specific. It gives us an example of the mocking. In 2 Peter 3:4, the mockers ask, "Where is the promise of His coming?"

Just a few years ago, there was a movie called *Rapture-Palooza*. That's an example of the world mocking "the promise of His coming." And we see quite a bit of that. It seems that people who know little about the specifics of the Second Coming are at least aware of it and have heard words like "Rapture" and "Armageddon."

But here's where the story becomes desperately sad. The world isn't where most of the mockery originates. Most who mock "the promise of His coming" are what we might call "church people." You may ask, "Isn't the Church built on the promises of God? Why would people of the Church mock God's promise?" According to this passage, the number-one motivation for mocking God's promise is that they want to walk according to the flesh. If you live in the expectancy of His return, you are far less likely to live according to the lusts of the flesh.

The mockers go on to say, "For since the fathers fell asleep, all things continue as they were from the beginning of creation." These people feel their infinitesimal level of knowledge qualifies them to attack the credibility of the Almighty, All-knowing God.

Their mocking attacks the very character of God. Jesus said He would come again, but they say, "No, He's not. It is stupid to actually think these parts of the Bible are to be taken seriously." "I've been hearing this stuff my whole life, everything is the same. He still hasn't come, and stop talking about this because He will not come."

But there is yet another reason the mockers are increasing. In 2 Peter, we read that, along with walking in their lusts, they are ignorant. In this case, their ignorance is seen as self-induced. The King James Version puts it like this: They are "willfully ignorant." They choose to forget, choose to ignore, choose to not study, choose to remain blind.

Second Peter 5 says, "For this they *willfully* forget: that by the word of God the heavens were of old" (emphasis added). They mock God's Word when they mock His promise. But by His word, He created the heavens and the earth. He said the words, "'Let there be light' and there was light" (Genesis 1:3).

The same God who spoke the universe into existence speaks of Christ's return. He promises it! He does so repeatedly and in dozens of different ways. When they mock His Word, they mock Him. How dare those who expect to go to Heaven based on His Word mock His Word!

What do Christians offer the world? Our message is that God has spoken. He spoke through prophets, and He eventually sent His Son into the world to speak with humanity face to face.

God the Son—preexistent with the Father and the Holy Spirit throughout eternity past—was born into the world. He walked among us.

The first chapter of John calls Him "the Word." Verse 1 identifies the Word as God. Verse 3 emphasizes He is God by saying twice that He created all things. Verse 14 says, "And the Word became flesh and dwelt among us, and we beheld His glory, the glory as of the only begotten of the Father, full of grace and truth." Verses 15 through 18 (and many others) identify the Word as Jesus Christ.

Every word Jesus spoke was the very word of God, because Jesus was and is God. He said, "Heaven and earth will pass away, but My words will by no means pass away" (Matthew 24:35). And He is coming back: "I will come again and receive you to Myself" (John 14:3); "I am going away and coming back to you" (John 14:28).

After the Lord's ascension, angels spoke to the witnesses there and said, "This same Jesus, who was taken up from you into heaven, will so come in like manner as you saw Him go into heaven" (Acts 1:11)

First Thessalonians 4:16–17 tells about the Rapture of the Church:

> For the Lord Himself will descend from heaven with a shout, with the voice of an archangel, and with the trumpet of God. And the dead in Christ will rise first. Then we who are alive and remain shall be caught up together with them in the clouds to meet the Lord in the air. And thus we shall always be with the Lord.

Scripture says mockers will come in the last days. Today, like never before in history, the mockers *have* come. They are here. They've arrived on the scene. And many are high-ranking members of Christian denominations. Mockers infest Christian colleges and seminaries. They teach our children as we send them to the Christian schools.

It's not surprising that American rapper Lil Nas X would depict himself and the devil having homosexual relations and that British singer/songwriter Sam Smith would try to glorify Satan at the Grammy awards. It's not even surprising that the Grammy awards' live audience of music-industry movers and shakers loved the performances. They embraced and applauded the evil.

But something *is* surprising. Not so long ago, major television networks and their advertisers were careful not to offend. In advance of the show, Smith tweeted pictures of a satanic rehearsal. CBS responded with the tweet, "We are ready to worship!"

A major television network was mocking God, His Word, and His people. They and the Grammy sponsors, including mega-corporations IBM, Google, MasterCard, Amazon, United Airlines, and Hilton fully and publicly embraced the message. Yet to a vast portion of their customers and potential customers, it is hate. It used to be about the money. But now the mockery has a life of its own. It is overwhelming, engulfing, and finally overtaking the advertisers' own self-interest.

Christians spend money, too. Christians buy advertisers' products, too. Why so deeply offend Christians and the people who love or even like their Christian friends and family? They are scared to say anything even remotely negative against much smaller groups of people. Yet CBS tweeted this evil, horrible insult to the Christian community. The age of mockery has dawned. The mockers of God are legion.

Scripture goes on to remind readers of God's judgment in the past, sending a great Flood during the days of Noah. Back in 2 Peter 3, verse 7, we read: "The heavens and the earth...are now preserved by the same word."

Mockers should realize they and the world are sustained by the Word they mock. Verse 7 goes on the say the earth is "reserved for fire until the day of judgment and perdition of ungodly men." Mock away, but judgment is coming! Denial of the truth doesn't negate the truth.

Verse 8 reminds us that "with the Lord one day is as a thousand years, and a thousand years as one day." If you try to put God on the clock, forget it. It doesn't work that way. Time to Him isn't the same as it is to us. Isaiah 57:15 calls Him "the High and Lofty One Who inhabits eternity."

Verse 9 says, "The Lord is not slack concerning His promise, as some count slackness." God always keeps His promises. He cannot lie. That verse goes on to say God is "longsuffering toward us, not willing that any should perish but that all should come to repentance."

I suppose that's what we need to remember the most right now. Regardless of mocking and ridicule, marginalizing and targeting followers of Christ, those who mock us still need to be saved, for their end is horrific—and it is for eternity. *Help us, Lord, to tell others about the great hope we have in You…our only hope.*

This Makes No Sense

On May 14, 1948, Israel declared its independence. United States President Harry Truman, against the advice of the State Department, immediately and officially recognized its independence. His action was followed by most of the world. As the Bible prophesied, a nation was born in a day (Isaiah 66:8). It was a miracle for the ages. God had said He would do it, and He did.

There are no precedents. No other nation has been exiled from its homeland and forced to disperse around the world, yet remained a distinct people. No other nation that has disappeared for two thousand years has been suddenly reborn—let alone a nation made up of the most hated of peoples.

Anti-Semitism permeated the world of the 1940s. The Nazis had just tried their "Final Solution of the Jewish Question"—which was to murder them all. The immediate aftermath of the Holocaust may have been the only moment in world history when a majority of nations would vote for the formation of an independent Jewish state. But that's exactly what the United Nations General Assembly did.

It was a miracle like no other. The Old Testament often reminds Israel of God's special relationship with that nation by identifying God as the One who delivered them from the land of Egypt. It's a reminder of God's miracle-working power on their behalf. The Exodus from Egypt featured a series of jaw-dropping miracles—the burning bush…the plagues…the Passover…the pillar of cloud by day and the pillar of fire by night…the Red Sea parting….

But God told the prophet Jeremiah the events surrounding the Exodus will not always be the great reminder of God's miracles on Israel's behalf. Jeremiah 16:14–15 says:

"Behold, the days are coming," says the Lord, 'that it shall no more be said, "The Lord lives who brought up the children of Israel from the land of Egypt," but, "The Lord lives who brought up the children of Israel from the land of the north and from all the lands where He had driven them." For I will bring them back into their land which I gave to their fathers.

That's amazing! God says the miracle of drawing Israel out of the nations and back into its promised homeland supersedes even the miracles of the Exodus from Egypt, including the parting of the Red Sea.

Christians should have been on their feet applauding at the miraculous rebirth of Israel. Before their eyes, God showed His unlimited power and fulfilled promises no one thought possible. But sadly, and unreasonably, most of Christendom refused to see the hand of God in these massive events—even though it had all been laid out in the Bible.

The Christian rejection of Israel boils down to three things—two doctrinal issues and an ancient prejudice. The first doctrinal issue is their belief that biblical Israel no longer exists. They believe God broke His word to the physical descendants of Abraham, Isaac, and Jacob by utterly destroying the nation of Israel and transferring its promises to the Church.

I don't have room here to go into detail on why they think God would do such an abominable thing, or give all the reasons we know they are wrong. But I will say this: According to Numbers 23:19, "God is not a man, that He should lie." In addition, 1 Samuel 15:29 says He "will not lie," and Titus 1:2 says God "cannot lie." That's not a restriction on His omnipotence, but an expression of it. Truth is God's nature. That's who He is. Jesus, God the Son, said in John 14:6, said, "I am…the truth." He said in Matthew 24:35, "Heaven and earth will pass away, but My words will by no means pass away."

Don't call Him a liar!

Other Christians reject the miracle because they don't think present Israel qualifies to receive it. They point to Scriptures about the Millennium that picture a regathered Israel that will be living for God and redeemed in Christ.

I live in a place surrounded by beautiful mountains. A friend was recently driving along, watching two ultralight aircraft. One of the ultralights appeared to be crashing. It flew into what looked like a small mountain and disappeared. A few moments later, it reappeared on the other side of the mountain as though it had flown right through it. As my friend got closer, he realized the mountain was actually two mountains. The tiny craft had simply flown between the two and come out on the other side. Two mountains in the distance can easily seem like one.

Prophecies about the Messiah spoke of a conquering king and also of a dying Savior. Before Jesus, no one could figure it out. They didn't realize they were looking at two mountains in the distance—a first coming of the Messiah and a second.

It's the same principle here. Some prophecies about a regathered Israel also speak of Israel being made spiritually whole. But a close look at Scripture shows Israel will be regathered in the Promised Land *before* it becomes spiritually whole.

Ezekiel 36:22: "Thus says the Lord God: 'I do not do this for your sake, O house of Israel, but for My holy name's sake.'" Verses 24 and 25 say, "I will take you from among the nations, gather you out of all countries, and bring you into your own land. *Then* I will sprinkle clean water on you, and you shall be clean" (emphasis added).

First, He gathers them, *then* He cleans them.

When they return, they're still spiritually dead. God illustrates this in the next chapter, Ezekiel 37. Here we find the famous valley of dry bones. The bones represent an unrepentant, spiritually dead Israel scattered on the earth.

God tells Ezekiel the bones are the "house of Israel." Verse 8 of Ezekiel 37 says, "The sinews and the flesh came upon them, and the skin covered them over; but there was no breath in them."

So here they are—human cadavers lying in the desert—still as dead as when they were merely a pile of bones. But they have been gathered. The parts are all there. They have human form, but they need more than form. They need life, and that comes from the breath of God.

They assembled while still spiritually dead! Israel will gather together while spiritually dead. First comes the return to the Promised Land, then—sometime after they've been reassembled—God will bring them alive spiritually.

Romans 11 addresses these issues. Verse 1 asks, "Has God cast away His people?" The context here leaves no doubt it's talking about the physical descendants of Abraham, Isaac, and Jacob. Then it answers the question: "Certainly not!" God hasn't cast away His people!

Verses 25 and 26 say after "the fullness of the Gentiles has come in...all Israel will be saved."

So, we have a picture of Israel being dispersed around the world, God drawing them back together, and God then giving them a spiritual rebirth. This is the work of God and not humanity. Israel doesn't suddenly become righteous and therefore go back to the land. But while they are yet sinners, God begins the regathering process.

This only scratches the surface of what makes this miracle so astounding—including the part we see happening before us now, the regathering of the nation of Israel from all over the world.

God's Word is being fulfilled exactly as the Bible says!

Chapter 12

PROFOUND PROPHETIC PONDERINGS

By Daymond Duck

General Editor's note: Daymond Duck has been a brother in Christ and close friend and associate for many years. His writing on Bible prophecy and the issues and events of these end-of-the-age days is eagerly sought by those who want sources that provide the most relevant and timely information guaranteed to be centered in the truth found in God's Word.

Anyone who's sat in on a Daymond Duck message will quickly tell you it's an experience they wouldn't have missed. His presentations, whether written or oral, always seem to grasp attention with special intensity, making the time pass too quickly. And there are certainly more than enough things of prophetic significance Daymond has to work with during these days. The contribution he has made will alert and inform, as if issued directly from Heaven's throne room. Daymond is indeed attuned to our Lord's desire to make those who will hear aware of the lateness of the prophetic hour.

✦✦✦

God has granted me and enabled me to write a weekly article for raptureready.com for more than twelve years. Below is a sampling of some of those articles.

Two Great Days

During one of his crusades, evangelist Dr. Billy Graham said:

> The first thought I have when I wake up in the morning is I wonder if He is going to come today. I would like to see Him come; what a day that's going to be. All of our aches and pains are going to be behind us, all of our tears are going to be behind us, all of our problems are going to be solved. What a day that's going to be!

Actually, many Christians believe two great days are coming. First, the day of the Rapture:

- Every *deceased* Christian will be raised from the dead with an incorruptible, immortal body like Jesus had when He was raised from the dead.
- The body of every *living* Christian will be changed into an incorruptible, immortal body like Jesus had when He was raised from the dead.
- Christians will see their saved loved ones in Heaven.
- Christians will be taken to Heaven for rewards.
- Christians will be presented to Jesus for the Marriage Supper of the Lamb.
- The Christian's prayer to be accounted worthy to escape the Tribulation period will be answered.
- The salvation of multitudes by the preaching of the 144,000 and two witnesses will be near.
- The blinding of Israel will soon cease, and all Israel will soon be saved.

Second, the day of the Second Coming:

- Satan will be bound, chained, and cast into the bottomless pit for one thousand years.
- Antichrist and the False Prophet will be cast into the lake of fire.
- The restoration of planet Earth will begin.
- Jesus will reign and be worshipped all over this Earth.
- There will be peace, justice, and righteousness on Earth.
- God's covenants with Israel will be fulfilled.
- Christians will reign with Jesus.

Christians should look forward to these two magnificent events taking place.

Rejoice

Following the selection of His original twelve disciples, and early in His earthly ministry, Jesus selected seventy men and sent them forth two by two from city to city to prepare the way for His ministry and a great harvest of souls (Luke 10:1–20).

He warned these men they would encounter opposition, hardship, and danger.

He empowered them to work miracles (heal the sick, etc.) in cities where they were received, and instructed them to tell people, "The Kingdom of God is nigh unto you."

He told them a day of judgment is coming, and the judgment of God will fall on those who reject the Kingdom message, because accepting or rejecting Jesus is the same as accepting or rejecting the God (Jehovah) who sent Jesus.

The seventy went forth and returned rejoicing that even the devils (demons) obeyed them in the name of Jesus. Jesus revealed that the obedience of demons in the name of Jesus is a foretaste of Satan being kicked out of Heaven (at the middle of the Tribulation period; see Revelation 12:7–12), and the ultimate victory and deliverance of those who trust Him.

He said to the seventy, "Rejoice not that the spirits are subject unto you; but rather rejoice because your names are written in heaven."

Christians concerned about what may happen in the coming weeks and months (forced vaccinations, tracking everyone, transition to a digital currency, persecution, losing stuff, etc.), should focus on spiritual matters.

Instead of rejoicing over our earthly freedoms, successes, etc. (in reality, gifts from God), let us rejoice:

- Because of the death, burial, and resurrection of Jesus for the sins of those who believe and put their trust in Him.
- Because our names are written in the Lamb's Book of Life in Heaven.
- Because our sins have been forgiven and we've been sealed by the Holy Spirit.
- Because we have eternal life, and nothing will be able to separate us from the love of God.
- Because we will not experience even one minute of the Tribulation.
- Because Satan's power and influence on earth will soon end.
- Because God will avenge the harm the lost inflict on His people.
- Because we will return to earth with Jesus at His Second Coming and reign with Him during His millennial Kingdom on earth.

Our Resurrected Body

Paul said:

Some men will say, How are the dead raised up? and with what body do they come? (1 Corinthians 15:35)

He first answered the question with an illustration from the *study of plants (botany)*: "That which thou sowest is not quickened [made alive], except it die."

When we sow a seed, it dies before it becomes a plant. If the seed doesn't die, it won't become a plant. If it doesn't disintegrate, a plant won't come out of it, the roots and leaves won't emerge, etc.

Paul added:

And that which thou sowest, thou sowest not that body that shall be, but a bare grain, it may chance of wheat, or of some other grain: But God giveth it a body as it hath pleased Him, and to every seed its own body.

With his words, Paul made three points:

- When we sow a seed, we bury a bare seed in the ground. It is a seed.
- God gives that seed a new body. We cannot give the seed a new body. It can't give itself a new body. But God gives the seed a new body.
- Every seed has its own body. A wheat seed receives one kind of body. A bean seed receives another kind of body. A corn seed receives another kind of body, etc. Different seeds receive different kinds of bodies.

So how are the dead raised? They are raised by God, and the process is like what happens to a seed. The seed dies and becomes a living plant. A little apple seed dies, and it becomes a big apple tree. The apple seed has one kind of body before it dies and another kind after it's brought back to life. Something inside the dead seed comes forth and makes a living plant. Something inside each of us comes forth, and God gives us a new body.

Paul continued with a second illustration from the *study of animals (zoology)*:

All flesh is not the same; but there is one kind of flesh of men, another flesh of beasts, another of fishes, and another of birds.
(1 Corinthians 15:39)

There are different kinds of flesh; humans are different from animals, beef is different from pork, fish is different from chicken, etc. There are even kinds of flesh we don't know anything about. God will make our resurrection bodies out of a different kind of flesh, a flesh unlike anything we know about right now.

Paul continued with a third illustration from a *study of the heavenly bodies (astronomy)*:

> There are also celestial bodies, and bodies terrestrial: but the glory of the celestial is one, and the glory of the terrestrial is another. There is one glory of the sun, and another glory of the moon, and another glory of the stars; for one star differeth from another star in glory. (1 Corinthians 15:40–41)

There are different kinds of heavenly bodies: asteroids, comets, moons, planets, stars, etc. God created all of these, but each one is different, and each one has different degrees of splendor and beauty. Some stars are large, some are small; some heavenly bodies give off light, some heavenly bodies reflect light, etc.

In the same way, there are different kinds of bodies; a human's body is different from an animal's, a cow's body is different from a pig's, a fish's body is different from a chicken's. Cows don't lay eggs, and fish don't have feathers. Our resurrection bodies will be different from our present ones in at least five ways:

1. We will be raised in incorruption (without a sin nature).
2. We will be raised with bodies that will never die.
3. We will be raised in glory (with a glorious body superior to anything we know about).
4. We will be raised in power (with a powerful body that will never become weak or frail).
5. We will be raised with a spiritual body (with one that's different from this physical body). We won't be ghosts, or vapor. We will have a spiritual body.

Choosing to Be an Abomination to God

On April 17, 2023, Benny Johnson (Turning Point USA) released a short clip of an interview he did with Florida Governor Ron DeSantis. Johnson asked DeSantis about men taking the role of women, and DeSantis said he believed the ideology is a total fraud, asking whether we're going to be a society based on truth or deceit.

"If you take a man and they dress up as a woman, and you tell me I have to accept that they're a woman, then you're asking me to be complicit in a lie, and I just refuse to do that," he said. "So, we've got to tell the truth, you know, I think the truth will set you free, and let's just be honest about what's going on here."

The book of Proverbs says:

> These six things doth the Lord hate: yea, seven are an abomination unto him: A proud look, a lying tongue, hands that shed innocent blood, an heart that deviseth wicked imaginations, feet that be swift in running to mischief, a false witness that speaketh lies, and he that soweth discord among brethren. (Proverbs 6:16–19)

God is a God of truth (Psalm 31:5). Jesus is truth (John 14:6). Satan is the father of lies (John 8:44).

A nation that chooses to abandon the truth and become a nation of fraud, lies, and deceit is also choosing to become a nation that is an abomination unto God.

A nation founded on the Scriptures cannot choose to abandon God to follow Satan and get away with it forever. God will call for repentance by allowing hardship to come upon that nation, but a lack of repentance will ultimately stir the wrath of God.

Beginning to Come to Pass

The book of Revelation begins with these words:

The Revelation of Jesus Christ, which God gave unto him, to show unto his servants things which must shortly come to pass; and he sent and signified it by his angel unto his servant John: Who bare record of the word of God, and of the testimony of Jesus Christ, and of all things that he saw. (Revelation 1:1–2)

The book of Revelation is:

- The Revelation of Jesus Christ.
- A list of things to show God's servants.
- A list of things that MUST happen.
- A list of things that MUST happen shortly (in God's timing).
- A list of things that an angel showed John.
- The Word of God.
- The testimony of Jesus Christ.

Here are five major signs in Revelation chapter 13 that must come to pass during the Tribulation period:

1. A global power must come into being.
- Revelation 13:7 says, "Power was given him [Antichrist] over all kindreds, and tongues, and nations."
- An unelected person [Antichrist] must be given power over all nations.
- This is the New World Order, the Great Reset, the coming world government.

2. A global false religion must come into being.
- Revelation 13:8 says, "And all that dwell upon the earth shall worship him [Antichrist], whose names are not written in the book of life of the Lamb slain from the foundation of the world."

- Every lost person *must* worship the Antichrist.
- This appears to be where the unbiblical global ethic is going (the LGBTQ+ agenda, the woke culture, abortion, etc.); the coming world religion; Mystery Babylon the Great, the Mother of Harlots and Abominations of the Earth.

3. There must *be a global population reduction.*

- Revelation 13:15 says, "And he [the False Prophet] had power to give life unto the image of the beast [a statue of Antichrist], that the image of the beast should both speak, and cause that as many as would not worship the image of the beast should be killed."
- This appears to be artificial intelligence, a computerized, talking statue that will reduce the population of the earth by ordering the death of all who refuse to obey their government and worship an idol.

4. There must *be a global marking system.*

- Revelation 13:16 says, "And he causeth all, both small and great, rich and poor, free and bond, to receive a mark in their right hand, or in their foreheads."
- There *must* be a global mark that identifies the lost supporters of world government; this is probably where face scans and hand scans are going.
- The desire for a mark to identify everyone who has been vaccinated appears to be a step in this direction.

5. There must *be a global economic system.*

- Revelation 13:17 says, "And that no man might buy or sell, save he that had the mark, or the name of the beast, or the number of his name."
- All must take the mark or they cannot buy and sell.

- Everyone must be required to support the government if they want to buy and sell.
- Replacing cash with a digital currency is the ultimate goal.

In Daniel chapter 4, we read that God caused King Nebuchadnezzar to lose his mind. The king's hair grew like feathers and his nails grew like claws. He crawled around in a pasture on all fours and grazing like an animal. His body stayed wet from the dew. This lasted seven years.

Why? So, "the living may know that the most High ruleth in the kingdom of men, and giveth it to whomsoever he will, and setteth up over it the basest of men" (Daniel 4:17, 25, 32). In other words, God allowed this to happen so the living would know:

- God is in control.
- God raises up leaders.
- God brings down leaders.
- God puts the leaders He want in charge.
- God even puts bad leaders in charge.

In response to a question about His Second Coming and the end of the age, Jesus said, "When these things begin to come to pass, then look up, and lift up your heads; for your redemption draweth nigh" (Luke 21:28). As the end of the age nears, there will be a generation that can see the signs beginning to come to pass (Matthew 24:32–33). The current generation is seeing the five major signs in Revelation chapter 13 beginning to come to pass. It is not a coincidence that these five major signs are shaping up. It is the revelation of Jesus Christ beginning to come to pass.

Warnings

On June 22, 2023, expert Bible prophecy teacher Amir Tsarfati said:

When many look at the world around us, they see chaos. I see something different. I see God warning the people of this world that His judgment is coming soon. The Bible shows us that this is the way He operates – warning, then judgment. God sent Noah to warn the world that His judgment was coming. He sent angels to warn Sodom and Gomorrah that judgment was coming. He sent prophets to Israel to warn them judgment was coming. And He told the whole church of the signs that judgment is coming.

On June 24, 2023, expert Bible prophecy teacher and fellow contributor to this book, Jonathan Brentner, said:

> A day is coming when the end time signs will become reality; then it will be too late for many.
>
> God will surely judge the wickedness of our world. It's a matter of when, not if.
>
> It's far better to heed God's warnings now, before they become reality.

Among other things, these two expert Bible prophecy teachers want people to know the prophetic signs being fulfilled today are warnings from God that His judgment is coming, and this is real news that should be immediately acted upon.

God didn't tell people to watch for the warnings (signs) to scare them. He told people to watch so we will know He exists, time is short, and we need to make our salvation sure (and encourage others to know and do likewise). He is a loving God who reveals what He intends to do before He does it (Daniel 2:27–30; Isaiah 46:9–10), and there are many undeniable warnings (signs) that He's preparing to judge the world:

Warning 1, concerning world government and deceit (the climate-change scam): On June 28, 2023, the World Net Daily (WND) staff reported that United Nations Secretary General Antonio Guterres called for the immediate and global destruction of the world's energy industry because, he claimed, fossil fuels are "incompatible with human survival."

Guterres said, "All of this action must be global. It must be immediate, and it must start with the polluted heart of the climate crisis—the fossil fuel industry."

He added, "The world must phase out fossil fuels in a just and equitable way, moving to leave oil, coal and gas in the ground where they belong and massively boosting renewable investment in a just transition."

Notice the terms "global destruction," "action must be global," and "the world."

Here is a warning (sign) to watch for: At the end of the age, an evil government will rule the world (Revelation 13:7b).

Here is an undeniable fact: Evil people at the UN, the World Health Organization (WHO), the World Economic Forum (WEF), the International Monetary Fund (IMF) global corporations, the media, and others think they need to create a crisis to bring in a world government by 2030 or sooner. It is my belief that the Bible clearly teaches the Rapture will happen before that.

The world uses energy to grow and transport food, heat and cool homes, run equipment in factories, cause vehicles to move, etc. The head of the UN calling for the global destruction of the world's energy industry should get our attention.

Warning 2: The Tribulation period will begin when Antichrist confirms (strengthens) an existing covenant with many for seven years (Daniel 9:27; 1 Thessalonians 5:3).

In late September of 2015, delegates from 193 nations unanimously approved a UN document called "Transforming Our World: The 2030 Agenda for Sustainable Development." This document, or "covenant," that was approved by many (delegates from 193 nations) went into effect on January 1, 2016. In essence, it calls for a transition to a world government by 2030.

In early June 2023, Guterres issued a progress report on the transition to world government, and his report says most of the world is behind schedule. It says the world is behind schedule and it has less than seven years to meet its goals by 2030. Guterres said delaying or giving up on the deadline to establish a world government by 2030 is not an option.

The UN scheduled a meeting called the SDG Summit for September 18–19, 2023, to discuss this problem. Guterres asked world leaders to commit to "seven years of accelerated, sustained, and transformative action, both nationally and internationally, to deliver on the promise of the SDGs" (the creation of a world government).

In my words, Guterres wants world leaders to agree (make a covenant) to speed up the formation of a world government by making more and faster changes over the next seven years. His desired agreement (covenant) to bring that to pass is generating questions.

Notice in Daniel 9:27 Antichrist will "confirm" (strengthen; make stronger) an existing covenant for seven years, and that will begin the Tribulation Period. People have been e-mailing me to ask if the UN vote for the nations to commit to world government in seven years could be the covenant Antichrist will confirm that starts the seven-year Tribulation. We don't know, but it's a legitimate question.

All the signs are converging. The Tribulation will begin with the confirmation (strengthening) of a seven-year covenant, and now the UN is calling for a seven-year covenant. Guterres believes the transition to a world government is behind schedule, and the Bible teaches that a Restrainer is holding back the rise of Antichrist (see 2 Thessalonians 2:5–8.). Many prophecy teachers, including myself, believe the Rapture will occur before the confirmation of the covenant, making this very interesting.

How the covenant will be strengthened is not clear, but we know there will be a brief rebellion by three of the ten kings, Antichrist will subdue them, and he will ultimately end up with total dictatorial power.

Warning 3, concerning a falling away or a departing from the faith at the end of the age (2 Thessalonians 2:3; 1 Timothy 4:1): On July 2, 2023, World Net Daily posted a "Daily Caller News Foundation

Article" stating People for the Ethical Treatment of Animals (PETA) had used artificial intelligence (specifically, ChatGPT) to rewrite the Creation story in the Bible. They changed the Word of God to promote their idea of animal rights.

For example, following Adam and Eve's sin, the KJV Bible says God made "coats of skins, and clothed them" (Genesis 3:21), but PETA's altered story says He made them clothes of hemp and bamboo (never mind the "coats of skins" might refer to the skin of a lamb, pointing to the Lamb of God who would die for their sin).

PETA's altered story adds that Abraham and Sara adopted a dog named "Herbie" from a shelter. To make matters worse, a PETA official said the organization may rewrite more books of the Bible in the future.

It is important to understand that the Bible was given by God. He chose the words to say what He wants people to know. He warned everyone not to add anything to or take anything away from the Scriptures (Deuteronomy 12:32; Revelation 22:18–19). Those who deliberately add, delete, or change just one word, even if it is to promote a good cause, could have the eternal judgment of God fall on them.

This is the danger of church denominations, seminary professors, pastors, church members, and others changing what the Bible says about LGBTQ+ issues. The changes will not end with just one or two issues. They will keep coming, and it's a slippery slope into the abyss with no way out.

Warning 4, concerning the return of Jews to the Promised Land at the end of the age: The largest concentration of Jews in the world today is in Israel, but there is still a large concentration of Jews in Russia and Ukraine. In late June 2023, two Jewish rabbis in Ukraine warned the Jews to leave Russia immediately. They said, "Whichever way this situation (the war) plays out, it's going to be very bad for you" (they could face an organized massacre of Jews).

Following the death, burial, and resurrection of Jesus, God used persecution to scatter the Jews and spread the gospel all over the world

(Acts 1:8; 8:1). He sometimes uses persecution today to cause the Jews to return to the Promised Land from all over the world.

Warning 5, concerning ungodliness, deceit, censorship, the loss of freedom of speech and the loss of freedom of religion at the end of the age: On June 27, 2023, a letter bearing the signature of more than 250 celebrities was sent to the heads of Facebook, Twitter (now called X), TikTok, and YouTube demanding the suppression of views critical of LGBTQ+ issues (deceitfully called trans healthcare).

If America is "one nation under God, with liberty and justice for all," is it legal for social media to suppress the views of those critical of LGBTQ+ issues? Is suppressing the freedom of religion and freedom of speech of Christians the beginning of forcing everyone on earth to support the views of Antichrist and the False Prophet? Will this suppression lead to denying people the right to buy and sell, or killing people to reduce the population of the earth? The denial of freedom of speech and freedom of religion for those who believe the Bible should not be taken lightly, but it looks like that's where this is headed.

Warning 6, concerning a global currency and the tracking and control of all buying and selling: In a speech at a WEF meeting on June 28, 2023 (called the "Summer Davos"), Cornell University Professor Eswar Prasad said (as I understand it, summarized in my words for simplicity):

- Everyone on earth could soon face the disappearance of physical money.
- Programmable Central Bank Digital Currencies (CBDCs) could soon become a global reality.
- Bank computers can be programmed to allow customers to make good purchases (buy food, medicine, etc.) or prevent customers from making bad purchases (buy porn, drugs, guns, ammunition, etc.), or to target people (make people obey the government; yield to government social policies such as abortion and the LGBTQ+ agenda; force people to

buy from approved places; deny them permission to buy from unapproved places, etc.).

- CBDCs could make the world a better place, but there is potential for the world to end up in a pretty dark place.

This is an admission that the world could soon have a global currency that can be tracked, controlled, and used to control everyone on earth. Concerning professor Prasad's remarks (posted on sociable.com), website editor Tim Hinchliffe reported comments of several influential people (again, as I understand it and summarized for simplicity):

- Christine Lagarde, president of the European Central Bank, said programming should be left up to commercial banks, but they should be allowed to put conditions on how the money is used.
- A Chinese official said governments should use programmability to control what people can own and how their money can be spent.
- India is studying a programmable currency that will expire.
- Nigeria is studying putting customers in brackets (based on obedience or whatever) with limits on how much they can spend in a day.

I believe many of the global elite are looking at ways to control everyone on earth.

Visit the following link to the Sociable article so you can form your own opinions: https://sociable.co/government-and-policy/governments-program-cbdc-restrict-undesirable-purchases-wef-summer-davos-china/.

Preparing for Antichrist

The word "antichrist" has two meanings: 1) "against the Christ," and 2) "instead of the Christ." Antichrist will be "against the Christ," meaning he will be an enemy of Christ, and he will try to "replace the Christ," meaning he will be a false Christ. In the New Testament, we read:

- Antichrist is called the "man of sin," "the wicked one," "the beast that ascendeth out of the bottomless pit," and "a beast" (2 Thessalonians 2:3, 8; Revelation 11:7, 13:1).
- Antichrist will oppose God and claim he is God (2 Thessalonians 2:4).
- Antichrist's coming will be the work of Satan, who will empower him with lying wonders that appear to be supernatural (2 Thessalonians 2:9).
- Antichrist will blaspheme God and everyone in Heaven (Revelation 13:6).
- Antichrist will be given power over everyone and every nation on earth (Revelation 13:7).
- Antichrist will be worshipped by everyone on earth whose name is not written in the Lamb's Book of Life, but all who refuse to worship him will be killed (Revelation 13:8, 15).

Many people have opposed Christ, but—other than Satan, who caused Him to sweat great drops of blood—there has never been a more sinister or worthy opponent of God on the face of planet earth than Antichrist. Many false Christs, false prophets, and deceivers have come and gone, but there has never been a greater or more evil deceiver than this man.

On August 29, 2023, LifeSiteNews posted an article by Michael Haynes about an interview with Catholic Archbishop Vigano. As I understand it, here are some of the things Vigano said (in my words and his):

- The rise of globalism is preparing humanity for the rise of Antichrist.

- The corruption of society is corrupting the Catholic Church.
- Globalism and satanism are remarkably similar.
- World leaders will serve Satan by surrendering the sovereignty of their nations to Antichrist.
- World leaders are trying to remove Christ from the institutions, culture, and life of citizens.
- Antichrist will be a dictator, and by the time world leaders discover what they have done, it will be too late to do anything about it.[132]

Trumpets

While the Hebrews were wandering in the wilderness, God told Moses to make two trumpets of silver, and to blow the trumpets:

- To signal the people to assemble
- To signal the people to march
- To signal the people at times of war
- To announce the feast days and sacrifices (Numbers 10:1–10)

God also told Moses what feast days to observe, when to observe them, and why they should observe them (Leviticus 23)

Concerning blowing the trumpets to assemble:

- God said, "When they shall blow with them, all the assembly shall assemble themselves to thee at the door of the tabernacle of the congregation" (Numbers 10:3).

Concerning blowing the trumpets to march:

- God said, "Make thee two trumpets of silver…for the journeying of the camps" (Numbers 10: 2).
- When Moses wanted the Jews to move to a new location, they were to start moving at the sound of a trumpet.

Concerning blowing the trumpets for war:

- God said, "If ye go to war...blow the trumpets and I will remember you" (Numbers 10:9).
- At Jericho, God told Joshua to march around the city once each day for six days and have priests blow rams' horns (shofars or trumpets; see Joshua 6:1–27).
- He told them to do it seven times on the seventh day, and on the seventh time the walls of Jericho fell.

Concerning blowing the trumpets for feasts and sacrifices:

- God said, "In the day of your gladness.... Ye shall blow with the trumpets over your burnt offerings, and over the sacrifices" (Numbers 10:10).
- Trumpets were blown to show that the Feast Days and sacrifices were special, not ordinary, days and events.
- They are special because they point to God and Jesus.

Concerning trumpets and the voice of God:

- The Israelites heard the voice of the trumpet when God came down to give them the Ten Commandments at Mt. Sinai (Exodus 19:16).
- When John saw Jesus on the Isle of Patmos, he heard a voice like a trumpet (Revelation 1:10).
- When John was called up into Heaven, he heard a voice as of a trumpet (Revelation 4:1).

Concerning trumpets when deceased Christians are raised from the dead:

- Paul said, "The Lord himself shall descend from heaven with a shout, with the voice of the archangel, and with the

trump of God: and the dead in Christ shall rise first" (1
Thessalonians 4:16).

Concerning an Old Testament picture of the New Testament
Rapture:

- Moses led the Jews to Mt. Sinai (Exodus 19:1).
- God told Moses He would come down in a thick cloud to
  meet the people (Exodus 19:9–11).
- Jesus will come down in the clouds to meet His people at
  the Rapture (1 Thessalonians 4:16).
- God wanted the Jews to hear His voice at Mt. Sinai (Exo-
  dus 19–9).
- Jesus will shout, and His people will hear His voice at the
  Rapture (1 Thessalonians 4:16).

Concerning what went on at Mt. Sinai three days later:

- "There were thunderings and lightnings, and a thick cloud
  upon the mount, and the voice of the trumpet exceeding
  loud" (Exodus 19:16).
- "And Moses brought forth the people out of the camp to
  meet with God" (Exodus 19:17).
- At the Rapture, the Church will be caught up to meet the
  Lord in the air (1 Thessalonians 4:17).

Concerning the last trump or great blast:

- "Mount Sinai was altogether on a smoke, because the
  LORD descended upon it in fire: and the smoke thereof
  ascended as the smoke of a furnace, and the whole mount
  quaked greatly. And when the voice of the trumpet sounded
  long, and waxed louder and louder, Moses spake, and God
  answered him by a voice" (Exodus 19:18–19).

- The last blast of the trumpet was the longest and loudest.
- Some of the religious Jews call the last blast the "last trump" or the "great blast."

Concerning assembling at the door:

- When the trumpets were blown a certain way in the wilderness, the Jews were to assemble at the door of the tabernacle (Exodus 19:13).
- When Jesus blows the trumpet, the Church will assemble in the air and go to the door of Heaven (1 Thessalonians 4:13–18; Revelation 4:1).

The feasts of Passover, Unleavened Bread, and First Fruits foretold the gospel (the death, burial, and resurrection of Jesus). Not all agree, but many prophecy teachers believe the feasts of Pentecost and Trumpets foretell the beginning and end of the Church Age, also called the Age of Grace. They believe the feasts of Atonement and Tabernacles foretell the Second Coming and the millennial reign of Jesus on earth.

New Phase of Accelerated Decline

What is your opinion of America today? Have you said or heard anyone say, "The America I am living in today is not the America I grew up in?" Have you said or heard anyone say, "I believe America is headed in the wrong direction?"

What is your opinion of the global situation today? Have you said or heard anyone say, "The world is in a mess?" Have you said or heard anyone say, "The UN has done a wonderful job of solving the world's problems for more than seventy years?" Come to think of it, the UN (I call it the "United Nothing") has done little, if anything, to solve the world's problems.

On October 30, 2008, presidential candidate Barack Obama said, "We are five days away from fundamentally transforming the United

States of America," and it seems to me America indeed has been going through a fundamental transformation (a spiritual, moral, and economic downward spiral).

In late September 2015, the UN released a document titled "Transforming our World: the 2030 Agenda for Sustainable Development," and UN Secretary General Ban Ki-moon called it the "start of a new era."

Considering that the fundamental transformation of America and the world were revealed before many of these fundamental changes started coming on the scene, it seems like the changes must be part of a plan.

Having said this, it's a little disturbing to know UN Secretary General Antonio Guterres thinks the fundamental transformation of the world needs speed up. It's even more disturbing to know that world leaders agreed with him, on September 18–19, 2023, and voted to do everything they can to complete the fundamental transformation of the world by 2030 or sooner.

They're calling the coming years "a new phase of accelerated progress." Get that? They called the September 2015 vote the "start of a new era" and the 2023 vote "a new phase of accelerated progress." Pardon me for being a skeptic, and I hope I'm wrong, but I tend to believe the next few years will turn out to be "a new phase of accelerated decline" (not progress).

As I understand the Bible, their "new era" will produce the Tribulation period, and Jesus said, "Except those days should be shortened, there should no flesh be saved" (Matthew 24:22).

FYI: God doesn't send anyone to Hell (all of us are born with a sin nature and destined to go to Hell because we sin), but has provided a way (Jesus) for everyone to go to Heaven (and He is the only way to get there; see John 14:6).

Finally, are you Rapture Ready?

If you want to be Rapture ready and go to Heaven, you must be born again (John 3:3). God loves you, and if you haven't done so, sincerely admit that you are a sinner; believe Jesus is the virgin-born, sinless Son of God who died for the sins of the world, was buried, and raised from the dead. Ask Him to forgive your sins, cleanse you, come into your heart, and be your Savior. Then tell someone you have done this.

Chapter 13

ISRAEL'S DARKENING SKIES

By Tim Moore

General Editor's note: Israel, the nation at the center of God's Word, is under excruciating pressure. The satanic rage has spawned hatred across America and the world unlike anything seen since the Holocaust perpetrated by the Nazi regime of Adolf Hitler's Germany.

Despite being blind to the truth that their Messiah is Jesus Christ, Israel looks for the Messianic figure they believe is on the way to rescue them and set up Jehovah's Kingdom on earth. They are blinded to the fact that the one they will accept, according to Jesus, will be a false Messiah. It will be Antichrist, written of by John the apostle and described by Daniel, Paul, and Jesus.

According to all we see developing, the time for Antichrist to come on the scene must be near indeed. Tim Moore, head of Lamb & Lion Ministries and host of the *Christ in Prophecy* TV program, takes on the task of informing about Israel, its myopic view of their Messiah, and what that blindness entails.

+ + +

The storm clouds of the Tribulation are gathering. The signs of the times are increasing in frequency and intensity. Even those who are spiritually blind can discern that our world is hurtling toward a chasm.

For those who are awaiting Jesus Christ—our Blessed Hope—even these foreboding signs point to the imminence of His return. As pastor and author Adrian Rogers once said, "It's getting gloriously dark!"

God's Word not only describes the societal trends and natural signs that point to the Rapture of the Church and ensuing Tribulation, it also documents a similar period in human history. Once before, darkness seemed to permeate before the Light of the World was born in Bethlehem.

We can draw insight from Jesus' First Advent even as we await His glorious Second Coming.

Between the Testaments

In the long, silent years following the completion of the Old Testament, Israel descended into a period of darkness. As prophesied, there was a famine for the Word of the Lord, because following Malachi there were no more revelations.

The Greek Empire rose and fell, eventually giving way to the Roman Empire. Positioned strategically at the crossroads of the ancient world—at the intersection of Asia, Africa, and what would later be known as Europe—Israel became a subject land. Short-lived revolts offered temporary relief, but by just over two thousand years ago, the heavy boot of Roman peace had crushed the religious and nationalistic hopes of most Israelis. Zealots were ready to take up arms and fight against Rome.

The Judean provinces represented an ongoing annoyance to the Roman overlords. Always bickering, and stubbornly resistant to embracing Roman gods (which had been largely appropriated from the preceding Greeks and simply renamed), the Jews insisted on worshipping their own God and stiffening their necks instead of going with the flow of Roman rule.

It was into this dark moment in human history—in a place important to the rest of the world only as a crossroads between other civilizations—that God sent His Son. We're all familiar with the Christmas story, even if some of the details we know are extrabiblical. Gabriel appeared first to John the Baptist's father, Zechariah, then to Mary. Joseph also had an angelic visitor who foretold Jesus' birth. Other than those three and Zechariah's wife, Elizabeth, there is no record in Scripture of Jesus' birth being prophesied to anyone else.

The night He was born, angels appeared in the sky above Bethlehem. They didn't come to proclaim the good news to the well-connected or religiously proud. They came to "some shepherds"—men on the very edges of society who slept in the fields by night. But, oh, what a sight the shepherds beheld when a multitude of the heavenly host burst into a song of praise above their heads. Advised of the Savior's birth, they hurried to Bethlehem to see the Baby. As they returned to their flocks, they went "glorifying and praising God for all that they had heard and seen, just as had been told to them" (Luke 2:20).

But there were two other people whom the Bible says were anticipating the Lord's Messiah. Simeon was a man looking for "the consolation of Israel"—a title referring to the promise that the Messiah would deliver Israel. And Anna was an eighty-four-year-old prophetess. She had been widowed for many years, but was at the temple night and day, fasting, praying, and waiting upon the Lord.

Luke describes how these two faithful Jews were given the blessing of meeting the Baby Jesus. The Holy Spirit had revealed to Simeon that he would not see death before he had seen the Christ (Luke 2:26). Anna, too, was spiritually discerning. She recognized Jesus as the Anointed One as soon as she saw Him, and gave thanks to God for allowing her to look upon the Redemption of Jerusalem.

Why Only Two

We might like to assume Simeon and Anna—a devout man and woman—were representative of a much larger group awaiting the Messiah. But I don't think that's the case. Matthew, whose Gospel was directed at a Jewish audience, tells us that Magi from the east came to Jerusalem seeking to find and worship the One who was born to be King of the Jews. He records that Herod was troubled—and all Jerusalem along with him.

Why was the Idumean king troubled, and why was the city upset along with him? Certainly not because they had missed the signs of Jesus' birth. The chief priests and scribes who assembled to respond to Herod's inquiry rightly said they Messiah would be born "in Bethlehem of Judea, for this is what has been written by the prophet" (Matthew 2:5). Scripture doesn't indicate *any* of them bothered to go to Bethlehem and see for themselves. Unlike the lowly shepherds who hurried to see Baby Jesus, they couldn't be bothered to trek the handful of miles to the city of David—literally on the outskirts of Jerusalem to the south.

Herod, too, was uninterested in going to see or worship the newborn King of the Jews. He sent the visiting Magi on their way and asked them to report back to him. Herod's professed desire to eventually worship was patently false, which is why God warned the wise men in a dream not to return to Herod.

No, the Idumean king of the Jews was troubled because the true King of the Jews—even as a small child in Bethlehem—represented a great threat to his reign. Herod had his beloved wife Mariamne and two of his own sons killed, just because his paranoia led him to think his power was at risk. So, given Herod's tendency to lash out at anyone who might undermine his claim to the throne, the entire city was on edge wondering how he might react when foreign emissaries came to worship the newborn Messiah.

Isaiah said the Messiah would be like a shoot springing forth from the root of Jesse (Isaiah 11:1), but that, like a "tender shoot" or a "root out of parched ground," He would have "no stately form or majesty" (Isaiah 53:2). Regarding the reference to parched ground, the four-hundred-year gap between the Old Testament and the New reflects that period of heavenly silence and demonstrates at least a partial fulfillment of Amos 8:11–12:

"Behold, days are coming," declares the Lord God, "When I will send a famine on the land, not a famine for bread or a thirst for water, but rather for hearing the words of the LORD.

People will stagger from sea to sea and from the north even to the east; they will go to and fro to seek the word of the LORD, but they will not find it."

The Anointed One born in Bethlehem wasn't the mighty warrior king many Jews were longing for. They wanted a savior to deliver them from Roman oppression and restore their national primacy, not a Savior to deliver them from their sins and restore their relationship with Almighty God. Indeed, the priests and scribes took great offense when Jesus dared to suggest that they would be deemed unworthy, or, even worse, that the grace of God would be extended to Gentiles instead of them.

Some point to Luke 2:38 and suggest others beside Simeon and Anna were eager to welcome the Messiah. Luke records that Anna spoke "to all those who were looking for the redemption of Jerusalem." But while they were eager for Jerusalem to be redeemed—delivered from Roman oppression—Luke doesn't say they were looking for the Anointed One. Many people today clamor to "make America great again," or restore our national prominence and pride. But how many are looking for the Messiah, honoring Him as Savior and Lord already? Then and now, people want the blessing of His Lordship without embracing Him personally.

No, from the time He was born, Jesus wasn't heralded by the masses. According to Scripture, there were only six Jews and a handful of Gentiles from the east who were looking forward to Jesus ahead of time, and "some shepherds" who were advised about His arrival. The rest of the Jewish society seems to have been fixated on going about their lives with no spiritual discernment whatsoever.

Consistent Pattern during His Ministry

As a child, Jesus wasn't just precocious, He was unlike anyone who had come before (understatement of all time!). When He was only twelve years old, teachers of the Law at the temple were "amazed at

His understanding and His answers" (Luke 2:47). After His public ministry began, He confounded the scribes and Pharisees by teaching as someone with authority. And still, people did not recognize Him for who He was.

Even Jesus' disciples were unsure what to make of Him. Multiplying loaves and fish; calming a stormy sea; healing the deaf, lame, leprous, and blind; releasing the demon-possessed from bondage; it still took the revelation of the Father in Heaven for Peter to finally confess, "You are the Christ, the Son of the living God" (Matthew 16:13–17).

Meanwhile, the masses, although drawn by miracles of nourishment and healing, were largely unaware Jesus was the prophesied Messiah.

For His own good reasons, Jesus did not broadcast that fact. More often than not, He told the people He healed to follow the Law, but not to tell anyone about Him. He even spoke in parables so the fullness of His meaning would be unrecognizable by the masses who had not really put their trust in Him. His words and the truth they revealed were for "those with eyes to see and ears to hear" (Matthew 13:16). In a very real sense, only the sheep who recognized His voice would hear and follow Him—then, and now (John 10:27–28).

What about Today?

If the anticipation of Jesus' First Coming was so sparse, what about today? Like society in ancient Judea, people still tend to fall into one of several different categories:

1. Some people literally don't know Jesus is coming again. They either don't know Him at all, or nobody has told them He is coming.
2. Others claim to know Him, but don't live as if He's had any impact on their lives. They manifest complete apathy about His return.

3. Other ostensibly faithful Christians are convinced He isn't coming anytime soon, or at least not in a glorious manner that will literally fulfill the prophecies of His coming. They're often ignorant or fearful of Bible prophecy, convinced it doesn't have any relevance to their daily lives.

4. But for some followers of Christ, the promise of His Coming resonates in our hearts and inspires our days. We wake up each morning hoping He will come *today*. We take communion and consider Paul's admonition that we commemorate Christ's death "until He comes" (1 Corinthians 11:26). We long for Jesus to come for us even as we seek to serve Him in this life.

The unbelieving world clearly fits in the first category. People who don't know the Lord or have rejected Him outright don't realize He is coming soon. They live carefree lives oblivious to the fact that they live on the brink of eternity and the wrath of God abides on them (John 3:36). Living in spiritual darkness, they say, "peace and safety," unaware that "destruction will come upon them suddenly like labor pains upon a woman with child" (1 Thessalonians 5:3–4). Like most of the people living in the time of Noah, they will be swept away when God's wrath is poured out upon the world.

Tragically, many professing Christians fall into the second category. Polls by the Pew Research Center, the Barna Group, and other Christian-affiliated organizations have proven that many self-declared Christians do not adhere to the basic tenets of the faith. They don't believe in Creation as described in the Bible, the virgin birth of Christ, the literal death and resurrection of Jesus, or the promise of His return. (Astoundingly, 20 percent of professing Christians say they don't even believe in the God of the Bible!)

We are witnessing a great falling away of these Christians of convenience as our society becomes increasingly hostile to genuine Christian faith. Without social capital to be gained from church membership, the roles have declined dramatically in many urban churches. The accelerating drift of lukewarm Christians toward secularism explains why whole denominations are hurtling toward apostasy, and "None" is the fastest-growing category of religious affiliation in the United States today.

Over the past several years, I've come to realize most churches fit into category 3 of the above list. Even vibrant churches full of sincere followers of Jesus Christ manifest an aversion to His prophetic Word. Disdainful of extremists who have sown division and fanatics who peddle the sensational and manipulate and misquote the Word of God, many pastors are leery of any presentation relating to Bible prophecy. But the signs of the times are so obvious that faithful Christians are beginning to clamor for teaching and preaching about Bible prophecy.

A growing number of Christians in category 4 embraces sound teaching on Bible prophecy and seeks to encourage one another—and all the more as we *see* the day drawing near (Hebrews 10:23–25).

Casting Our Crowns

When the Magi came from the East, they brought gifts to the newborn Jewish King. Scripture says they presented Him with gold, frankincense, and myrrh—rich gifts suitable for a king. Over time, song and lore envisioned these wise men as kings, and assumed there were three of them because that was the number of their gifts. But the Bible doesn't specify that detail, and it is unlikely they were rulers in the classical sense.

What we do know is the wise men had probably studied the writings of Daniel. They discerned a sign in the heavens and undertook a long and difficult journey to see the Messiah. Their quest to encounter the Holy One of Israel—along with their determination to have something of value to present to Him—offers a model for us.

I opened this chapter focusing on Simeon and Anna, the only two Jews recorded in the Gospels as eagerly anticipating the Messiah other than Jesus' parents, Zacharias, and Elizabeth. Scripture tells us John, full of the Holy Spirit, also leapt for joy while still in his mother's womb in the presence of his unborn Lord (Luke 2:41).

We believe the wise men learned of the coming Messiah from the Hebrew Scriptures and from the testimony of faithful Jews who lived in the pagan kingdom of Babylon. In that regard, they had the same prophetic Word we have in the Old Testament—although we have the complete canon of the Old Testament prophets. And, like John, followers of Christ have the gift of the Holy Spirit dwelling in us, illuminating God's Word in our hearts.

So why aren't we as determined to watch for the signs the Lord is revealing all around us today? The signs of the times are multiplying before our eyes—and converging as never before. Soon—perhaps very soon—He will burst from the sky. We won't have to follow "yonder star" to find His humble birthplace, He will come in radiant glory to reign upon the earth.

Have you ever wondered what you will give Him when you first see Him? That is a question worth pondering.

Scripture speaks of several crowns we will be awarded in Heaven:

- An imperishable crown (1 Corinthians 9:24–25)
- A crown of exultation or rejoicing (1 Thessalonians 2:19)
- A crown of glory (1 Peter 5:4)
- A crown of life (Revelation 2:10)

Paul also says there is a crown of righteousness laid up for all who have loved Jesus' appearing (2 Timothy 4:8). That is one crown reserved just for those who have been eager to see the Messiah, like Simeon and Anna.

I've always wondered what I would do with a crown. Then, reflecting on the Magis' gifts and turning to God's prophetic Word, it dawned on me. Like the elders described in Revelation 4:10, we will cast our crowns before the throne of the Lamb and say:

Worthy are You, our Lord and our God, to receive glory and honor and power; for You created all things, and because of Your will they existed, and were created.

Oh, how I want those crowns! Not for my own glory—or to give me what biblical scholar and evangelist David Reagan describes as an eternal neck ache!! I want all five crowns to be able to cast them before my Lord and Savior. For the imperishable body He gives me will be like His resurrected body. My rejoicing is due to the song He put in my heart. Any glory I experience will be a reflection of the glory that is His. The eternal life I enjoy will be thanks only to His death and resurrection. And, the righteousness manifest in the crown I receive will be credited to me from His infinite righteousness and holiness. Even the crowns He gives me belong to Him, and they will become the very gifts I will be thrilled to lay at His feet.

Looking Forward

If you haven't put your trust in Jesus Christ as your Savior and Lord—confessing your sinfulness and accepting His eternal forgiveness—then the wrath of God abides on you.

Soon, every Christian will be gathered to Heaven in the twinkling of an eye. Shortly thereafter, the world will descend into a seven-year period of horrific suffering as God's righteous wrath is poured out. Do not wait another day or hour to flee from the wrath to come, and into the loving arms of our Savior.

Christ—and the promise of Rapture—is indeed the Christian's Blessed Hope. I believe that some reading this book soon after it is published will not see death before the Lord's Messiah comes (Luke 2:26). Are you praying earnestly for Jesus to rend the heavens and come down? Do you wake up each day crying out, "Maranatha! Come quickly, Lord Jesus!"

The "Light of revelation the Gentiles and the glory of [God's] people

Israel" has come. He is coming again—not as a humble Babe to be wrapped in swaddling clothes, but in power and glory.

The last stanza of "We Three Kings" sounds the expectant, triumphal chorus of the Second Coming:

> Glorious now behold Him arise;
> King and God and sacrifice:
> Alleluia, Alleluia,
> sounds through the earth and skies.
> Amen. Come Lord Jesus!

Chapter 14

APOCALYPTIC ANXIETY

By Dr. Randall Price

General Editor's note: Dr. Randall Price is one of today's leading scholars in Bible prophecy from the premillennial, pre-Tribulation view, the true view from God's Word. But he is also one of the world's top hands-on explorers within biblical archeology. He has undertaken numerous expeditions into areas important to human history and to God's dealing with humankind.

Randall's many trips to Mt. Ararat in search of Noah's ark and his exploration of the Temple Mount and surrounding areas, as well as of many other places, such as Qumran and the Dead Sea region, would be the stuff of legend, if his exploits were not true in every case. All this history makes my friend more than qualified to inform our readers here of that era of the worst time in history that is quickly approaching.

The Tribulation can be a complex matter. So we are blessed to have Dr. Price examine for us what it means to this judgment-bound world, and where we stand on God's prophetic timeline.

+++

The world today lives in fear of the apocalypse. These fears appear to be justified as we survey the world scene. As the US totters under impossible debt, massive recession, and social unrest, globalists no longer hide their agenda, but proclaim a "Global Reset" date with the move to a cashless society, worldwide depopulation, and invasive controls in every area of life. To this is added the threat of an expansive

war in the Middle East backed by Iran with its allies Russia and Turkey, and a Third World War with the newly ascendant global power of
China. Everywhere, people and nations fear we are the terminal generation and the age of apocalypse is upon us. However ominous and
terrible the global forecast may be to modern observers, the worst has
not yet been witnessed. That will come when Hell literally breaks forth
on earth and the people of earth enter the Tribulation, when there will
be a universal experience of the Apocalypse.

Tribulation or Tribulations?

How will we know when the Age of Apocalypse has arrived? After all,
people feared the end of the earth had come many times in the past,
but those crises came and went without apocalyptic fulfillment. But
Jesus taught, based on the Old Testament predictions, that "there will
be a great Tribulation, such as has not occurred since the beginning
of the world until now, nor ever shall" (Matthew 24:21).133 This
statement indicates that all of the world's greatest disasters are nothing by comparison to the Great Tribulation that will one day engulf
our globe. The event is to be unparalleled, both in extent (universal)
and experience (extraordinary). This understanding also eliminates
the temptation of those undergoing tribulations to consider themselves already in the Tribulation. Jesus said to His disciples: "In the
world you have tribulation" (John 16:33). Jesus' statement concerned
the present and continued condition of life (note the present active
tense) for believers in this world system. In fact, "tribulations" are
not viewed in Scripture as an option for the Christian life, but as the
expected outcome: "And indeed, all who desire to live godly in Christ
Jesus will be persecuted" (2 Timothy 3:12). Throughout the subsequent two millennia, these words have found fulfillment as Christians
have endured unbelievable hardships, persecution, pogroms, torture, indignities, and myriad forms of martyrdom. Examples of such
"tribulations" in past ages have been passed on in part through the
well-known *Foxes Book of Martyrs*. Yet, the passage of time, with

its supposed civilizing of society and technological advances, hasn't lessened the atrocities against the faithful. It has been stated by missiologists that the last century on earth has witnessed more martyrdom and persecution of Christians than in all the centuries since the time of Christ combined! Evidence supporting this claim has been documented in James and Marti Hefley's modern account of martyrdom in their book, *By Their Blood: Christian Martyrs of the 20th Century*, and ongoing global attacks of Christians are reported by such organizations as Voice of the Martyrs.

However, those who rightly divide the Word discern that the present experience of tribulation in the world is to be distinguished from the future experience by the world of the Tribulation. One major distinction is that, during this age, those who suffer tribulation do so in the absence of God's wrath. Today there is no direct display of divine justice on the earth in recompense for the injustices inflicted on the just. By contrast, those who suffer tribulation in the future age of the Tribulation will do so in an environment that witnesses God's judgment poured out on earth in unprecedented measure, culminating with the return of the Judge Himself to the earth (Revelation 19:11). In fact, it is the "tribulations" of those at present as well as their brethren in the Tribulation that will call forth God's wrath, as the prophetic Scriptures indicate. In 2 Thessalonians 1:5–8 we read concerning those persecuted in the Church Age (verse 4):

> This is a plain indication of God's righteous judgment so that you may be considered worthy of the kingdom of God, for which indeed you are suffering. For after all, it is only just for God to repay with affliction those who afflict you, and to give relief to you who are afflicted and to us as well when the Lord Jesus shall be revealed from heaven with His mighty angels in flaming fire, dealing out retribution to those who do not obey the gospel of our Lord Jesus.

In like manner, concerning those who are in the company of the saints during the Tribulation (Revelation 14:12), we read in Revelation 6:10 with 19:1b–2 (compare 11:18; 16:5–6):

> How long, O Lord, holy and true, wilt Thou refrain from judging and avenging our blood on those who dwell on the earth? ...Hallelujah! Salvation and glory and power belong to our God; because His judgments are true and righteous; for He has judged the earth with her immorality, and He has avenged the blood of His bond-servants on her.

Another distinction between the tribulations of today and the Tribulation of tomorrow is the description concerning believers during these periods of trouble. Believers in "tribulations," especially those affecting the whole of the Christian community, such as the first-century persecutions, were described as better for the experience:

> And after you have suffered for a little while, the God of all grace, who called you to His eternal glory in Christ, will Himself perfect, confirm, strengthen and establish you. (1 Peter 5:10)

Believers were, therefore, not to seek to avoid such trials, but welcome them as opportunities to grow in grace:

> Consider it all joy, my brethren, when you encounter various trials, knowing that the testing of your faith produces endurance. (James 1:2–3; compare 1 Peter 4:13–14).[134]

By contrast, those believers in the Tribulation are described as being able to endure only because their experience will be reduced:

> And unless those days had been cut short, no life would have been saved; but for the sake of the elect those days shall be cut short. (Matthew 24:22)

They're not counseled to abide in their sufferings, but commanded to flee for their safety (Matthew 24:16–20; Revelation 12:6). This last point reveals a distinct disadvantage to being a believer in the Tribulation as opposed to any other crisis period in history. Since post-tribulationists contend the Church must go through the Tribulation and believers will be preserved from the divine wrath unleashed during that period, we need to briefly consider these claims.

Who Will Live in the Age of Apocalypse?

It is clear that those who inhabit the Age of Apocalypse will be divided, as now, into two distinct camps comprised of unbelievers and believers. Both camps appear to have members who are Jewish135 and Gentile, although a larger company of Jews are believers (Revelation 7:1–8; 11:1; 12:13–17; Matthew 24:30 with Zechariah 12:10–14; compare Romans 11:26), leaving Gentiles ("the nations") as the largest representation of unbelievers (Revelation 11:2, 9; 12:5; 14:8; 16:19; 18:3, 23; 19:15; compare Matthew 25:32). This first division of unregenerate humankind is most often referred to in the book of Revelation as "those who dwell on the earth" or "the earth-dwellers" (Revelation 3:10; 6:10; 8:13; 11:10; 13:8, 12, 14; 17:2, 8). This term describes their origin (natural birth) and character as "earthly" as opposed to believers whose origin (new birth) and character is "heavenly." They belong to the earth, and since the earth is to be destroyed in judgment, they are destined to be destroyed with it (2 Peter 3:7; Jude 10; Revelation 11:18). Another term used for them is "whose name has not been written in the book of life from the foundation of the world" (Revelation 17:8), emphasizing their unrepentant and reprobate nature. The second division of believing humankind is most often referred to as "the saints" (Revelation 11:8; 13:7, 10; 14:12; 16:6; 17:6; 19:8), "bond-servants" (Revelation 7:3; 11:18; 19:2, 5; 22:3), "redeemed" (Revelation 5:9; 14:3–4), and "brethren" (Revelation 6:11; 12:10; 19:10), and are described with respect to their triumphant faith as "overcomers" (Revelation 12:11; 21; 21:7). The one term that does not appear for these believers after Revelation chapter 3 (until Revelation 22:16) is "church." This is strange, since many of the other terms for believers such as "bond-servants" (Revelation 2:20) and "overcomers" (Revelation 2:26; 3:5, 12, 21) do reappear.136 But if, as dispensational futurists contend, the Church is shown to be in Heaven (i.e., raptured) in Revelation 4:4–11, as God reveals to John "what must take place after these things" (Revelation 4:1), that is after the completion of God's dealing with the churches in Revelation 2–3, then the Church is the company of believers in Heaven throughout the Tribulation who are joined by the martyred Tribulation saints. This identification removes the Church from the Tribulation, as many texts indicate (1 Thessalonians 1:10; 5:19; 2 Thessalonians 2:2–3; 2 Peter 2:9; Revelation 3:9–10), while understanding that a believing company (who apparently came to faith after the Rapture and through the later witness of the 144,000 and the two witnesses) will go through the Tribulation.

Nevertheless, posttribulationists, who argue that the Church will go through the Tribulation, often state this is necessary in order to purify it from its carnal ways. However, such a view does injustice to the Christian martyrs who have been through their own tribulations as part of the Church. In democracies like the United States, where being a Christian is at present a protected lifestyle, there may appear to be fewer struggling to survive than under atheistic communism or Muslim terrorism. Even so, God has commanded those in the Church Age to pray for their governments (who can restrain persecution): "kings and all who are in authority, in order that we may lead a tranquil and quiet life in all godliness and dignity" (1 Timothy 2:2). If the Church were in the Tribulation, this would require believers to intercede for Satan, Antichrist, and the False Prophet who, as the ruling authorities, are the agents of believers' persecution (Revelation 12:12–13, 17; 13:7–10; 15–17). This would constitute a contradiction in conduct, for, according to Scripture, believers are ordered to resist and overcome them (James 4:7; 1 Peter 5:9; 1 John 2:14; 4:1–4; Revelation 11:5–6;

12:17; 13:7, 10; 14:12). The only recorded prayers of the Tribulation saints with respect to these evil entities are for their soon destruction (Revelation 6:10; 11:18; 8:2–5; 15:2–4; 19:1–6; compare 16:5–7).

As to those who experience the wrath that falls upon the earth, although it comes with the purpose of judgment on unbelievers, the consequences must affect everyone alive. If God presently judges our American nation because of its leaders' sins and our society's sins of apostasy, pornography, abortion, infanticide, homosexuality, etc., will not every Christian living in the country also suffer simply because they're citizens? Hasn't this been the case for Christians living in nations such as Germany and Great Britain, once the center for the Reformation and Christian missions, but now filled with anti-Semitism and sorcery? Protection during the Tribulation is selectively afforded the 144,000 virgin Jewish saints, the divinely appointed "two witnesses," and part of the believing Jewish remnant ("the woman who gave birth to the male [child]," i.e., the Jewish people). These are sealed and protected (Revelation 7:3–4; 9:4; 11:4–6; 12:6, 14–16) to perform their unique witnesses. Nevertheless, even the 144,000 and the two witnesses are permitted to be killed once their missions are complete (Revelation 11:7; 14:1), and the rest of the Jewish believers are left open to Satan's attack (Revelation 12:17). All other believers during this period are apparently able to be killed in earthquakes (Revelation 11:13) or savaged by Antichrist (Revelation 13:7–10). It is for this reason the plagues are sent "to avenge the blood of the saints" (Revelation 16:6; 18:20; 19:2). Jewish believers during this time will particularly suffer, as Zechariah 13:8 notes: "It will come about in all the Land [of Israel], declares the Lord, that two-thirds will be cut off and perish." Just as the perpetrators of the Nazi Holocaust did not discriminate between believing and unbelieving Jews, so it will also happen in this future holocaust of the Tribulation. We're not given a clear picture of what happens to Gentile believers, but they, too, are part of those martyred, appearing in Heaven as a great company from "every tribe and tongue and people and nation" (Revelation 5:9; 7:9).

Furthermore, the plagues that come with the sixth trumpet kill a third of all humankind. Since no special protection is said to be given the general population of Tribulation saints, we must assume many are also killed by the plagues. The difference, of course, is the plagues are designed to punish unbelievers and bring their repentance or cause their deaths and seal their doom (Revelation 6:15–17; 9:20–21; 11:13; 16:8–9, 21), whereas for believers they deliver them beyond the reach of Antichrist and his oppressions and increase their rewards in Heaven. This is especially stated in Revelation 14:13:

> "Blessed are the dead who die in the Lord from now on!"
> "Yes," says the Spirit, "that they may rest from their labors, for their deeds follow with them." (compare Revelation 7:14–17; 11:18; 12:11)

Yet another eschatological option is offered by preterists who attempt to fit the details of the book of Revelation into the past event of Jerusalem's destruction by the Romans in AD 70. They have to radically minimalize the wrath of God, both in its extent and severity, in order to limit it geographically to Jerusalem and agree with the recorded siege and captivity of its Jewish citizenry.[137] Aside from the fact that Zechariah (12–14), Daniel (12:1), the Olivet Discourse (Matthew 24:13, 22; Mark 13:13, 20; Luke 21:27–28), and the book of Revelation (1:7; 6:15–17; 7:1–8; 11:18; 12:12–16; 15:3–4; 16:14; 19:15, 19) all depict an opposite scenario—Gentiles as the object of wrath and Jews as the object of salvation—Revelation clearly reveals that in the Tribulation judgments, the "wrath of God is finished" (Revelation 15:1). The culmination of divine judgment comes with the final seven plagues, which in form resemble the plagues against the Egyptians at the Exodus (Exodus 7–10). Just as those judgments were sent to deliver Israel and punish their oppressors, so these will complete God's promise to "judge the world in righteousness" (Acts 17:31; compare 2 Thessalonians 1:6–10). Since the plagues of the seventh bowl judgment are the "last" and end the wrath of God, they can only conclude with the final judgment of the wicked in the lake of fire (Revelation 20:12–15). This cannot be construed in any eschatological scheme to be fulfilled in the past or reduced to a remnant. As biblical scholar and author Robert Thomas correctly observes:

> No amount of rationalization—such as some theonomists practice to soften the tone of ultimacy, absoluteness, and universality in finding a fulfillment of these plagues in the AD 70 events surrounding the destruction of Jerusalem—can mitigate the force of this language regarding the finality of these plagues.[138]

The apocalyptic wrath of preterism can only account for one judgment against a small portion of the Jewish population (most of whom were living comfortably outside the land of Israel at the time), while leaving the unjudged world free from a divine wrath exhausted two thousand years ago! Yet, even the prophet Daniel saw in Daniel 12:1–2 that the magnitude of this "time of distress" was so pervasive and final it had to be followed by the resurrection of the righteous (Revelation 20:4–6) and wicked (Revelation 20:5). Therefore, to appreciate the unparalleled nature of the Tribulation, let us survey what Scripture reveals life will be like for those who will inhabit this most terrible time in all of history.

Life in the Age of Apocalypse

The beginning of wrath (the Day of the Lord) is seen in the first seal judgment with a rider on a white horse going out "conquering and to conquer" (Revelation 6:2). Pre-wrath advocates hold that wrath is reserved for the last quarter of the Tribulation and isn't present here. However, this depends on what ones sees as indicative of the wrath of God. The first use of the term "wrath" (*orges*) appears in Revelation 6:16–17 at the time of the sixth seal judgment, where the text reads: "the great day of their wrath has come." However, the Greek verb *elthen* ("has come") used in verse 17 is aorist indicative and therefore looks back on wrath that has previously arrived. This could be that portrayed in the sixth seal's terrestrial and celestial disturbances in the form of earthquakes, atmospheric pollution, and a meteor/asteroid assault (Revelation 6:12–14), but it could as easily encompass the previous five seals in which world conquest is initiated and global warfare ensues (Revelation 6:2–4), followed by worldwide famine with one-fourth of earth's population destroyed (Revelation 6:5–8). According to Romans 1:18, "the wrath of God is revealed from heaven against all ungodliness and unrighteousness of men," and has been evidenced in cultures where idolatry and homosexuality have been tolerated (the continued cancerous presence of these lifestyles being part of the judgment itself). The result of this corrupted society is that it is "worthy of death" (verse 32). If the figure on the white horse in the first seal of Revelation 6:2 is Antichrist, then his assault on the world to bring it under his corrupt control is the culmination of a sinful society ripened for wrath. Since 2 Thessalonians 2:3–12 connects the rise of Antichrist with worldwide lawlessness and deception (verses 4, 8, 10–12), the usurpation of deity as the climax of idolatry (verse 4), and the activity of Satan (verse 9), it shouldn't be difficult to see Antichrist's foray for world conquest as the commencement of divine wrath on a humanity worthy of death. This is especially the case with the extensive and extraordinary manner of deaths that result from military slaughter, starvation, viral epidemic, and wild animal attack (Revelation 6:4–8). Among the casualties of these violent opening months of the Tribulation are believers killed because of their faith who cry out for greater wrath to be sent to judge and avenge their deaths (Revelation 6:9–10). Therefore, from the beginning of the Tribulation (with the rise of Antichrist seen in the signing of a covenant with the Israelis; see Daniel 9:27), God's wrath is progressively and increasingly unleashed on earth. With the conclusion of the sixth seal, the world's unbelieving population, from the poorest to the richest, convinced that what they're experiencing is God's judgment, believe the apocalyptic age has come and the end of the world is at hand (Revelation 6:15–17). But the worst is yet to come.

As we move into the seventh seal, which includes the trumpet and bowl judgments, we find with the trumpet judgments that one-third of the world's vegetation is burned (Revelation 8:7), one-third of earth's oceans and fresh water sources are polluted, and one third of all ships are destroyed (Revelation 8:8–11). Further, one-third of the luminaries are affected so that the world experiences unprecedented darkness (Revelation 8:12), a horrendous and unbelievably painful demonic attack occurs for five months (Revelation 9:1–12), one-third of earth's population is killed (Revelation 9:15–18), and an earthquake accompanied by huge hailstorm ravages the planet (Revelation 11:19). Adding to these disasters, the bowl judgments plague humanity with loathsome and malignant sores (Revelation 16:2), completely destroy all life in the seas and the waters of the lakes, rivers, and springs (Revelation 16:3–4), burn humans severely with increased radiation from the sun (Revelation 16:8–9), and cover the earth with deep darkness (Revelation 16:10). Demonic spirits gather the nations of the world for war, the battles of Armageddon (Revelation 16:12–16), which include an initial attack and final siege against Jerusalem (Zechariah 12:3–14:3). There is widespread destruction through earthquakes and one hundred-pound hailstones; the catastrophic climax will be the burning of the world's commercial center, Babylon (Revelation 16:18–21; 18:2–19).

To this catalog of catastrophes we must add the horrors of life under the government of a demonic, power-mad ruler with a god complex, Antichrist (Revelation 13:1–10), who will enslave the nations of the world (Daniel 11:36–40), invade the land of Israel, desecrate the Jewish Temple, persecute the Jewish people (Daniel 11:41–45; Matthew 24:15–16; Mark 13:14–15; 2 Thessalonians 2:4; Revelation 11:2), and make war on all the saints (Revelation 13:7). He is joined by his deputy of deception, the False Prophet, who will work deceitful miracles and require complete allegiance to Antichrist or otherwise death (Revelation 13:11–15). However, taking the mark of identification with Antichrist will be tantamount to renouncing God, thus dooming oneself forever (Revelation 13:16–18). Overshadowing all of these figures is the evil one himself, Satan, who, having been cast down to the earth during the Tribulation, will come with wrath against the world, knowing his time is short (Revelation 12:12). This indicates that those who live in the Tribulation will have spiritual encounters with demons as well as dramatic demonstrations of God's wrath. No one in that day will be able to deny the existence of God or the supernatural, but neither will they be able to avoid the deceptive signs and wonders that will lead them to embrace Antichrist and their damnation (2 Thessalonians 2:9–12). Today the presence of the Holy Spirit through the Church permits a restraint of such evil, the advent of Antichrist, and the deception of the devil (2 Thessalonians 2:6–7). However, once the Church is raptured, its influence will be ended, and all hell will literally break loose. Though at first the lack of such restraint may seem like a new peace for the world, it will be a pseudo peace that will fast foment the formation of the world around one wicked will. Today, the worst war, the most terrible tyrant, the most dreadful disasters, and the most pernicious pestilences are nothing by comparison to what awaits in the Age of Apocalypse.

Life in the Tribulation

Since the Lord first revealed through His prophets and apostles the coming conditions of the Age of Apocalypse, people have thought through the last two millennia that various local and global crises might be the apocalyptic age. As early as the first-century epistle to the Thessalonians, we read that the widespread persecutions and problems they faced (1 Thessalonians 1:6–7; 3:3–5; 2 Thessalonians 1:4–5) influenced many to panic and even alter their lifestyle in fear that the end was at hand (2 Thessalonians 2:2; 3:6–12). This has followed suit in every like situation, whether influenced by famine, plague, world wars, atomic bombs, petroleum shortages, environmental and population crises, or Y2K. However difficult these days have been, they were but the experience of life in a fallen world and will pale by comparison with the Age of Apocalypse when it finally arrives. Nevertheless, the catastrophes of the Tribulation are not extinction-level events. The world and all those who inhabit it during this time will suffer greatly, but God still has a plan for the planet (the millennial Kingdom), and its eventual destruction will be followed by new heavens and a new earth (2 Peter 3:10–13; Revelation 21:1; compare Isaiah 65:17; 66:22).

During the present age of the Church, believers should expect "tribulations" in this world (1 Thessalonians 3:3–4; 1 Peter 4:12), and face them with faith instead of fear (1 Corinthians 15:58; 1 Thessalonians 3:2–3; 2 Thessalonians 2:2; James 5:8; 1 Peter 4:12–14, 19; 5:9–10), "for it is time for judgment to begin with the household of God; and if it begins with us first, what will be the outcome for those who do not obey the gospel of God?" (1 Peter 4:17). For such people, "the present heavens and earth by His word are being reserved for fire, kept for the day of judgment and destruction of ungodly men" (2 Peter 3:7). When the Tribulation commences with the signing of a covenant between "the prince that shall come" (Antichrist) and the "many" (the nation of Israel), as noted in Daniel 9:27a, the world will enter a time of unparalleled deception (2 Thessalonians 2:10–12) followed by unprecedented destruction. Like those in the days when Noah was building the ark, most of the world's population will not understand the severity of their condition until the flood of God's judgment has come and swept them all away (Matthew 24:37–39). However, for those who accept Jesus Christ today as God's ark of safety, trusting in His death for their sins on the cross as God's promise of escape from wrath, they will be removed from earth before the Age of the Apocalypse begins (1 Thessalonians 1:10; 4:13–5:11; 2 Thessalonians 2:1–5; Revelation 3:9–10). Their life until that time may be one of "tribulations," yet supported by a confidence in the Lord's strength and salvation for every trial. And their life after that time will be one of unending joy and pleasure in the Lord's presence (Psalm 16:11; Revelation 21:4; 22:3–5). But for those reading these words who have never believed the warning of the Apocalypse or fled to Christ for refuge, their lives will be lived (for however long they can endure) in these darkest of days of the Tribulation. Some may feel these are scare tactics used to frighten people into faith, but everyone must first come to understand the wrath of God they deserve, before they can accept the love of God they do not deserve. The Scriptures reveal that God Himself became a man (Jesus Christ, God's Son), and He was made subject to His own wrath so He "might deliver those who through fear of death were subject to slavery all their lives" (Hebrews 2:15). Therefore, to warn us of our imminent end and give us an opportunity to escape the wrath to come, God has made the message clear:

> Inasmuch as it is appointed for men to die once and after this comes judgment, so Christ also, having been offered once to bear the sins of many, shall appear a second time for salvation without reference to sin, to those who eagerly await Him. (Hebrews 9:27–28)

According to this promise, Christ came once to die for sinners, and He will return to judge them. Those who fear this judgment and flee to Him in faith will find the rest of that promise: Their horror of His coming will be replaced by a hope in His coming. He has promised a "blessed hope" (Titus 2:13), the Rapture, to those who trust Christ as Savior. His purpose is for them to be "delivered from the wrath to come" (1 Thessalonians 1:10).

These days have now been described for you; if you haven't already, will you come to Christ for His promised salvation? Now is the time to escape the hell that is coming on earth and for eternity. Christ is coming…are you going?

SECTION V

RAPTURE READYING

Chapter 15

BITTER ROOTS OF THIS FALLING AWAY

By Jim Fletcher

General Editor's note: Satan has worked through the minds of fallen humanity to concoct every form of false religious evil. We have for the most part fallen victim to this prevarication. The authors of the lies in the matter of origins, etc., have been obviously chosen by the "father of lies" because of their gifted intellectual prowess, in many cases. The masses seem easily persuaded by such "superior" thought, as we see, for example, considering the Age of Reason and the Renaissance.

People's demands to self-govern have pushed God's governance aside since the Fall in Eden. But Heaven's truth shines through all the luciferian darkening of humanity's understanding of God's desired relationship with us. Jim Fletcher, one of today's top authors in Bible prophecy, here looks upon the issues and events of these troubled times. He delves deeply yet with clarity into the satanically inspired attempt at the clouding of the truth regarding God's relationship with us.

And I saw, and behold a white horse: and he that sat on him had a bow; and a crown was given unto him: and he went forth conquering, and to conquer. (Revelation 6:2)

The scraping of crates on the floor of Yale's venerated Peabody Museum of Natural History caused Thomas Huxley's heart to race. The already legendary evolutionist had crossed the Atlantic to see, among other things, the extensive fossil collection housed at Yale by his friend, O. C. Marsh…the "Bone Collector."

Marsh, whose perpetual fixed stare resembled one of those portraits with eyeholes with which to spy on unsuspecting visitors, stood nearby and watched Huxley in silence.

The gloomy Londoner felt like the hopelessly curious boy he'd once been as he pondered the possibilities. On the heels of his famous "horse evolution" theory and subsequent papers and lectures, Huxley now had in his hands the pieces he needed to put flesh on his musings about life on ancient Earth.

Marsh nodded at an assistant when Huxley called for yet another box of bones, and the gruff fellow known as "Darwin's Bulldog" mixed and matched piece after piece, intent on providing physical evidence of his theory that horses had in fact evolved and had not, as now widely believed, appeared fully developed in the Garden of Eden.

Both Huxley and Marsh well knew what no one else would: The former would fit the evidence to fit his theory. According to Barry Werth in *Banquet at Delmonico's*:

Darwinians had learned, in large part from engaging with Agassiz, not to rely too heavily on fossil records, which were well recognized as hosting too many dead ends, anomalies, and missing links. And Huxley resisted departing from his own popular theory. He pored over box after box of Marsh's bones, assiduously, challenging him again and again, calling for a hoof from this ancient species or a molar from that one. With each challenge, Marsh beckoned an assistant to fetch another crate. "I believe you are a magician," Huxley finally blurted. "Whatever I want you just conjure up." Huxley declared the collection "the most wonderful thing I ever saw," telling Marsh: "The more I think of it, the more clear it is that your great work is the settlement of the pedigree of the horse."[139]

And there you have it. Quite apart from being objective scientific inquiry rooted in irrefutable evidence, evolution itself was in fact just another subjective worldview. Ever since, Darwin's theory has brought devastation and brutality to the world, and in particular has left the West without moral principles with which to lead.

To understand what is happening in our culture today—everyone agrees it is ailing—it's critical to understand why things are the way they are. Otherwise, corrective solutions are at best unorganized and less effective than solutions born of knowledge and understanding.

From public education to law, media, and politics, most would agree evolution has been imprinted on Western civilization (not to mention being the catalyst for totalitarians like Mao, Hitler, and Stalin). Public education turns out automatons steeped in moral relativism. Constitutional government is being replaced by a court system committed to ever-evolving societal mores. Even entertainment sources (*Inherit the Wind, Contact*, etc.) implant Darwinian ideology and propaganda into the public consciousness.

The results, as noted by the great creationist organizations, are predictable and poignant. Most have a feeling today that civilization is cracking up, and the near future feels ominous, as school shootings, anarchy in major cities, and rapidly changing government institutions threaten to alter America irrevocably. In 1999, one of the Columbine shooters, Dylan Klebold, announced in a message he left that he and his killer cohort had simply evolved to a higher state of being, therefore had the right to take human life at random.

As John Morris has stated, "Most people believe in evolution, because most people believe in evolution."

The thing Huxley "created" in the bowels of the Peabody Museum? The creature bore no resemblance to reality, except the reality Huxley summoned in his mind. He wanted to find a missing link, and because his real genius lay in his marketing abilities, he and Darwin and their small circle of science friends in London were able to mainstream evolutionary thought to the masses.

Thus was born the X Club, a group of a dozen men who met regularly for thirty years in the shadows of a London supper club. There they discussed evolution, the Bible—and, for our purposes today, ways to market their philosophical worldview to society as a whole.

Huxley, Darwin, and their colleague, Herbert Spencer (who coined the term "survival of the fittest") exported their views to America, beginning in earnest in 1881, when Spencer was hosted—incredibly—by America's most famous preacher, Henry Ward Beecher.

It was into this environment that influencers like the writer H. G. Wells were born, and stories like *The Time Machine* imprinted the idea of long ages on readers. Additionally, famed industrialists like Andrew Carnegie were so enamored of the ideas of Social Darwinism they built titanic industries on the backs of faceless workers. In fact, Carnegie himself was so taken with Spencer's militant brand of Social Darwinism (roughly, that a privileged few have the right to determine the fates of millions) that he wrote what some have described as love letters to the British sociologist.

By 1925 and the so-called Scopes Monkey Trial, evolutionary theory became accepted reality.

Tragically, it was and will always be only...philosophy. That is the key, and it is critical to understand that.

Upending the End

So, then, what happens to the Bible when you knock out the underpinnings of Genesis?

The great prophetic passages—including, of course, Jewish history—are cast as myth, legend, or metaphor. This has laid the groundwork for today's dearth of prophecy teaching in the churches. It is a cultural rot that targeted the Church. When I worked in the Christian book publishing industry as an editor, I first was fascinated by the main attacks on the doctrine of Creation. Later, I began to see that the new attack priority was Bible prophecy.

Specifically, the Rapture.

Most of Christian media despise Bible prophecy. *Christianity Today,* thought to be the flagship periodical of evangelicalism, is steeped in liberal thought and has been for decades. *Relevant* magazine, targeting evangelical Millennials, loves nothing more than to poke fun at Rapture teachings. Famous pastors like Rick Warren downplay (at best) prophecy teaching. Why? I think because it comes up against his Kingdom Now/ We're Going to Hand off a Triumphant Church to Christ movement that arrogantly believes humans can help themselves and, gross, help God.

I've been out of active publishing for fifteen years, and I see the attacks on the Rapture growing stronger. A very well-known prophecy teacher told me recently that anything to do with Israel on his podcast results in low ratings. People seem uninterested.

This is all incredibly ironic when you consider that *everyone* in the world feels the current instability is about to really unravel in an apocalyptic way.

And the Church stands silent.

Unable to provide answers to seekers, church leaders are left running what amounts to community centers. What began in the nineteenth century as attacks on the Bible and congregations was launched in the seminaries and by, as I mentioned, philosophers who hated God.

Because of this, the modern Church cannot tell people where they came from, why they're here, and where they're going.

I'm a Boomer, so I remember the "glory days" of Bible prophecy. Growing up in Oklahoma City, there was a prophecy conference somewhere in town every weekend. Southwest Radio Church was right down the road. Prophecy in the News, the same. Our church was pro-Israel and Rapture ready. Pastors were bold.

I remember believing the coming storm of evil would include a one-world religion, coordinated between the Vatican and the New Agers. Certainly we watched Israel like a hawk.

Charles Darwin, Herbert Spencer, and Thomas Huxley created the conditions to destroy people's confidence in our history and our destiny. They hated prophecy as much as they hated Creation doctrine. They were simply men who hated the God of the Bible. The spiritual ancestors of these British thinkers didn't embrace the philosophy of naturalism because they came to scientific conclusions that the earth is very old (in contrast to the Genesis account). They developed and promoted Darwin's theory of evolution because it gave them a rationale to reject God.

All these men, by the way, shared a common tragedy: Their fathers destroyed them by teaching them to hate Christianity. Darwin's father and grandfather (Erasmus) were already familiar with ancient concepts of evolutionary theory. They simply passed it on to a young Charles, who in turn handed it to unfortunate generations that came after him.

No Shalom

All this reminds me of one of the last songs Johnny Cash wrote and recorded: "The Man Comes Around." It is a vivid and haunting picture of the end of time, when Jesus Christ comes back in victory and glory. The third verse is compelling:

Till Armageddon, no shalam, no shalom
Then the father hen will call his chickens home
The wise man will bow down before the throne
And at his feet, they'll cast their golden crowns
When the man comes around.[140]

Cash was of a generation that actually believed the Bible. He's been gone twenty years, and subsequent generations hate what he loved.

It's interesting to note that dispensationalists, Christians who believe in Bible prophecy, the promises to the Jews, and warnings about last things, are often excoriated by fellow Christians who dislike talk of eschatology. This division is increasing, as I constantly speak to Christians who report that teaching about Bible prophecy is on the decline in churches.

A major reason for this is the rise of the emergent church, the group seeking common ground even with other religions. Ironically, its proponents "break bread" with adherents of other religions, but profess frustration with Bible-prophecy advocates. This group includes Tony Campolo, Jim Wallis, Brian McLaren, Mark Noll, and the editorial board of *Christianity Today* magazine.

As Jan Markell of Olive Tree Ministries has astutely pointed out, many of these leaders espouse the following views:

- Prophetic Scriptures are denied or fulfilled in AD 70 (as is also the belief of preterism).
- The Church is the new Israel.
- Armageddon is the ongoing battle between the forces of light and darkness.
- Antichrist is a spirit, not a person.
- We're already in the Tribulation, but at the same time, we're in the Millennium. (It doesn't get any stranger! It's one or the other.)
- Rather than following traditional Bible prophecy, they follow "new revelations."
- Modern-day prophets must be obeyed and not judged for their inaccuracy.

Do you understand that the scoffers who deny the biblical warnings of the last days unknowingly confirm the very passages they deny?

Many of them like to entangle the whole issue in terms of exegesis, the study of biblical interpretation. Some say the "end-times" passages are ambiguous. Some say they were meant for the times in which the prophets lived. Some say they are twisted out of context by the bloodlust of "doomsday preachers" who teach about Bible prophecy.

No, the bottom line is that they hate a God who sets the rules and is above His creation.

From a Brian McLaren blog post:

Thanks for the encouragement. One slight tweak—in Chapter 18, I talk about the meaning of the word "parousia." I explain that the term "second coming" isn't found in the biblical text. It's a term like "the Fall"—developed in extra-biblical theological literature, and then read back into the text (and sometimes put there by "translators" who are actually interpreters). That doesn't mean it's wrong—just that the term itself is subject to questioning. When Jesus speaks of coming back or again, sometimes he's referring to the resurrection...sometimes he may be referring to his coming to be with us via the Holy Spirit at Pentecost...and sometimes he may be referring to the coming of a new era and "the end of the (current) age" centered in holy city, temple, priesthood, and sacrifice. He may also be referring to some ultimate judgment day...but the more I read the New Testament, the fewer of those references I think there are. More and more, it seems, Jesus was referring to things that were very close at hand, and so in that way, it turns out both Jesus and Paul were right: the cataclysm they predicted would happen "before this generation passes."[141]

McLaren particularly hates eschatology—at least the version that glorifies our Great King, the Lord Jesus Christ.

The Roots of Rapture Hatred

Several years ago, I read a book that I rank in the top five I've read from the Christian community. Occasionally, you find one that really unlocks a lot of mysteries. In my case, I wondered how the Church had gotten so off track, particularly as it relates to Bible prophecy.

Paul Smith's *New Evangelism* is one of those brave books authored by someone unafraid of the enemy. In his case, some of the enemies were from within his own camp. Smith, the brother of Calvary Chapel founder Chuck Smith, was more of a behind-the-scenes guy. His wisdom and counsel were invaluable to his brother, from the late sixties until Chuck's death in 2013.

Paul was also a master researcher. He had all the receipts, as it were, from his perch in Southern California. He had, for instance, access to materials from Fuller Theological Seminary, began by Charles Fuller in 1947, but now a left-wing (my words) institution. Today, for example, Fuller is likely to send student groups (as does their ideological twin in the Midwest, Wheaton) to "Palestine," where their heads are filled with PLO propaganda. That might shock you, but it's true.

Why did this happen?

As Paul explains, early on, Fuller's son, Daniel, went to Europe to study theology. Among his mentors was German scholar Karl Barth. He was the change agent who coined the inane term "true myth." In other words, there are portions of the Bible that, while not historically true, have "truths" to teach us.

This is of course blasphemy. But Fuller the Younger was exposed to it. Not surprisingly, he came home changed. The biggest change in his thinking was in eschatology.

In a 1960 letter to Dr. Harold Lindsell, Charles Fuller wrote the following:

In correspondence with my son, Daniel, he has helped me appreciate the fact that there are difficulties with the dispensational interpretation of prophecy and that we should not be dogmatic about details of eschatology (when the rapture will take place; whether there is a millennium or not) which has unhappily divided Christians in our day. Of course we know that God's Word plainly teaches that the Lord Jesus is coming in person and power to establish His glorious kingdom. Dan has given me a respect for Calvinism and I hope that in our theology department this point of view will always have a fair representation. In other words, I want our school to be true to the great Protestant, orthodox, and evangelical tradition with no limitations that would prevent our having the finest faculty that it is possible to get, of men committed to the Word of God and the gospel of grace in these latter days.

As is often the case with big ministries, here the son is influencing/mentoring the father. That's *always* a recipe for disaster. Notice what this letter excerpt tells us.

Daniel "helped" his father sees "difficulties" with dispensationalism. Via Karl Barth. It was here Charles should have had a cup of coffee with sonny boy and told him to keep his liberalism out of Fuller. Not only did he not do that; he continued to allow Daniel to pollute the institution. Eventually, the son would become president of the seminary!

Next, Daniel helped Father appreciate Calvinism. Bingo. Explains so much. This was part of the contribution to where we are now. If I can be blunt, Calvinism has hijacked the Southern Baptist Convention, once a bastion of conservative thought and love for the Rapture, Israel, and Bible prophecy overall. Now the SBC is dominated by men who do not like our brand of eschatology.

In short, Charles Fuller was naïve at best. And his son Daniel was a change agent. He died in 2023, at 97. His lifelong work resulted in turning Fuller from ostensibly a solid institution into yet another garden variety liberal think tank. Saddleback Church founder Rick Warren obtained his doctorate from Fuller in 1980.

The Tentacles of the Church-Growth Movement

When Warren began ministry, there were about fifty "megachurches" (congregations of two thousand members or more) in the country.

Today there are five thousand.

This church-growth movement—birthed in places like Fuller—is also responsible for the downturn in prophecy teaching in our churches. In his mega-book, *The Purpose-Driven Life* (published in 2002), Warren bares his fangs for prophecy teaching:

> When the disciples wanted to talk about prophecy, Jesus quickly switched the conversation to evangelism. He wanted them to concentrate on their mission in the world. He said in essence, "The details of my return are none of your business. What is your business is the mission I have given you. Focus on that!" (p. 285)

Warren's publisher, Zondervan (perhaps the most liberal "Christian" publisher out there), worked a deal to get the book into all forty-five thousand SBC churches.

Do you see yet?

Never mind the fact, Dr. Warren, that Jesus spent a good deal of time talking to His followers about Bible prophecy. But what is Warren's ace in the hole? The churches he's helped craft discourage people from bringing their Bibles on Sunday, and they have instead pushed "cell groups" that teach from studies sanctioned by the Mother Church. That way, they blanket the country with their anti-prophecy worldview.

The late Dr. Noah Hutchings of Southwest Radio Church Ministries also clued me in on all this several years ago, when he showed me hundreds of letters in his files from distraught church members who saw their local church hijacked by Warren clones.

Here's another interesting statement from Paul Smith:

> Our current generation has witnessed two eschatological markers with our own eyes. The first one was the Jews returning to their Promised Land and forming the nation of Israel in 1948. The second marker is the Emerging church paradigm that gave birth and will inadvertently host, through accommodation,

compromise, and a postmodern mindset, a platform suitable for the coming one-world religion as clearly prophesied in the Bible.

This statement is crystal-clear true. Yet it is hated by the majority (my hunch) of modern American pastors.

End Game

Our job, our mandate, is to keep the flame of our blessed hope held as high as we can, for as long as we can. Although the things I've written about are depressing, we are in fact privileged to live in this time! We live in the time when the Jews have reentered history. We live in the time of the great apostasy. Painful realities, to be sure, but our Lord has gifted us with this perch at this time.

So, to bring it all home:

Darwin influenced Henry Ward Beecher, the famous New England preacher of the last quarter of the nineteenth century. And who did Beecher influence? Harry Emerson Fosdick, who preached liberalism for a half-century in New York City. And who did Fosdick influence? Norman Vincent Peale, the leftist positive thinker. And who did Peale influence? Rick Warren.

There you have it.

We are in for a very bumpy ride until The Man Comes Around. But He will, praise God.

Maranatha!

Chapter 16

MOST IMPORTANT APPOINTMENT!

By Wilfred Hahn

General Editor's note: The answer you and I give to the question Jesus asked the Apostle Peter—and us as well—are the most important words we will ever utter in this life: "Who do you say that I am?"

At the basis of the Lord's question is: "Do you believe?"

"Believe" what?

Wrapped up in that name—Jesus—is the Truth of every human being's fate.

Jesus said: "I am the way, the truth, and the life. No man comes to the Father but by me."

You and I must believe Him. There can be no "maybe" to the answer we give. The answer is either "yes" or "no." It is "belief" in His name that determines our eternal destiny.

Peter answered Jesus: "You are the Christ, the Son of the Living God."

We, too, must give this answer in our own words, and mean it. If so, we immediately become a child of God forever. We will then go instantly to Heaven when we take our last breath or when He Calls believers in the Rapture.

My friend Wilfred Hahn, one of the foremost Christian writers on God's Word and the truth found therein, weighs in on how important our decision for Christ is to us and to those we love.

+++

The Hebrews were to be a "a light for the Gentiles" (Isaiah 49:6, Deuteronomy 4:6).

They failed abysmally. And, there was a heavy consequence. They were dispersed across the globe…punished and despised.

At least, to date.

A worldwide evangelization by the Jews will yet occur, but not without supernatural help. In Revelation 14:3, we read that 144,000 men will be redeemed from the earth—selected and sealed (protected) by God (Revelation 7:4)—as they will go about this mandate before the end of first half of the Tribulation.

But this matter may be relative.

Possibly, even more so than the Jews, the Church (the greatest recipient of grace to date) has failed. How so? Amongst many shortcomings, it has failed to teach and preserve the Rapture doctrine—the great blessed hope of the Church (Titus 2:13, Romans 8:24) and the appearing of the glory of our great God and Savior, Jesus Christ.

This has brought much tragedy these past two millennia. And the worst fallout of this mortal oversight is yet to come. The coming devastation falling on many people in the Tribulation would be entirely indescribable due to its scale were it not detailed in the Scriptures. Uncountable numbers of people will be slaughtered, which otherwise would not need to have happened, as we will explain.

As applied to the Hebrews, the Church, too, has been tasked as a "light to the world" (Matthew 5:14). Yes, Christ is in charge of building His Church (Matthew 16:18). Yet, when He returns, He will find "little faith on earth" (Luke 18:8). The great shock is so few saints will be in the Church. This is already the case today.

But is it balanced to say the Church's shortcomings are greater than those of the Jews? Readers may judge this question for themselves at this chapter's conclusion. However, surely, the list of scriptural derelictions is long—among many, replacement theology; "best life here and now" theology; prosperity gospel, and as mentioned, the robbing of the "great hope." All these distortions have little truck with the

Rapture and are spiritually deadly. The fact is that both the Hebrews and the Church failed many times, requiring necessary interventions (and dispensations) by God. The Rapture counts as one of these for the Church, as also the First Resurrection for the tribulational Christians.

Consider this statement carefully: The saints of the Tribulation are a number "that no one could count" (Revelation 7:9). Here the Bible is referring to earth-dwellers in the first half of the Tribulation period, who come to acknowledge Christ and refuse to bow to the Beast. They become Christians…literally, so to speak, just under the wire. They are distinct and not part of the Church, as it has already been raptured away at this point. These tribulational Christians will ALL be killed (as we will yet prove.)

To confirm, the text from Revelation 7:9 clearly establishes it is actually those who are saved (and slaughtered) in the first half of the Tribulation that are beyond number.

By comparison, those who earlier ascend in the Rapture are not without number. They are a smaller group—namely, stragglers—as there is little faith on earth at this time. This account parallels Christ's words to the Philadelphian church. It is weak (small in population). However, Christ says, "Since [they] have kept my command to endure patiently, I will also keep you from the hour of trial that is going to come on the whole world to test the inhabitants of the earth" (Revelation 3:10). This verse anticipates the Rapture.

Just how many candidates for the Rapture are there today? It would be impossible to estimate. Only Jesus Christ can know the answer. But if we're allowed to hazard an opinion, it would be simply to say that whatever their number, it will be surprisingly low.

Whatever the case, the failure to teach the imminent expectancy of the Rapture will lead to the greatest human and demonic atrocities and suffering of all time.

The consequences will be horrific, to put it flatly. How so? All who refuse to bow to the Beast and ignore the lure of economic security will be pursued, pilloried, persecuted, and killed. All who turn to

Christ will die and be martyred! This will happen to many people… many more than would have been the case had the Church taught the Rapture with the Gospel.

Would it be too extreme to draw this conclusion? All those who didn't bow to the Beast may carry a grudge against the Church. They could have been raptured had they known ahead of time, had they been evangelized earlier and taught to expect an imminent Rapture.

But are we correct that all Christians will die in Tribulation period (specifically, in the first half)? There is opposition to and questioning of this position. Can we know with certainty that all tribulational saints will be martyred? We make the case that this indeed happens— we believe beyond doubt.

In doing so, we discover that this proof provides an indisputable doctrinal anchor for placing the timing of the Rapture event to a pre-Tribulation time frame.

Why Are the Saints Overcome?

Allow us to first address one other question before launching into the proofs of martyrdom. We read about a situation in the Bible where the "holy ones" are given over to be defeated by Antichrist, the latter also known as the "little horn." This statement is found in the seventh chapter of Daniel. The prophet tells us: "As I watched, this horn [the 'little horn'] was waging war against the 'holy ones' and defeating them" (verse 21). Again, not to miss this, it says, "defeating them." We may wonder why this is allowed to happen to the "holy ones," as it seems unjust. It would seem unconscionable that God will allow "holy ones" to be overcome by the devil during that time. Here again, the proof of this action is indisputable.

Any lingering doubt of this occurrence is quickly dispelled, as this defeat of the "holy ones" is described at least five more times in the Bible.

A few verses later (Daniel 7:25), we read that Antichrist "will speak against the Most High and oppress his 'holy ones'…the 'holy ones' will be delivered into [Antichrist's] hands for a time, times and half a time." Here we learn this ordeal faced by the "holy ones" will last three and a half years in the Tribulation.

But that's not all. There are yet additional and similar prophecies in the book of Daniel stating the "holy ones" would be overcome. A later vision of Daniel interpreted by an angel informs us that "He [Antichrist] will cause astounding devastation and will succeed in whatever he does. He will destroy those who are mighty, the 'holy ones'" (Daniel 8:24).

Lastly, in Daniel 12:7, it says again: "It will be for a time, times and half a time. When the power of the 'holy ones' has been finally broken, all these things will be completed."

We see here that even though the "holy ones" are said to be "mighty," they will be destroyed.

Crucially, these above-mentioned statements from Daniel in the Old Testament all align with prophecies written in the book of Revelation…in the New Testament.

There, we read: "People worshiped the dragon because he had given authority to the beast, and they also worshiped the beast and asked, 'Who is like the beast? Who can wage war against it?'" (Revelation 13:4). "[The Beast] was given power to wage war against God's 'holy ones' and to conquer them" (Revelation 13:7).

These are the exact words Daniel wrote centuries earlier. These "holy ones" mentioned in the Old and New Testaments are of the same identity. Daniel and John, the Revelator, are in perfect alignment. The Beast's supremacy cannot be in doubt.

Also, they agree with the period over which the defeat of the holy ones will take place—forty-two months: a "time, times and a half"; three and a half years. This same period is mentioned both by Daniel and the Apostle John. Given these confirming references from both Testaments, there can be no doubt. For three and a half years (in our interpretation, this must be in the first half of the Tribulation period) the holy ones are going to fall prey to Antichrist.

They not will only be defeated; the Bible also says they will be destroyed (Daniel 8:24). A plain interpretation would therefore suggest ALL are destroyed, a perspective that aligns perfectly with proofs from the New Testament.

Identity of the Holy Ones

Just who are the "holy ones" being overcome in the previously quoted texts?

We identify them as the tribulational Christians.

There is an ironclad case supporting this conclusion. At the outset, importantly, we must note that the concept of the Church was yet hidden at the time of Daniel and other OT prophets. The Messiah had not yet appeared, nor had He yet been rejected by the Jews.

The identity of the "holy ones" seems fairly clear, as it is referring to a future time when "holy ones" would exist. This certainly applies to the tribulational Christians. The "holy ones" being shown as vanquished and destroyed in Scripture are Tribulation saints. This means those who have come to recognize Jesus as the Messiah and Savior during the first half (forty-two months) of the seven-year Tribulation began. As such, this all unfolds after the Rapture has taken place.

None of the aforementioned prophecies apply to the saints of the Church Age. Why? All members of the Church are taken up in the Rapture before the Tribulation. Post-Rapture saints have a much different timeline to salvation...this requiring that the saints be martyred in the Tribulation.

Many misinterpret these accounts of saints being destroyed as evidence the Church-age Christians will not be raptured and therefore will be required to go through the Tribulation. This is an incorrect conclusion on several counts.

Tracing the Trail of Holy Ones

Where do the holy ones come from? The Bible tells in no uncertain terms.

John says when Jesus Christ opened the fifth seal:

I saw under the altar the souls of those who had been slain because of the word of God and the testimony they had maintained. They called out in a loud voice, "How long, Sovereign Lord, holy and true, until you judge the inhabitants of the earth and avenge our blood?" (Revelation 6:9)

Then each of them was given a white robe, and they were told to wait a little longer, until the full number of their fellow servants, their brothers and sisters, were killed just as they had been. (Revelation 6:9–11)

Next, at the time of the sixth seal, John says:

After this I looked, and there before me was a great multitude that no one could count, from every nation, tribe, people and language, standing before the throne and before the Lamb. They were wearing white robes and were holding palm branches in their hands. (Revelation 7:9)

Who were they? The angel answered:

These are they who have come out of the great tribulation; they have washed their robes and made them white in the blood of the Lamb. (Revelation 7:14)

There we have our answer: The great multitude are tribulational Christians...so-called holy ones. The "multitude" identified at the time of the sixth seal is, in fact, the fulfillment of the prophecy given at the time when the fifth seal was opened.

As well, we can deduce here that many Christians were martyred from before the time of the fifth seal. Just as Daniel prophesies, they will all have been "destroyed" (martyred).

We now note a pivotal point: After the sixth seal, the terms "saints," "servants," "Christians," "God's people," or "multitudes" are never mentioned again in Revelation's timeline. Crucially, no mention is made of more Christians having arrived in front of the heavenly altar during the Tribulation. Why? Because all have been martyred, we maintain. We will present further scriptural sources providing confirmation of this view.

Why All Tribulational Christians Die

How can we know all tribulational Christians will die, as we assert to occur in the first half of the Tribulation? There are a number of proofs, both scriptural and deductive. Given that our view—that ALL tribulational Christians will be martyred—is such a critical factor in the Rapture debate, we want to firmly prove the veracity of this position. We next present further proofs for this view.

Consider that the second Beast shown in Revelation 13 only offers two options—one or the other. Worship the image of the first Beast or die. No other option is on offer. There is no allowance for exceptions: "All who refused to worship the image [are] to be killed" (Revelation 13:15). (Again, see Revelation 20:4.) All means ALL, not some. The Bible also says this about these Tribulation saints:

> They triumphed over him [the dragon] by the blood of the Lamb and by the word of their testimony; they did not love their lives so much as to shrink from death. (Revelation 12:11)

What happens to those who do worship the image? Could they change their minds at some later date? Revelation 14:9–11 is clear:

> If anyone worships the beast and its image and receives its mark on their forehead or on their hand, they, too, will drink the wine of God's fury, which has been poured full strength into the cup of his wrath. They will be tormented with burning

sulfur in the presence of the holy angels and of the Lamb. And the smoke of their torment will rise for ever and ever. There will be no rest day or night for those who worship the beast and its image, or for anyone who receives the mark of its name.

Once having made the election to worship the image of the Beast and to take the mark, there is no recourse or recanting. To believe otherwise would be inconsistent with the character of God. Once He unleashes His wrath, it's too late to repent. After all, His wrath only comes after repeated entreaties and warnings. Then comes the point of no return...of no further grace.

Next, consider Revelation 13:8:

All inhabitants of the earth will worship the beast—all whose names have not been written in the Lamb's book of life, the Lamb who was slain from the creation of the world.

We're told here ALL inhabitants of the earth will worship the Beast. That can only mean that at this point there are no remaining tribulational Christians. They will be gone from the face of the earth by the time of the sixth seal, this being near the midpoint of the seven-year Tribulation.

Further, consider Revelation 13:15:

The second beast was given power to give breath to the image of the first beast, so that the image could speak and cause all who refused to worship the image to be killed.

Again, note the word "all." ALL who refuse to worship the Beast will be killed. For that to take place, no Christians can remain. ALL are martyred. The Bible couldn't be clearer on this point.

To further support our case, we must also consider the elements of the Apocalypse—namely, the trumpet and bowl judgments. Why?

Because these all unfold in the second half of the Tribulation. Since, as we argue, the martyrs are all eradicated by the time of the sixth seal and none survive after this point, there can be no hint of their presence during these trumpet and bowl judgments.

Not surprisingly, try as we might, we find no trace of any Christians being on earth during the time of the trumpet and bowl judgments… this during the early second half of the Tribulation. First, we will examine the fifth and sixth trumpet judgments, followed by the bowl judgments.

A Deduced Absence

At the fifth trumpet blow (first woe; Revelation 9:1–6), perhaps midway into the second half of the Tribulation:

> Out of the smoke locusts came down on the earth and were given power like that of scorpions of the earth. …They were not allowed to kill earthdwellers but only to torture them for five months. And the agony they suffered was like that of the sting of a scorpion when it strikes.

Only those who didn't have the seal of God were allowed to be tormented. The only group with a seal placed upon them at this point are the 144,000 servants. As such, were Christians still on earth at the time of this judgment, they would be expressly allowed by God to be tortured. Any Christians on earth during this woe would be selected to face God's wrath. Shown here is that God can and does exclude one group to be protected from His wrath (namely the 144,000). Then, why would He choose not to do so with his children? "Which of you fathers, if your son asks for…an egg, will give him a scorpion?" (Luke 11:11–12).

Thus, we can draw one of two conclusions. There are no Christians on earth at the time of the first woe; or, if yes, then God expressly chooses to torment them. Only the former perspective aligns with the character of God.

Can Christians Curse God?

At the call of the sixth trumpet, one-third of the world's population is wiped out; two-thirds remain who then ALL curse God. Revelation 9:20–21:

> The rest of mankind who were not killed by these plagues still did not repent of the work of their hands; they did not stop worshiping demons and idols.... Nor did they repent of their murders, their magic arts, their sexual immorality or their thefts.

Could Christians be counted in this number of survivors? Not if all of the survivors are said to "curse God," "refuse to repent," and keep "worshipping demons and idols." Clearly, then, there can be no Christians survivors upon earth at this point. After all, salvation is impossible without repentance. At this time, note that no one is repenting. Rather, they are condemning God. Therefore, this number could not include Christians.

Conclusion? Either no Christians are upon earth at the time of this woe, or God expressly makes sure that, while one-third of the earth's population dies, it would mean ALL Christians would die at this time. But, again, it would be absurd to believe God in His wrath would wipe out ALL remaining Christians at this juncture, favoring instead other godless earth-dwellers.

We can reasonably deduce that no Christians exist upon earth at the time of the fifth and sixth trumpet judgments.

No Christians to Be Found

Further buttressing our case, we next review the period of the bowl judgments.

The first bowl is mentioned in Revelation 16:2:

> The first angel went and poured out his bowl on the land, and ugly, festering sores broke out on the people who had the mark of the beast and worshiped its image.

Specifically, this only can apply to non-Christians, namely, those "who had the mark." Christians aren't mentioned because they aren't there. To consider that they might still be on earth, we would need to assume some land wasn't affected by this judgment—or that the festering sores are non-communicable. There is no basis for such positions.

Next, we review the fourth bowl, described in Revelation 16:8–9:

> The fourth angel poured out his bowl on the sun, and the sun was allowed to scorch people with fire. They were seared by the intense heat and they cursed the name of God, who had control over these plagues, but they refused to repent and glorify him.

Given the nature of this judgment, the scorching and searing sun will affect all earth-dwellers. But no repentance occurs...not at all. In fact, ALL do not repent and ALL curse God. Were Christians still on earth or were people still being converted into saints, there would be instances of repentance. But this isn't indicated at all. This provides uncontroversial proof no Christians are on earth at that time.

During the fifth bowl judgment (Revelation 16:10–11), similarly, there is no repentance:

> The fifth angel poured out his bowl on the throne of the beast, and its kingdom was plunged into darkness. People gnawed their tongues in agony and cursed the God of heaven because of their pains and their sores, but they refused to repent of what they had done.

Turning to the seventh bowl, we read:

> The seventh angel poured out his bowl into the air, and out of the temple came a loud voice from the throne, saying, "It is done!" Then there came flashes of lightning, rumblings, peals

MOST IMPORTANT APPOINTMENT!

of thunder and a severe earthquake. No earthquake like it has ever occurred since mankind has been on earth, so tremendous was the quake. The great city split into three parts, and the cities of the nations collapsed. ...Every island fled away and the mountains could not be found. From the sky huge hailstones, each weighing about a hundred pounds, fell on people. And they cursed God on account of the plague of hail, because the plague was so terrible. (Revelation 16:4–21)

Obviously, it would be impossible to segment Christians from nonbelievers, given the scale of pandemics and destruction during this period. More than anything sealing our conviction here is that, for the third time, earth-dwellers curse God. Again, we conclude that these cannot include Christians.

Ironclad Time of the Rapture

We conclude the above arguments (as well as others made earlier in this chapter) prove no Christians will survive the Tribulation period; all will become martyrs by its midpoint. This fact leads to several additional perspectives and findings that are crucial.

Above all is the resultant case for the timing of the Rapture. This now becomes clear.

Put simply, since no Christians are alive on earth as of the middle of the Tribulation, there can be no mid-Tribulation Rapture or end-of-Tribulation Rapture. Why? No one would remain to be raptured.

The only time point Scripture allows is a pretribulational Rapture.

That makes for great urgency! The Rapture can happen at any time—it is imminent, yes, at the very door front.

Thoughts to Ponder

The Lord is faithful and true (Psalms 33:4). What He says He will do, He will do. He has said He will bring His reward (Revelation 22:12)

255

and that He will spare us from the Tribulation (Revelation 3:10). His wrath will not fall upon the true Church (1 Thessalonians 5:9). He will take us up individually to be with Him. Our bodies will be transformed into the incorruptible.

Make no mistake! For those who haven't acknowledged Jesus Christ is Lord and the Son of God, having redeemed His children from sin through His death on the cross, their future is grim and dire. They will not be raptured.

Instead, they face eternal damnation and the Tribulation—a terrible period like never before experienced in human history.

The Rapture can come at any time. It will most certainly occur before the Tribulation begins. There will be no final warnings, other than perhaps a general recognition of the season and times to those who are watching. This is an irreversible and binary event: Either you are in—or not. What occurs then is unchangeable.

Yet, true to His nature, the Lord provides one more chance for his Creation to attain salvation. He doesn't want anyone to perish (2 Peter 3:9). He is compassionate. For a period of forty-two months, He will allow earth-dwellers an opportunity to reject the mark of the Beast, to refuse the Beast's demand to worship him, and to stay steadfast and true to the testimony of Christ.

While this is wonderful, the persecution of tribulational Christians by the Beast, the Dragon, and the False Prophet—the Trinity of Doom—escalates ferociously. All who have come to salvation will be martyred. All.

What should we make of the Rapture naysayers who maintain there is no Rapture to be expected at all? To take this position means all of humankind (including Church Age Christians) will go into the Tribulation period. More Christians would then be added to their number through conversions during the earlier stages of the Tribulation. The question then arises: Why would God allow ALL Church Age Christians in the world to be killed during the Tribulation?

First Thessalonians 5:9 states: "God did not appoint us to suffer wrath but to receive salvation through our Lord Jesus Christ." Therefore, if ALL Christians (from the time of before and during the Tribulation) will be annihilated on earth, this is a "wrath" of a different gospel. This is not congruous with the character of what God has said.

Conclusively, a naysayer's view must endorse a very nonsensical sequence of events. They must maintain that ALL Church Age Christians go into the Tribulation so ALL will be slain so they ALL can be given resurrected physical bodies at the First Resurrection so they ALL will come back to life in the Millennium.

This sequence of events seems unnecessarily cruel...and inefficient. What about the saints who have died before the Tribulation period? The Rapture naysayer must take the position that these saints need to wait another thousand years for the Second Resurrection, as they will not be eligible for the First Resurrection. Scripture doesn't support these confused perspectives (more could be presented). Rather, it expressly says "the dead in Christ will rise first" (1 Thessalonians 4:16).

Glorious is the fact that raptured Christians are spared the first death and second death and are also spared "the hour of trial" (Revelation 3:10); they will be in Heaven with the Lord while the Tribulation takes place upon earth.

Raptured Saints "will be with the Lord forever" (1 Thessalonians 4:17) in their translated, resurrected, incorruptible bodies. Whether on earth or in Heaven, wherever Jesus will be, that is where the raptured Christians will be. They "will be with the Lord forever."

Surely the Tribulation is a terrible period...as none ever before in human history. Nevertheless, there is good news to celebrate: For ALL Christians, there will be no second death. Whether a Tribulational or raptured Christian, we will all be given eternal life (no second death).

Wonderfully, after the Tribulation, the Lord, "will wipe every tear from their eyes. There will be no more death or mourning or crying or pain, for the old order of things has passed away" (Revelation 21:4).

The pre-Tribulation Rapture view, as we have shown, is consistent with Scripture.

Consider that there is no incentive for Christians to attempt to survive the Tribulation since all will be killed anyway, and all are then resurrected at the start of the Millennium. Why prolong physical suffering if one can look forward to the First Resurrection after the Tribulation?

Therefore, whether amongst those who will be raptured or those saved during the Tribulation, there are no physical preparations to be made—nothing to buy and no "escape getaways" to arrange. There is no need to pay for survival supplies or to build an underground bunker.

For now, given that the Rapture still lies ahead, we remain part of the generation that "continue[s] in him, so that when he appears we may be confident and unashamed before him at his coming" (1 John 2:28).

It cannot be emphasized enough: A horrible time awaits all tribulational Christians. Pray that anyone you know will not miss the Rapture!

> Look, I am coming soon! My reward is with me, and I will give to each person according to what they have done (Revelation 22:12).

CONCLUSION

By Mondo Gonzales

General Editor's note: Mondo Gonzales, television cohost of *Prophecy Watchers*, has brilliantly, in my opinion, encapsulated all I intended for this book in this summation of things involved in God's rescue of believers out of the worst time in human history.

His insight portrays with pinpoint precision what we authors intended to convey through this book. Thus I chose his contribution for the book's conclusion.

Indeed, this generation is quickly "running out of normal." Business as usual is about to come to a stunning end. The sudden catastrophic intervention by the Lord Jesus Christ will happen at an unknown moment. We are the generation on the cusp of experiencing Christ's foretelling as recorded in Luke 17:28–30.

+++

How soon is the Rapture? One week? One month? One year? One decade? Inquiring minds want to know! One of the objections to those waiting for the blessed hope of the return of Jesus at the Rapture (Titus 2:13) is continually repeated by mockers and is clearly predicted by Peter. He says:

> Knowing this first of all, that scoffers will come in the last days with scoffing, following their own sinful desires. They will say, "Where is the promise of his coming? For ever since the fathers fell asleep, all things are continuing as they were from the beginning of creation." (2 Peter 3:3–4)

Ultimately, the objection of the mockers is that people have been "waiting" for the rapture for almost two thousand years; therefore, we should give up on the whole idea as being a false hope.

It's not faithless to acknowledge that the Church has been looking for the Rapture for quite a while. Jesus said the timing of the beginning of the sequence of end-time events is in the hands of the Father (Acts 1:7; Mark 13:32). However, Paul reveals that we certainly can be aware of the seasons (1 Thessalonians 5:1–8). In addition, Jesus gave us much information and encouraged us to be watching (Mark 13:37). If we're meant to be clueless, then why would Jesus tell us repeatedly to watch for indicators?

One of the goals of this book is to share various indicators that the Day of the Lord Tribulation and seventieth week of Daniel is quickly approaching. One of the ways to measure how soon the Tribulation will arrive is to examine in detail two often-overlooked eschatological passages found in the Gospel of Luke: 12:35–48 and 17:20–37. Based on a harmony of the Gospels, it is reasoned that Jesus preached the words recorded in Luke 12:35–48 approximately five months before His full exposition of end-time events as recorded in the Olivet Discourse (Matthew 24–25; Mark 13; Luke 21). As His passion week came closer, He preached the message recorded in Luke 17:20–37 about two weeks or less before He gave the longer Olivet Discourse two days before His death. This is important as we compare the particular themes and angles each Gospel writer intended. What I mean is, we often jump ahead to the Olivet Discourse and read the material there without recognizing that Jesus had already introduced much of the specific language, parables, and concepts earlier. It is wise hermeneutics (biblical interpretation) to examine the places where theological concepts are introduced, then consider later revelation in comparison.

"Therefore, you also must be ready, for the Son of Man is coming at an hour you do not expect" (Luke 12:40; Matthew 24:44). Remember, this teaching appears in two different Gospels and two different periods. Each author is writing from his own perspective and intentions, with specific overall themes. It is always good hermeneutics to identify the intended audience of the speaker and writer. When contemplating the Matthew version of this verse, it's logical to ask who Jesus is talking to here. Is He giving this as an admonition to the world? To unbelievers? To believers? In the Olivet Discourse and two days before His death, Mark 13:3 reveals that Peter, James, John, and Andrew asked Jesus privately, while on the Mount of Olives, to explain His comments about the Temple being destroyed. In a narrow sense, Jesus was speaking to those four privately. This reveals that the primary (but not the only) intended audience for the Olivet Discourse was believers.

Who is Jesus' audience in the other parallel passage? The Luke 12:40 version reveals exactly who Jesus is addressing. Notice the likeness in language and further expansion by Luke:

> "But know this, that if the master of the house had known at what hour the thief was coming, he would not have left his house to be broken into. *You also must be ready, for the Son of Man is coming at an hour you do not expect."* Peter said, *"Lord, are you telling this parable for us or for all?"* And the Lord said, "Who then is the faithful and wise manager, whom his master will set over his household, to give them their portion of food at the proper time? Blessed is that servant whom his master will find so doing when he comes. Truly, I say to you, he will set him over all his possessions." (Luke 12:39–44, emphasis added)

I am so glad Peter asked who the intended audience of the parable was supposed to be. No doubt, there are truths and warnings for everyone in general, but Jesus responds with an answer, albeit indirectly. The parable is for the one who is claiming to be and/or seeks to be a "faithful and wise manager" of the master's household. Unbelievers don't claim or seek to be wise managers of Jesus's household. This parable is for those claiming to be believers. Now, here's the point. Jesus makes it clear we have the responsibility to be ready so His coming is not like a thief to the wise and faithful manager. Nowhere in Scripture does it say He will come like a thief upon believers who are ready. At the same time, Jesus said He is coming at an hour we do not expect. How can this be true? Even though we know the general times and seasons (1 Thessalonians 5:1–4) and that the Tribulation (Day of the Lord) will not surprise us, there is still an element spoken of by Jesus that His coming will be at an hour when we do not expect it.

To get to the bottom of this puzzle, the next question we need to explore is whether Jesus is referring to His coming at the Rapture or His Second Coming in great glory at the end of the Tribulation.

Let's begin by examining the context and teaching of Luke 17:20–37. It's possible to outline this sermon as follows:

- The preface concerning the days of the Son of Man (Luke 17:20–25)
- The pattern concerning the days of the Son of Man (17:26–30)
- The perspective concerning the days of the Son of Man (17:31–33)
- The payoff concerning the days of the Son of Man (17:34–37)

Luke writes:

Being asked by the Pharisees when the kingdom of God would come, he answered them, "The kingdom of God is not coming in ways that can be observed, nor will they say, 'Look, here it is!' or 'There!' for behold, the kingdom of God is in the midst of you." (Luke 17:20–21)

Jesus makes sure the Pharisees know the Kingdom of God arrived in the person of Jesus Himself. He declines to reveal to them any more information about the nature of the Kingdom, but does turn to explain more details to His disciples. One of the most important aspects of this Kingdom comes in what He describes next. Note the more important points in italics in the passage below:

> And He said to the disciples, "The days are coming when you will desire to see one of the *days of the Son of Man*, and you will not see it. And they will say to you, 'Look, there!' or 'Look, here!' Do not go out or follow them. For as the lightning flashes and lights up the sky from one side to the other, so will the Son of Man be *in His day*. But first He must suffer many things and be rejected by this generation." (Luke 17:22–25, emphasis added)

The phrase "days of the Son of Man" (using a plural for "days") only occurs in 17:22 and 17:26. It is vital to connect this idea with the next illustration about Noah and Lot. But first, Jesus shares with the disciples standing in front of Him that they would long to see the events of the Second Coming, but they wouldn't observe it. It would be far into the future—after their deaths. This helps us understand what He meant by telling the Pharisees the Kingdom had already come in some way. Yet He reveals that indeed the Kingdom has come, but the end-of-the-age fulfillment of it ("the days of the Son of Man") would occur in the distant future. Therefore, they shouldn't be deceived if someone tells them it has arrived in their lifetimes. Jesus assures them it will not, but when it does happen in the distant future, it will be unmistakable.

Further, Jesus reveals that the concept of His future (second) "coming" happens over a period of "days." This isn't accidental and can only be interpreted in parallel within the subsequent context. The entire theology of the Second Coming of Jesus is equated to be a period Jesus labels as "the *days* of the Son of Man." Before giving the comparison with Noah and Lot, Jesus warns a future generation against being deceived that His coming in great glory would be in secret (17:23). In fact, His final return will certainly occur on a specific day ("in His day"—Luke 17:24) and will involve tremendous luminescent displays of cosmic glory (like lightning) in the midst of darkness (cf. Matthew 24:27–30). Yet He reminds them that even though He will come in glory on a future specific day, He must first be killed by that generation (17:25). What we learn from this passage so far is that the entire scope of Jesus's Second Coming involves a period of "days" up to and including the final culmination of His return on a specific single day. Jesus continues by providing an illustration to help us understand the nature and conditions of the "days of the Son of Man."

> *Just as* it was in the *days of Noah*, so will it be in the *days of the Son of Man*. They were eating and drinking and marrying and being given in marriage, until the day when Noah entered the ark, and the flood came and destroyed them all. *Likewise, just as* it was in the *days of Lot*—they were eating and drinking, buying and selling, planting and building, but on the *day* when Lot went out from Sodom, fire and sulfur rained from heaven and destroyed them all. (Luke 17:26–29, emphasis added)

Even though Matthew brings up Noah in his version of the Olivet Discourse (Matthew 24:37–39), this is the only place where Lot occurs in the context of comparison to the *period of time* involving Jesus' Second Coming. The "days" of each person Jesus mentions includes descriptions of the immediate period of time before judgment, but also includes the judgment itself. The Flood judgment came in the days of Noah. The fire and brimstone judgment came in the days of Lot. The judgment of the Son of Man (the Tribulation) arrives in the days of the Son of Man. Jesus provides the two illustrations of Noah and Lot and summarizes the "days of Son of Man" when He says, "It will be *just the same* on the *day* that the Son of Man is revealed" (Luke 17:30). Some people can get confused as to why Jesus switches to the singular "day" in this verse. We already know from the context of 17:22 that Jesus is discussing the "*days* of the Son of Man." He began by using a plural to guide the rest of the discussion and is also confirmed by the pattern. Additionally, it is well known in the Old Testament that the coming Tribulation (day of wrath) is called the "*day* of the Lord," but typically reflects a period of time and not just one day. This same usage is found in the New Testament and includes the entire seven-year Tribulation that comes as a thief in the night on an unsuspecting world (1 Thessalonians 5:2; 2 Peter 3:10). We're not left guessing about Jesus' use of the singular "day," because He explains how we're to interpret it in the two illustrations of Noah and Lot.

In 17:30, we read, "It will be just the same," translated from the Greek *kata ta auta*. It literally reads "according to the same," which refers to Noah and Lot. Another way to translate it is "according to this pattern." The Greek *auta* is plural and helps show that the pattern involves that which is more than one. The phrase only occurs three times in the entire New Testament; the other two instances are also in the Gospel of Luke, which is helpful in understanding Luke's meaning. Luke 6:23 and 6:26 both discuss the manner/pattern in which the Jewish forefathers operated. Notice how the New King James Version translates the phrase as *kata ta auta*. I will italicize the Greek phrase in the following as it appears in English:

> Rejoice in that day and leap for joy! For indeed your reward is great in heaven, for *in like manner* their fathers did to the prophets. (Luke 6:23)

In other words, "according to this pattern" of the ancient forefathers is how many believers will be persecuted, which results in great reward.

To summarize, in Luke 17:30, Jesus uses a plural (*auta*) in describing that to understand the pattern of the *days* of the Son of Man in His final return, the illustration of the *days* of Noah and the *days* of

Lot involves a pattern that has *plural* points of similarity. Let's see how these plural points in the pattern and parallelism look visually in the following chart:

	Description of Daily Life	Description of Rescue	Description of Direct Judgment
Days of Noah	Eating, drinking, marrying, being given in marriage—normal activities were taking place.	Noah and family were commanded to enter the ark.	Judgment began only after Noah went into ark, but came quickly and *interrupted daily normal life.*
	Noah preached in the time period prior to judgment (2 Peter 2:5).	They escape and were rescued from judgment.	Windows of Heaven opened; rain began on a certain day and lasted forty days.
Days of Lot	Eating, drinking, buying, selling, planting, building—*normal activities* were taking place.	Lot and his family were commanded to leave Sodom.	Judgment began only after Lot fled the city, but came quickly and **interrupted daily normal life.**
	Lot was vexed in the time period ("day to day") prior to judgment (2 Peter 2:6–8).	They escaped and were rescued from judgment (except Lot's wife, who was left behind).	Fire from heaven came on a certain day.

	Description of Daily Life	Description of Rescue	Description of Direct Judgment
Days of the Son of Man	The pattern shows that before the judgment comes, people will be living normally. Two types of people will be living side by side under these normal conditions. The pattern shows one group of people will be preaching and also vexed prior to the judgment arriving.	The pattern shows that there should also be a group to be rescued and escape coming judgment. The Rapture generation is commanded "to be ready at all times." They will escape and be rescued from the coming judgment.	The pattern shows that the judgment will begin only after believers are rescued, but will come quickly and interrupt daily normal life. The heavenly judgment begins on a specific day and will last seven years, based on other passages.

This chart shows a clear plurality in the pattern, parallelism, and consistency in Jesus' description of the days of the coming of the Son of Man. These days include the description of people experiencing relatively normal lives, the rescue of a specific group, and the quick beginning of direct judgment by God from Heaven, which interrupts daily normal life and then brings destruction to the many left behind.

We've examined the *preface* and the *pattern* of this mini-sermon, but Jesus goes on to explain that those who seek to be rescued need to have the proper *perspective* (or attitude). Jesus gives an illustration in verse 31 about the need to be single-minded in regards to Kingdom readiness. Jesus tells us to "remember Lot's wife" (17:32), then He goes on to say, "Whoever seeks to preserve his life will lose it, but whoever loses his life will keep it" (17:33). This phrase has occurred previously in Luke 9:24 in the context of being a true, committed disciple. Our attitude at all times should be so single-minded we will not be double-minded like Lot's wife. She was led outside of Sodom by the angels with the rest of her family, but she lingered behind as Lot and the two daughters continued without her to the city of Zoar (Genesis 19:16, 26). She sought to preserve her own life and lost it. We need to have the proper perspective so when the days of the Son of Man arrive, we will follow the pattern and be among those who are taken away and rescued. If we have this perspective, we'll always be ready and avoid being caught by surprise when the Son of Man does indeed come when we don't expect it.

The conclusion to Jesus' mini-sermon involves the *payoff*, which will happen in the days of the Son of Man. Jesus discusses two types of people in 17:34–35: one who is *taken* and another who is *left*. Both words are used in a passive sense. Jesus says:

> I tell you, in that night there will be two in one bed. One will be taken and the other left. There will be two women grinding together. One will be taken and the other left.

This language appears also in the Olivet Discourse of Matthew 24:40–41. The question is commonly asked, "Is the taken one saved or is the one left behind saved?" Jesus just encouraged us to remember Lot's wife (17:32). With that imagery in mind, the answer becomes obvious when comparing Lot and his wife. Clearly, Lot was *taken* to refuge (salvation) and his wife was *left* to judgment. This is the classic left-behind scenario, and it also applies to Noah and his family. Noah was *taken* in the ark (in salvation) and the others were *left* to the judgment of the Flood. Darrel Bock, in his massive commentary on Luke, notes that this understanding of "taken" and "left" is consistent with Luke's use of the Greek words elsewhere. In Luke 13:35, the leadership of Israel was "left" for judgment because they rejected Jesus (Luke 13:35; cf. Matthew 23:38). Also, other disciples who were "taken along" denotes a close relationship or association in a positive sense (Luke 9:10, 28; 18:31). This isn't the only way to interpret these words, for sure, but in the context of this passage and in the Gospel of Luke itself, it makes good sense.

Jesus finishes the *payoff* section by answering a question from the disciples:

And they said to him, "Where, Lord?" He said to them, "Where the corpse is, there the vultures will gather." (Luke 17:37)

This phrase also appears in the Matthew Olivet Discourse (Matthew 24:27–28). There, the context is referring to the end of the Tribulation as Jesus is returning in great glory. Here, in Luke, it is in reference to the judgment of a seven-year Tribulation period that certainly will involve much death. Jesus tells the disciples through His illustrations that the group "left" to die in judgment (like Lot's wife) will be where the birds gather to feast. Context is important; when people die and are left on the ground, we're very aware that vultures or other birds gather around to eat the carrion.

As I conclude this teaching, the point I want to help us understand is that we're watching the world progress quickly to NON-NORMAL living. There is a stark difference between relatively normal living conditions taking place when the rescue occurs (similar to the conditions during the days of Lot and Noah) and the descriptions of "life" inside the seven years of Tribulation.

Revelation 6–18 "living"	Olivet Discourse "living"	The day and hour "living"
• War • Massive inflation (two loaves of bread will cost a full day's wage) • One-fourth of the world being killed by sword, hunger, disease, martyrdom, great earthquakes, and cosmic astronomical disturbances. • One-third of earth being burned up • The sea turning to blood • Sea creatures • Ships being destroyed • Wormwood • More cosmic disturbances in sun, moon, and stars • Five months of a demon locust plague so intense that people will seek death • Two hundred million demons will kill one-third of humanity • Painful sores on those with mark of the beast • All sea creatures die • Rivers and springs turn to blood • The sun scorches humanity, • Periods of darkness • Greatest earthquake in history • Seventy-five-pound hailstones • People will be cursing God	Birth pains will increase in frequency and intensity. These include: • Great earthquakes in various places • Famines • Pestilences • Fearful sights and great signs from heaven • Nation against nation • Kingdom against kingdom • Tribulation • Betrayal by family • Hatred of one another • False prophets and deception • Love of many growing cold • People fainting from fear • Jews fleeing into the mountains to hide from Antichrist • Greatest time of tribulation in the history of the world—so bad that if God did not limit its duration, all of humanity would be eliminated • Great signs and wonders to deceive • Final war before Jesus returns	Matthew 24:37–39 Noah's Day—"In the days before the flood"— • Unaware (oblivious) • Eating • Drinking • Marrying • Giving in marriage Luke 17:26–27 Noah's Day: • Eating • Drinking • Marrying • Giving in marriage Luke 17:28–29 Lot's Day: • Eating • Drinking • Buying • Selling • Planting • Building • Normal, everyday living

Think of it. Jesus says that, in the future, this time of unprecedented Tribulation (Mark 13:19) will arrive on an unsuspecting world as a trap (cf. Luke 21:34–36) when people are planting their crops, planning weddings ("putting deposits down on the wedding venues," in modern parlance), making business plans, having celebrations, building new barns, adding landscaping. We could go on and on. There will always be times of generic "trouble" in our world (John 16:33). Yet the descriptions seen in the examples Jesus gave are the relatively *normal* circumstances He said would be occurring at the time of the coming of the Son of Man. His coming involves a rescue, the arrival of the Day of the Lord, judgment, and sudden destruction. If we compare this normal living with the living happening during the Tribulation period right up until Jesus' Second Coming in great glory, there is no comparison. Life is anything but normal at the end of the Tribulation.

We are running out of normal living, and this means the coming Rapture/rescue is soon approaching. It is my prayer that anyone who hasn't put their faith and trust in Jesus as Savior will do so immediately.

No one should want to be caught off guard and left behind.

Maranatha!

ENDNOTES

1   "Buckle Up: Greyerz—The Dark Years for the World Are Now Starting in Earnest," *King World News*, Rapture Ready News, March 12, 2022.

2   Isaiah 28:14–22; Daniel 9:27

3   Ezekiel 20:33–38; 22:17–22; 36:22–24; Isaiah 11:11–12:6; Zephaniah 2:1–2, 7–18. Isaiah 11:11–12:6 notes there will be two worldwide regatherings of Israel: One worldwide return in unbelief before the Tribulation for the judgment of the Tribulation and a second one by the Messiah Himself and His angels at the Second Coming after the remnant of Israel has been scattered by Antichrist during the Tribulation.

4   Deuteronomy 29:1–30:20

5   https://carolineglick.com/david-wurmser-the-u-s-is-treating-israel-like-a-vassal-state/

6   https://carolineglick.com/vdh-hamas-and-hezbollah-think-the-u-s-will-not-help-israel/

7   https://www.timesofisrael.com/un-condemned-israel-more-than-all-other-countries-combined-in-2022-monitor/

8   https://www.theguardian.com/us-news/2024/jan/11/ilhan-omar-gaza-ceasefire-joint-letter

9   https://www.npr.org/2024/01/11/1224126552/court-hearings-genocide-charges-israel

10 https://www.jewishpress.com/news/jewish-news/antisemitism-news/report-dramatic-rise-in-global-antisemitism-after-october-7/2024/01/31/

11 Ibid.

12 Ibid.

13 Ibid.

14 Ibid.

15 Ibid.

16 Woke ideology (i.e., cultural Marxism) views Israel as the oppressor and the Palestinians as the victims. The ideology also views Israel and Jewish people as having white privilege; according to Victor Davis Hanson, over the last ten years, colleges and universities have imported more than one million Middle Eastern students whose tuition is paid by Gulf oil money and are served by programs funded by Middle Eastern studies programs where political operatives and activism against Israel are found. https://carolineglick.com/vdh-hamas-and-hezbollah-think-the-u-s-will-not-help-israel/

17 Ibid.

18 https://carolineglick.com/david-wurmser-the-u-s-is-treating-israel-like-a-vassal-state/

19 Ibid.

ENDNOTES

20 https://www.breitbart.com/middle-east/2024/01/31/report-blinken-biden-considering
    -unilateral-recognition-of-palestinian-state/https://israel365news.com/382242
    /sovereignty-conference-oct-7-put-nail-in-coffin-of-two-state-solution/

21 https://www.wsj.com/articles/iran-10-billion-biden-administration-sanctions-iraq
    -israel-hamas-72bfc33a

22 https://www.jns.org/column/iran/23/8/31/315367/

23 https://freebeacon.com/national-security/iran-has-made-80-billion-in-illicit-oil-sales
    -since-biden-took-office/

24 https://www.jewishpress.com/multimedia/video-picks/douglas-murray-interviews
    -benjamin-netanyahu/2024/01/30/

25 Ibid.

26 https://www.timesofisrael.com/liveblog_entry/gun-permit-requests-rise-dramatically
    -since-hamass-oct-7-massacre/

27 https://www.timesofisrael.com/surveillance-soldiers-warned-of-hamas-activity-on
    -gaza-border-for-months-before-oct-7/

28 Ibid.

29 Ibid.

30 Ibid.

31 Ibid.

32 Ibid.

33 Ibid.

34 https://www.politico.eu/article/israel-border-troops-women-hamas-warnings-war
    -october-7-benjamin-netanyahu/

35 https://carolineglick.com/aharon-haliva-has-got-to-go-now/

36 Ibid.

37 Ibid.

38 Ibid.

39 https://www.jewishpress.com/indepth/opinions/death-to-israel-irans-plan-to-attack
    -israel/2023/04/17/

40 https://www.nytimes.com/2023/11/30/world/middleeast/israel-hamas-attack
    -intelligence.html

41 Ibid.

42 Ibid.

43 https://www.tabletmag.com/sections/israel-update/articles/israel-update-episode-6

44 https://www.theguardian.com/world/2023/nov/28/israeli-military-had-warning-of
    -hamas-training-for-attack-reports-say

45 https://www.timesofisrael.com/egypt-intelligence-official-says-israel-ignored-repeated
    -warnings-of-something-big/

46 https://www.jewishpress.com/special-features/israel-at-war-iron-swords/netanyahu
    -i-was-misled-by-military-intelligence-shin-bet/2023/10/29/

47 https://carolineglick.com/israels-isolated-generals/

48 Ibid.

49 Sura 2:14; 2:27, 2:44; 2:55; 2:61; 2:63-65; 2:74–75; 2:79; 2:87–88; 2:91; 2:93;
    2:100–101,174; 2:109; 2:247; 3:21; 3:75, 78; 3:112; 3:181; 3:183; 3:120; 4:46–47;

4:51–53; 4:155; 4:161;5:13; 5:18; 5:41; 5:59–60; 5:64; 5:66; 5:70; 5:79; 5:82; 7:166; 8:58; 9:29–30; 59:13–14.

50 https://www.usnews.com/news/best-countries/articles/2023-10-10/how-much-aid -does-the-u-s-give-to-israel

51 https://www.ft.com/content/763bb384-a974-4222-996f-8aecfbc32074

52 https://www.worlddata.info/asia/israel/tourism.php#:~:text=In%202021%2C% 20Israel%20ge nerated%20around%202.43%20billion%20US, of%20all%20 international%20tourism%20receipt s%20in%20Western%20Asia.

53 Fruchtenbaum, A. G. (2003). *The Footsteps of the Messiah: A study of the Sequence of Prophetic Events,* Rev. ed., (Tustin, CA: Ariel Ministries) p. 199.

54 Stephen D. Snobelen, *Statement on the Date 2060,* June 2003, at: https://isaac -newton.org/statement-on-the-date-2060/

55 Ibid.

56 Sarah Starkey, "Press Release: Doomsday Clock Remains at 90 Seconds to Midnight," January 23, 2024. https://thebulletin.org/2024/01/press-release-doomsday -clock-remains-at-90-seconds-to-midnight/

57 Bryan Jung, "G20 Announces Plan to Impose Digital Currencies and IDs Worldwide," Epoch Times, September 12, 2023. https://www.theepochtimes.com/article /g20-announces-plan-to-impose-digital-currencies-and-ids-worldwide-5489947

58 David Bowen, "FedNow Goes Live, Paving the Way to a Central Bank Digital Currency," September 20, 2023. https://harbingersdaily.com/fednow-goes-live-paving -the-way-to-digital-currency/

59 Michael Snyder, "While Barely Anyone Was Watching, Leaders at the UN Made A 7 Year Agreement to Implement a Single Global Agenda," September 21, 2023. https://endoftheamericandream.com/while-barely-anyone-was-watching-leaders -at-the-un-made-a-7-year-agreement-to-implement-a-single-global-agenda/

60 Terry James, *Midnight Hour* (Crane, MO: Defender Publishing, 2024). p. 23.

61 Jean M. Twenge, "Have Smartphones Destroyed a Generation?". https://www.the atlantic.com/magazine/archive/2017/09/has-the-smartphone-destroyed-a -generation/534198/

62 Victoria Barret, "A New Label for Kids Today: The Distracted Generation." https:// www.forbes.com/sites/victoriabarret/2012/11/01/a-new-label-for-kids-today-the -distracted-generation/#790f0e6958ec

63 Ibid.

64 Ibid.

65 Twenge.

66 Ibid.

67 "Number of Network Connected Devices Per Person around the World from 2003 to 2020," *Statista,* November 30, 2016. https://www.statista.com/statistics/678739 /forecast-on-connected-devices-per-person/

68 "Internet Stats & Facts (2020)." https://hostingfacts.com/internet-facts-stats/

69 Ibid.

70 Ibid.

71 Laura Nichols, "Poll: Gmail Dominates Email Use Among Millennials, Gen X," *Morning Consultant*, June 21, 2017. https://morningconsult.com/2017/06/21/poll -gmail-dominates-email-use/

72 "Quotes." https://www.quotes.net/mquote/679654

73 John Dyer, *From the Garden to the City: The Redeeming and Corrupting Power of Technology* (Grand Rapids: Kregel, 2011), p. 22.

74 Craig Loscalzo, *Apologetic Preaching: Proclaiming Christ to a Postmodern World* (Downers Grove: InterVarsity, 2000), p. 10–12.

75 Maryam Mohsin, "10 YouTube Stats Every Marketer Should Know in 2020," Ober-lo. https://www.oberlo.com/blog/youtube-statistics

76 Kevin Anderton, "Research Report Shows How Much Time We Spend Gaming," *Forbes,* March 21, 2019. https://www.forbes.com/sites/kevinanderton/2019/03/21 /research-report-shows-how-much-time-we-spend-gaming-infographic/

77 Dave Chaffey, "Global Social Media Research Summary 2020," Smart Insights, April 17, 2020. https://www.smartinsights.com/social-media-marketing/social -media-strategy/new-global-social-media-research/

78 Ibid.

79 Steve Turner, *Popcultured: Thinking Christianly About Style, Media and Entertainment* (Downers Grove: Intervarsity, 2013), p. 8.

80 Rick Richardson, *Evangelism Outside the Box: New Ways to Help People Experience the Good News* (Downers Grove, IL: InterVarsity Press, 2000), p. 23.

81 "American Pastor Delivers Sobering Message of Coming 'Dark Wave' of Persecution, All Israel News, October 19, 2022.

82 "Competing Worldviews Influence Today's Christians," May 9, 2017, Barna, last accessed October 29, 2020. https://www.barna.com/research/competing-worldviews -influence-todays-christians/

83 Ibid.

84 "American Worldview Inventory 2020—At a Glance…Release #3: Perceptions of God," April 21, 2020, *Cultural Research Center, Arizona Christian University*, last accessed October 29, 2020. https://www.arizonachristian.edu/wp-content/uploads /2020/04/CRC-AWVI-2020-Release-03_Perceptions-of-God.pdf

85 "How We Got Here: Spiritual and Political Profiles of America," May 23, 2017, Barna, last accessed October 29, 2020. https://www.barna.com/research/got-spiritual -political-profiles-america/

86 "A Snapshot of Faith Practice Across Age Groups," July 23, 2019, Barna, last ac-cessed October 29, 2020. https://www.barna.com/research/faithview-on-faith -practice/

87 "Sharing Faith Is Increasingly Optional to Christians," May 15, 2018, Barna, last accessed October 29, 2020. https://www.barna.com/research/sharing-faith -increasingly-optional-christians/

88 "Almost Half of Practicing Christian Millennials Say Evangelism Is Wrong," Febru-ary 5, 2019, Barna, last accessed October 29, 2020. https://www.barna.com/research /millennials-oppose-evangelism/

89 "51% of Churchgoers Don't Know of the Great Commission," March 27, 2018, Barna, last accessed October 29, 2020. https://www.barna.com/research/half-churchgoers-not-heard-great-commission/

90 "Silent and Solo: How Americans Pray," August 15, 2017, Barna, last accessed October 29, 2020. https://www.barna.com/research/silent-solo-americans-pray/

91 "American Worldview Inventory 2020—At a Glance…Release #11: Churches and Worldview," October 6, 2020, *Cultural Research Center, Arizona Christian University*, last accessed November 4, 2020. https://www.arizonachristian.edu/wp-content/uploads/2020/10/CRC_AWVI2020_Release11_Digital_04_20201006.pdf

92 "The State of Theology," a survey conducted by Ligonier Ministries and LifeWay Research in March of 2020, findings released September 8, last accessed October 29, 2020, https://thestateoftheology.com/. Note that not all of these statistics are covered on the "Key Findings" tab. One wishing to observe the list in its entirety must click on the "Data Explorer" tab at the top right of the main study page.

93 Ibid.

94 Nichols, Stephen, as quoted in: Michael Foust, "'Drifting Away' from Scripture: 30 Percent of Evangelicals Say Jesus Was Not God, Poll Shows," August 27, 2020, *Christian Headlines*, last accessed October 29, 2020. https://www.christianheadlines.com/contributors/michael-foust/drifting-away-from-scripture-30-percent-of-evangelicals-say-jesus-was-not-god-poll-shows.html.

95 John Stonestreet and Shane Morris, "Self-Constructed, Build-a-Bear, Buffet-Style Christianity Is No Christianity at All," September 14, 2020, Breakpoint, last accessed October 29, 2020. https://www.breakpoint.org/self-constructed-build-a-bear-buffet-style-christianity-is-no-christianity-at-all/

96 "Two-Thirds of Christians Face Doubt," July 25, 2017, Barna, last accessed October 29, 2020. https://www.barna.com/research/two-thirds-christians-face-doubt/

97 "2013 Church Budget Allocations, Learning Priorities, and Quarterly Financial Trends," *Evangelical Christian Credit Union* (ECCU), https://www.eccu.org/resources/advisorypanel/2013/surveyreports20; preserved by *The Wayback Machine Internet Archive*, last accessed September 27, 2019. http://web.archive.org/web/20141019033209/https://www.eccu.org/resources/advisorypanel/2013/surveyreports20.

98 "Financial Score Conversions and Tables," *Charity Navigator*, last accessed September 27, 2019. https://www.charitynavigator.org/index.cfm?bay=content.view&cpid=48; emphasis added.

99 Josiah Aden, "New York Presbyterian Church Hosts Pagan Deity," September 12, 2019, *Juicy Ecumenism*, last accessed January 10, 2020. https://juicyecumenism.com/2019/09/12/binghamton-presbyterian-sviatovid/.

100 Kimberly Chastain, in an untitled, public response to Josiah Aden's article over the United Presbyterian Church of Binghamton Facebook account on September 13, 2019, at 5:38 in the evening. Last accessed October 10, 2019. https://www.facebook.com/UPCBinghamton/posts/1387642211411481

101 Sherisse Pham, "Hallelujah! Christians Pole Dance for Jesus in Texas," March 22, 2011, ABC News, last accessed October 30, 2020. https://abcnews.go.com/US/hallelujah-christians-pole-dance-jesus-texas/story?id=13194891

102 "'Pole Dancing for Jesus' Taking Off Among Churchgoing Women—and Men" September 15, 2011, *Daily Mail*, last accessed October 30, 2020. https://www.daily mail.co.uk/news/article-2037915/Pole-Dancing-Jesus-taking-churchgoing-women--MEN.html

103 "The Connected Generation," 2020 survey report conducted by the Barna Group and World Vision, "Key Findings," last accessed October 29, 2020,.https://the connectedgeneration.com/key-findings/

104 "In U.S., Decline of Christianity Continues at Rapid Pace," Pew Research Center, last accessed October 29, 2020. https://www.pewforum.org/2019/10/17/in-u-s -decline-of-christianity-continues-at-rapid-pace/

105 "State of the Church: One in Three Practicing Christians Has Stopped Attending Church During COVID-19," July 8, 2020, Barna, last accessed October 29, 2020. https://www.barna.com/research/new-sunday-morning-part-2/?utm_source=News letter&utm_medium=email&utm_content=Barna+Roundup%3A+One+in+Three +Practicing+Christians+Has+Stopped+Attending+Church+During+COVID -19&utm_campaign=BU_07-08-20_Roundup

106 "American Worldview Inventory 2020—At a Glance...Release #10: Worldview in the Millennial Generation," September 22, 2020, *Cultural Research Center, Arizona Christian University*, last accessed October 29, 2020. https://www.arizonachristian .edu/wp-content/uploads/2020/09/CRC_AWVI2020_Release10_Digital_01 _20200922.pdf

107 J. Gresham Machen, *Christianity and Liberalism* (New Edition; Grand Rapids, MI; Cambridge, UK: Eerdmans, 2009), p. 113.

108 Ibid., 6.

109 Ibid.

110 "Global Christianity—A Report on the Size and Distribution of the World's Christian Population," December 19, 2011, Pew Research Center, last accessed October 29, 2020. https://www.pewforum.org/2011/12/19/global-christianity-exec/

111 As quoted in Margaret M. Poloma and John C. Green, *The Assemblies of God: Godly Love and the Revitalization of American Pentecostalism* (New York and London; New York University Press, 2010), 1. Original source: Steve Rabey, *Revival in Brownsville: [the Charisma Revival], Pentecostalism, and the Power of American Revivalism* (Nashville, TX: Thomas Nelson, 1998), p. 4–5.

112 Bob Jones, "The [Charisma] Revival: Shaken or Stirred?" *World Magazine*, December 20, 1997, accessed online February 28, 2020. https://world.wng.org/1997/12 /the_pensacola_revival_shaken_or_stirred.

113 Ibid.

114 Joe Horn, *Everyday Champions: Unleash the Gifts God Gave You, Step into Your Purpose, and Fulfill Your Destiny* (Crane, MO: Defender, 2019), p. 90, 94–97.

115 Thomas Horn and Donna Howell, *Redeemed Unredeemable: When America's Most Notorious Criminals Came Face to Face with God* (Crane, MO: Defender, 2014), p. 118–120.

116 As quoted in Joseph S. Exell (n.d.), *The Biblical Illustrator: I. Corinthians Vol. 2* (New York, NY: Anson D. F. Randolph, 1887), p. 365.

ENDNOTES

117 This is a small list, compiled from only two books: Steven Bancarz and Josh Peck, *The Second Coming of the New Age: The Hidden Dangers of Alternative Spirituality in Contemporary America and Its Churches* (Crane, MO: Defender, 2018); Dr. Thomas Horn, *Shadowland: From Jeffrey Epstein to the Clintons, from Obama and Biden to the Occult Elite: Exposing the Deep-State Actors at War with Christianity, Donald Trump, and America's Destiny* (Crane, MO: Defender, 2019). However, readers are encouraged to look beyond just these titles.

118 Bancarz and Peck, *Second Coming*, 324.

119 "Globalist Think Tank Laid Out Scenario Where Virus Outbreak Prompts Authoritarian Crackdown," Rapture Ready News, March 28, 2020.

120 David Sidman, "Ex British Prime Minister Calls on World Leaders to Form 'One World Government'," *Breaking Israel News*, March 26, 2020.

121 Dov Lipman, "Unity Government Formed: Netanyahu Stays in Charge…For a Half Term," *Breaking Israel News*, March 27, 2020.

122 Ibid.

123 Ibid.

124 Rhoda Wilson, "Klaus Schwab Wants to Stop the Retreat of Globalization and Global Governance with a New Form of Globalization and Global Governance," Expose-news.com, December 19, 2023.

125 Ibid.

126 "Russia, Syria, Turkey and Iran hold high-level talks in Moscow," *Al Jazeera*, May 10, 2023.

127 https://www.theguardian.com/commentisfree/2023/nov/03/war-israel-hamas-conflict-peace-extremists

128 https://www.gatestoneinstitute.org/20106/palestinian-authority-hamas-massacre

129 Ibid.

130 https://www.nytimes.com/2023/11/01/world/middleeast/israel-palestine-two-state-solution.html

131 https://www.out.com/news/dodgers-pride-night-drag

132 https://www.lifesitenews.com/news/archbishop-vigano-globalism-is-satanic-preparation-for-the-rise-of-the-antichrist/?utm_source=digest-world-2023-08-31&utm_medium=email

133 For a listing and discussion of the Old Testament uses of this phrase indicative of unparalleled Tribulation, see my chapter "Old Testament Tribulation Terms" in *When the Trumpet Sounds*, eds. T. Ice & T. Demy (Eugene, OR: Harvest House, 1995), p. 69–70, 82.

134 While present sufferings are said to be of present benefit only to pretribulational believers, both those believers who suffer in tribulations and in the Tribulation have the benefit that their sufferings demonstrate they are worthy (as a result of belonging to Christ) of entrance into the Kingdom of God (2 Thessalonians 1:5; Revelation 1:9; 7:9–17).

135 According to Ezekiel 20:33–38, there will be a company of Jewish rebels purged in the judgment. This indicates there will be Jewish unbelievers as well as Gentile unbelievers.

ENDNOTES

136 Non-dispensational futurists argue that this point indicates the Church is present since these terms were also used to refer to it previously and the global church is never mentioned in Revelation at all, so it should not be expected when the shift turns from the local churches to the world scene. However, the fact that the word "church" is used in Revelation 22:16 in a universal sense—"the churches"—and that the company of believers in Heaven during the Tribulation appear to be this "church," argues against the notion that Tribulation believers are to be identified as members of the church. They are called "fellow brethren" an expression of their common faith and testimony and perseverance in Jesus.

137 For example, see David Chilton, *The Days of Vengence* (Fort Worth, TX: Dominion Press, 1987), p. 383–84.

138 Robert L. Thomas, *Revelation 8-22: An Exegetical Commentary* (Chicago: Moody press, 1995), p. 231.

139 Barry Werth, *Banquet at Delmonicos: Great Minds, the Gilded Age, and the Triumph of Evolution in America* (New York: Random House, 2008).

140 Johnny Cash, "The Man Comes Around," from *American IV: The Man Comes Around*, released in 2002 by the American Recordings Universal label.

141 https://brianmclaren.net/blog/

www.ingramcontent.com/pod-product-compliance
Lightning Source LLC
Jackson TN
JSHW032126110225
78851JS00006B/15